# Remaking Red Classics in Post-Mao China

# Media, Culture and Communication in Asia-Pacific Societies

The Asia-Pacific region houses some of the richest and most diverse cultural, media and social practices in the world, with much of it yet to be analysed or uncovered. At the same time, there is a growing scholarly interest in understanding the breadth and depth of culture and media/communication practices in Asian societies. The aim of this series is to support this quest by enabling high-quality accessible and emergent scholarship on culture, media and communication in the Asia-Pacific to be published. It showcases innovative research produced in the region to a global readership with an eye to generating dialogue that will spark new ideas and enhance social and cultural understandings.

## Series Editors

Terence Lee, Associate Professor, Communication & Media Studies at Murdoch University, Australia

Susan Leong, Research Fellow, School of Media, Culture and Creative Arts, Curtin University, Australia

## Titles in the Series

*Media Power in Indonesia: Oligarchs, Citizens and the Digital Revolution*
Ross Tapsell

*Activism and Digital Culture in Australia*
Debbie Rodan and Jane Mummery

*The Tastes and Politics of Inter-Cultural Food in Australia*
Sukhmani Khorana

*Willing Collaborators: Foreign Partners in Chinese Media*
Edited by Michael Keane, Brian Yecies and Terry Flew

*Transnational Migrations in the Asia-Pacific: Transformative Experiences in the Age of Digital Media*
Edited by Catherine Gomes and Brenda S. A. Yeoh

*Digital Media in Urban China: Locating Guangzhou*
Wilfred Yang Wang

*Remaking Red Classics in Post-Mao China: TV Drama as Popular Media*
Qian Gong

# Remaking Red Classics in Post-Mao China

## TV Drama as Popular Media

Qian Gong

ROWMAN & LITTLEFIELD
London • New York

Rowman & Littlefield
4501 Forbes Boulevard, Suite 200, Lanham, Maryland 20706, USA
With additional offices in Boulder, New York, Toronto (Canada), and Plymouth (UK)
www.rowman.com

**British Library Cataloguing in Publication Data**

A catalogue record for this book is available from the British Library

ISBN: HB 978-1-78660-925-0

**Library of Congress Cataloging-in-Publication Data**

Names: Gong, Qian, 1968- author.
Title: Remaking red classics in post-Mao China : TV drama as popular media / Qian
    Gong.
Description: London : Rowman & Littlefield, [2020] | Series: Media, culture and
    communication in Asia-Pacific societies | Includes bibliographical references and
    index. | Summary: "In the 1990s, China's economic reform campaign reached a
    new high. Amid the eager adoption of capitalism, however, the spectre of revolution
    re-emerged. Red Classics, a historic-revolutionary themed genre created in the high
    Socialist era were widely taken up again in television drama adaptations. They have
    since remained a permanent feature of TV repertoire well into the 2010s. Remaking
    Red Classics looks at the how the revolutionary experience is represented and
    consumed in the reform era. It examines the adaptation of Red Classics as a result
    of the dynamic interplay between television stations, media censorship and social
    sentiment of the populace. How the story of revolution was reinvented to appeal
    and entertain a new generation provides important clues to the understanding of
    transformation of class, gender and locality in contemporary China"—Provided by
    publisher.
Identifiers: LCCN 2020054913 (print) | LCCN 2020054914 (ebook) |
    ISBN 9781786609250 (cloth) | ISBN 9781538153277 (paperback) |
    ISBN 9781786609267 (epub)
Subjects: LCSH: Television programs—Social aspects—China—History. |
    Communism and culture—China.
Classification: LCC PN1992.3.C6 G66 2020 (print) | LCC PN1992.3.C6 (ebook) |
    DDC 791.450951—dc23
LC record available at https://lccn.loc.gov/2020054913
LC ebook record available at https://lccn.loc.gov/2020054914

# Contents

# Contents

# Acknowledgments

My interest in the Red Classics was sped on by the paradoxical views toward this topic. Friends and peers who were university educated are often curious why I would be researching on a subject so "outdated" and out of sync with contemporary Chinese life. On the other hand, television adaptations of the Red Classics have a firm grip on its market niche and continue to attract millions of viewers. In a decade or so, I immersed in this project, trying to make sense of this cultural heritage that is complex, elusive, but nonetheless hugely influential to contemporary Chinese life. During the course of the project, the adaptation of the Red Classics has continued to evolve. The uncertain nature of the project makes the journey all the more exciting and enriching.

My deepest gratitude goes to my mentor and friend Wanning Sun, whose intellectual acuity and theoretical vision has remained a constant source of inspirations. Zhao Yuezhi's critical stance has helped shaped this book. Jenny Chio, Paola Voci, Zhang Xiaoling, and David Goodman all read the whole manuscript and their constructive engagement. Many people have read the chapters at various stages or enlightened me with their thoughts, critiques, or conversations in one way or another: Krishna Sen, Bai Ruoyun, Song Geng, Rosemary Roberts, Michael Keane, Louise Edwards, Louisa Schein, Richard King, Li Yang, and Li Li. Without the encouragement of Susan Leong and Terence Lee and their editorial advice, this project would not be possible. I also thank all my interviewees who generously shared their thoughts and feelings with me.

Earlier versions of chapters 3, 4, and 5 were published as "Remoulding Heroes: The Erasure of Class Discourse in the Red Classics Television Drama Adaptation." In *Chinese Television in the Twenty-First Century: Entertaining the Nation*, edited by Yuoyun. Bai and Geng. Song, 158–174. Oxon: Routledge, 2015; "Red Women and TV Drama." In Contemporary

Chinese Visual Culture: Tradition, Modernity, and Globalization, edited by Christopher Crouch, 295–315. Amherst, New York: Cambria Press, 2010; and "Living Red: Production, Consumption and Local Memory of Revolutionary Culture in Linyi." In *Mapping Media in China: Region, Province, Locality*, edited by Wanning Sun and Jenny Chio, 172–196. London: Routledge, 2012. Routledge and Cambria Press granted permissions to reproduce these publications.

Special thanks to my friend Andrew McDonald. Andrew was often the first reader of the manuscript, and being a comedian and an artist, he made comments on the language side in a good-natured, humorous way. Finally, this manuscript would not have come to fruition without the understanding and unwavering support of my immediate family, Wei, Tianchi, and Olivia, who have been through the emotional ups and downs with me and have remained my cheerleaders throughout all these years. My father died in 2008; however, I am painfully aware that it was he who encouraged me to think critically from a very young age. He was an independent-thinking person all his life, and I hope his spirit will run on in my blood.

# Introduction: Revolution and TV Drama

## *The Uneasy Bedfellows in the Reform Era*

Revolution is undoubtedly the key word for understanding Chinese history in the short twentieth century. In the rather traumatic encounter with imperialism and colonialism, revolution gave birth to a sovereign modern nation. The ensuing decades saw the canonization of a body of literary and art works that forms the heart of revolutionary culture. The core of works, referred to as Red Classics, narrates the founding myth of the nation, articulates the socialist utopian vision, and provides stories that communist doctrines, ideas, ethics, and virtues can be based. Officially endorsed and supported, revolutionary canonical works played the main role in shaping ordinary Chinese cultural experience in their everyday life till the end of the Cultural Revolution (1966–76). In tempering a socialist subject with the right class consciousness, the revolutionary culture also helped construct the "structure of feelings"[1] for the generations of Chinese growing with it.

Revolutionary culture represented by the Red Classics had fallen by the wayside with the end of the Cultural Revolution, when the intellectuals and the public reflected on the dire consequences of the Leftist aberrations, particularly the reification of the class struggle. The grand narratives of revolution were criticized for their repressing of humanity and denial of subjectivity. The 1980s proved to be a brief period of time when the whole nation, coming out of an ideological stricture, was engaged in some serious reckoning of liberation of individual, private ownership of property, legal rights, citizenship, freedom of speech, and human rights. This discussion, however, largely happened within a tacit recognition and under the framework of the socialist values such as independence, liberty, equality, and social justice, represented by China's revolution. The broad-based public debate of post-socialist China resulted in the 1989 political and social movement, which, ironically, put an abrupt end to the national discussion.

ix

The violent ending of the June 4th crisis dampened down the public enthusiasm and autonomy in political participation. What followed was hedonism and materialism as the political contract between individual and state lost its significance, degenerating into pure administrative and economic relations of reward and punishment.[2] The consensus on reform no longer existed. The Chinese Communist Party (CCP) now had to derive its legitimacy not from the communist orthodoxy but economic performance. Concurrent with the receding political enthusiasm and political imaginary in the public, the CCP adopted a pragmatic "no ideological debate" stance, prioritizing economic development. Its attitudes toward revolution are contradictory: as the beneficiary of revolution, the Communist Party affirms revolutionary legacy rhetorically for its own legitimacy to rule. In practice, the CCP leadership has quickened the pace to integrate with global capitalist economy and embraced the market economy, justified in the theory of "Socialism with Chinese characteristics."

The 1990s saw reform and opening up further deepened. The Western world was relieved that China has farewelled revolution and has increasingly become "one of us," and this was the "end of history."[3] In the cultural field, literary and artistic practice became intensely commercialized. The entertainment industry flourished in answer to the needs of consumer culture. However, revolution heritage made a spectacular comeback. Literary and art works of the Mao era made their way back across different cultural domains. Of particular interest was the adaptation of the canonical works into television drama, the most important narrative form and chief medium for delivering entertainment for the nation since the early 1990s. What drives this revival of revolutionary culture? In adapting these stories for TV drama in postrevolutionary China, how are the hegemonic symbolic terms of rules negotiated and rewritten in the narratives? What are the social and economic motives, consequences, and ramifications of the rewriting?

This is an important story of how the largest socialist nation seeks to survive and grow in the face of the failure of socialist experiments on a global scale and the triumphant advance of capitalism worldwide. This book argues that television adaptation of the Red Classics represents as well constitutes the fragmentation and commercialization of revolutionary ideology and culture in post-Mao China, and China has entered a postrevolutionary age. The focus of the argument is on how each of the quadripartite concepts of class, gender, place, and faith was negotiated in the production and consumption of the TV drama adaptions under the sway of different stakeholders, such as the market, the state, the party, the viewers, and the intellectual elites. Through textual analysis and audience research, I demonstrate that in adapting the Red Classics for popular entertainment, different forces form contingent alliances and adversaries, often contrary to seemingly logical assumptions. In this process, revolutionary heritage is constantly repudiated, replaced, and transformed, yet it still stubbornly manifests itself, albeit in a multitude of ways different from its original state.

## RED CLASSICS: PAST AND PRESENT

Since the late-1990s, the term "Red Classics" (*hongse jingdian*) began to appear with regularity in the Chinese media. The concept comes from an invention of CCP historiography. It generally refers to a body of politicized artistic productions created in line with the famous talks by Mao Zedong in 1942. In response to what he saw as the irrelevance of the artistic works, Mao Zedong gave his landmark speech on the Symposium of Literary and Art Circles held in Yan'an, calling for literary and art workers to engage in creative work for the common people, setting the tone of cultural policy in the whole Mao era from the 1940s to the 1970s.[4] The post-1949 Chinese art works in line with the policy were characterized by overt politicization, mainly engaged with the theme of class and class struggle, the efforts, and sacrifices which the peasants, factory workers, and soldiers made for the socialist cause. The result is a large number of literary, musical, and cinematic texts that provide a series of cultural imaginaries in keeping with the needs, ideals, and directives of the CCP.

Despite being widely used, there is no consensus on the exact body of works the term refers to. Most believe the concept first appeared in contemporary Chinese literary studies and was accepted and promoted by the state ideological apparatus.[5] In 1997, People's Press published a series of revolutionary-themed novels created from 1949 to 1966 under the title of "Red Classics Series," and this selection constitutes the core publications that later people referred to as the narrow scope of "Red Classics."[6] A short list of these Red Classics commonly referred to includes *Tracks in the Snowy Mountains* [*Linhai xueyuan*], *The Red Detachment of Women* [*Hongse niangzijun*], *Shajiabang* [*Shajiabang*], and *Struggles in the Old-line City* [*Yehuo chunfeng dou gucheng*]. Some scholars[7] tend to more vaguely define the genre as revolutionary-themed literary writing or creation characterized by grand narratives such as heroism, patriotism, and nationalism and extend the scope of the genre to include not only Chinese literary works but also canonical revolutionary novels written by Soviet Union writers.[8] Others push the boundary even further to include not only literary works but also fine arts, films, and theatrical productions. The term is also appropriated commercially as product brand. In the circular issued in May 2004, the then State Administration of Radio, Film, and Television (SARFT, 1998–2013) defined Red Classics as "revolutionary or historical themed literary works which evoke nationwide repercussions."[9]

The coinage of the phrase "Red Classics," however, is a recent phenomenon. "Classics" normally refers to works that attain canonical status over a
long period of time. In this case, the red classics were created in the modern
era, a conscious endeavor by the Chinese state to create a revolutionary
culture which would mold socialist society. The word "red" is directly associated with the communist revolution in modern Chinese history. The term
"Red Classics," however, is a distinctive postsocialist coinage. The revolutionary works it refers to were known neither as "red" nor "classics" in the
1940–1970s, when the majority of these works were produced. A revolutionary theme was the norm then, and they were not viewed as classic at the time,
but rather were a series of modern works created after 1942. The term "Red
Classics" thus is a postsocialist attempt to define a socialist genre.[10]

A few factors contributed to the popularity of Red Classics in the socialist
era. Created at a moment when China started its modernization project, the
Red Classics were designed to promote socialist ideals. The popularization of
these works was consequently backed by state promotion and encouragement,
even though some of them went through a few cycles of rewriting to suit
the political and ideological needs of the state at that time. Many were later
adapted in a variety of genres such as film, theater, ballet, musical, and other
folk art forms, reaching an ever-greater proportion of audience while enhanc-
ing their reputation through constant exposure. Second, the Red Classics
came into being when China was in the process of establishing revolutionary
hegemony after the turmoil of major warfare with Japan and other Western
nations as well as subsequent civil wars. The epic style that narrates the birth
of a nation and the revolutionary grand narratives of the Red Classics works
were in keeping with Chinese national sentiment. Third, the Red Classics
defined themselves against traditional literary classics by criticizing and
negating the latter, but at the same time, they incoporated the resources of
traditional folk culture which are readily embraced by the populace.

The first decade of reform brought phenomenal economic growth.
However, very quickly the consensus around reform no longer existed. With
marketization continuing to deepen in the 1990s, it became apparent that not
all benefited equally from the reform. Social ills such as official corruption,
imbalanced development between regions, and widened gaps between the
rich and the poor began to manifest themselves more clearly. An angry public longed for the socialist era, now fondly remembered as a "pure" society,
less corrupted, and more egalitarian. Around the same time, Red Classics
experienced a revival. Populist sentiments helped kick start the revival, but
the cultural phenomenon is complex, fluid, and contingent on many factors.

First of all, in the official cultural realm, the CCP updated its propaganda
technology, packaging Party moral education and socialist ideals in commercial publicity gambits designed to make it more attractive and entertaining.[11]

While state propaganda has continued to promote "saintly" Party members as role models for citizens to emulate, these party heroes' human nature and goodness has been exalted with great emphasis given to their compassion for the less fortunate, dedication to their cause, and necessary moral struggle at significant moments. In the meantime, the public nostalgia for the Mao era allowed the Party to see an opportunity to reconfirm its legitimacy by re-broadcasting original Red Classics films, performances, and music through official media, especially TV. China Central Television's (CCTV) film channel has, consequently, been regularly featuring the original Red Classics movies.

In the avant-garde arena, red culture is the key component of a successful formula. Traditionally, unofficial culture defines itself in opposition to state ideology, repression, and censorship, as demonstrated in the case study of rock music.[12] However, since the 1990s, commercialization and commodification have seriously eroded the boundary of the dichotomy. The Party symbols and icons were repackaged into political pop in the push to go international, the work's visibility guaranteed because of its perceived anti-state, subversive nature in the eyes of foreigners, even though the bottom line was usually the main concern for the producer. In the meantime, the avant-garde appropriation of revolutionary symbols and cultures has also created a "more inclusive official culture" over the years.[13]

In the popular cultural scene, revolutionary nostalgia has featured prominently since the late 1980s. Revolutionary symbols, as well as well-known forms of revolutionary culture such as collective singing, have never ceased to be in circulation, and the "structure of feeling" accompanying the lived experience in consuming the Red classics remains intact. As the turn of the twenty-first century saw China further abandoning its commitment to socialist revolution and integrating into global capitalism, paradoxically, popular memory of revolutionary history has been in ascendance and grown into a sizable industry.[14] Starting from the "Mao Fever" of the 1980s, memory of revolution proliferates in different media and sites, ranging from print media (books and magazines) to electronic media (television and films) and the new digital media. In the book market, the publication of personal memoirs of the Cultural Revolution often tops the bestseller lists.[15]

Repackaging the Red Classics in the popular arts realm is "as much a state-mandated propaganda campaign as a market-oriented commercial operation."[16] The products were necessarily hybrids, tentatively toeing a middle ground between out-and-out commercialization and orthodox Party style. Revolutionary songs were now packaged in karaoke style, sung by popular singers with modern electronic accompaniment. Popular TV shows such as *American Idol* inspired singing competitions of "Red Songs" in cities with long revolutionary histories. The phenomenon of "Red Tours," which are either organized or self-sponsored tours to pay homage to revolutionary sites, has drawn its popularity from the new middle-class traveling fad, revolutionary nostalgia, as well as Party educational tours. In all these cultural practices, there is a strong tendency toward cross-fertilization between state culture and commercial culture, in terms of content, form, style, and the organization and funding models.

## THE RED CRAZE AND TV ADAPTATION
## OF THE RED CLASSICS

To appreciate how widely the revolutionary legacy is appropriated in China's commercialized culture, one just needs to look at TV drama. With the influence of literature and film dwindling in the new millennium, TV has become the most popular and influential medium in providing entertainment for today's China, the true "bard" for reform-era China.[17] Despite the proliferation of TV formats and genres, TV dramas remain the most popular narrative format among ordinary Chinese daily viewers[18] as well as the top revenue generator in this cultural industry.[19] In this age of what Korean scholar Yim Choon-sung termed "dramacracy," audiences' understanding of life comes from TV drama. TV drama, as a special mode of story-telling, interacts with the stories themselves to produce certain subjectivities. If Red Classics participated in the constructing the "structure of feeling"[20] for the mass through theater, film, songs, dances, and rhythmic talk in the high socialist era, TV drama is no doubt the main medium that shoulders the task in the reform era. Television's broad audience and wide engagement with social life, and its capacity for meaning-making make it arguably the most important medium to reshape ideology and historiography.[21]

Revolution is monumental in Chinese life and retelling revolutionary history features prominently in TV drama's genre pool. TV drama played a significant role in repackaging and promoting sanctioned official culture along the lines determined by the Party.

Revolutionary, historical-themed prime-time TV series made up about 45 percent of the total TV drama output during the 1999–2001 period.[22] The momentum has shown no sign of decreasing. A brief survey of the prime-time drama programs on CCTV's Channel One seems to confirm this trend. From June to August 2010, CCTV has screened three revolutionary, historical-themed drama series. These include the thirty-episode *Behind the Shooting* [*Qiangsheng beihou*], a story about how communists upset a plot by Nationalist undercover agents to blow up a major power plant; followed by twenty-eight-episode *The Red Guard on Honghu Lake* [*Honghu chiwei-dui*], an adaptation of a 1961 musical film on how the Red Army organized local people to rise against the despotic landlord, and immediately after, the thirty-episode *Sister Jiang* [*Jiang jie*], another adaptation of the Red Classics novel on an undercover communist agent who died a martyr in 1948. The preeminence of this genre lies not only in its sheer quantity but also in its popularity. Some of the series are smash hits and odds-on favorites for the annual official awards. A few examples of the series passionately embraced by audiences include *Days of Burning Passion* [*Jiqing ranshao de suiyue*] in 2001, *Sky of History* [*Lishi de tianchong*] in 2004, *Sword Show* [*Liang jian*] in 2005, and more recently *Lurk* [*Qian fu*] in 2008.

Judging by their origin, these serial dramas tend to fall into two types: those adapted from novels written by contemporary writers and those adapted from the Red Classics produced in the pre-reform era. While both categories have their fanatical fans, it is the latter that is more constrained by the "moral economy"[23] of the individual viewers and the larger community, as well as the sponsorship and policing of the state. According to Linda Hutcheon's theorization, adapting a classic work into another genre offers pleasure in consuming the familiar and the unfamiliar variation at the same time.[24] In the early 2000s when the TV drama industry was hungry for indigenous content, Red Classics provided readily available texts, a potential audience niche, official approval, and therefore promise of financial return. However, the appropriation of Red culture is complex. What can and cannot be changed and how this transcoding is done are contested and controversial fundamental issues.

During the process of translating those classical texts into another medium, the Red Classics correlates to the unique historical, social, political, and cultural conditions of post-socialism. This special context is characterized by the coexistence of China's revolutionary experience and global capitalism. Deng Xiaoping's "no argument" over capitalism or socialism has in essence delinked the theoretical arena from the economic terrains. However, the developmentalism that underlay Mao's modernization project was effectively inherited by Deng's economic reform thrust.[25] At a time when China is plagued by serious social disintegration, the division between the rightist camp's reliance on the market and the leftist's insistence on social equality have once again pushed to the fore the question of how the historical, revolutionary experience could be constructed and represented to the public. Issues revolving around revolutionary culture are gaining more political and ideological significance in the evolving cultural politics of contemporary China. The adaptation of the Red Classics exemplifies the contestation.

An account of how Red Classics was transmogrified into TV drama product to appeal to post-Mao audiences provides a chance to tease out the complexity of the production and consumption of the revolutionary legacy in post-Mao China. Although the dynamics between the state and market set the scene for cultural production and consumption in post-Mao China, the relationships between the two forces have been recognized as much more complex than the "antagonistic" one used by analysts in the early stage of the political and economic reform. This book has the goal of debunking the notion that a state versus market dichotomy determines the outcome of the transformation of Red Culture. Such a view is not only too simple but also ideological. It failed to take into consideration several factors, including the state's role in initiating the marketization, the tensions between various state agencies, and the inhibiting potentials of the commercial media due to ownership concentration and the bias of advertising.[26]

The Red Classics have been at the center of the nation-building project of the Party. They were a state project that provided the language of liberation to the subaltern—those of inferior ranks and stations, such as the peasants, workers, and women under the feudal system—even though this language of rebellion against the ruling class was crude and too focused on official class discourse.[27] Throughout this time, revolutionary culture has been deeply ingrained in the living experience of the ordinary Chinese due to its hegemony in the Mao era. The Red Classics is deeply entangled with the people's identity and the Party's legitimacy to rule.

It serves as the cultural barometer of the Party's ideological control, as well as the ethos of society in different time periods. In particular, the television adaptation of the Red Classics provides a case to study how cultural boundaries change. This process of "translating" the Red Classics into TV drama, the most popular entertainment genre for popular consumption, thus became extremely interesting. In the eye of literary scholar Tang Xiaobing, "the Chinese culture and history after midcentury privilege us to witness an extraordinary metamorphosis of mass culture, with its socialist past ingeniously cannibalized by ever more voracious consumerism."[28] While I agree with Tang on the magnitude of the changes, I would argue that the outcome of the changes is not the total withdrawal of the socialist past. In the context of the Red Classics, the genre is transformed, and both embody and reflect the realities of a different social construction. The transformation involves a multiplicity of social actors and the process is a negotiation of their inclinations. The end product often reflects the differences, conflicts, and compromises between the state and the commercial segments, the intellectual elite and the viewers. Instead of showing how a revolutionary past is continuously being defeated and giving way to the all-engrossing capitalism and consumerism, this book is about how the Red Classics, created in a very different social and political environment, speak to a reform-era China, how it was negated, fragmented, and transformed, yet at the same time remains relevant and inspiring.

In his seminal work, *The Analysis of Culture*, Raymond Williams[29] has distinguished three levels of culture: the lived culture, the recorded culture, and the culture of the selective tradition. The recorded culture is one that survives in its records, while the selective process is one that absorbs the records into a selective tradition. By this definition, the Red Classics could be regarded as a body of works that serves as the record for the high socialist period. The TV adaptations, which connect the lived culture of today and the recorded culture of the socialist era, constitute the selective tradition. Williams further argued that the selective tradition "will be governed by many kinds of special interest, including class interest"[30] and that it will not only be a result of selection, but interpretation made for our own purposes.

Williams' argument is of particular relevance to my discussion of the transformation of the Red Classics. TV's take on the original revolutionary texts must undergo the process of secularizing the revolutionary in order to appeal to popular sentiment. This is nearly the opposite of the reifying process of revolutionary culture during the socialist era. To demystify the hero, to glamourize revolution, or to parody the sacred is a sign of modernity in post-Mao China, and the adaptations certainly must reflect the zeitgeist. According to Williams, reinterpretation, or reading the past work through contemporary experience, is inevitable.[31] The Red Classics genre has now been integrated into the cultural industry as a cultural product. The values the genre promoted—patriotism, nationalism, and self-sacrifice—are only identified with in a fragmented way by a quasi-capitalist society. Replacing these values are individualism, entrepreneurism, self-improvement, materialism, and a post-socialist humanity. The embellishment, distortions, and reinterpretations made in the TV adaptations of the Red Classics reflect and are governed by these historical changes and the development of the society.

Carrying out cultural analysis of the TV adaptations entails understanding and laying bare this selective process—how old boundaries are transgressed, broken, or redrawn. The significance of analyzing the TV adaptations is not to show the deviations in order to seek a "truer" interpretation of the original Red Classics, but to make TV's interpretation process conscious and, in doing so, illuminate the contemporary values which underlie the TV adaptations.

## THE SPECTRUM OF THE RED: HYBRIDIZING
## THE REVOLUTIONARY CULTURE

The Red Classics received a period of cold treatment in the decades immediately following the Cultural Revolution. Tired of the incessant political campaigns, the public dismissed these works as mere politicized products to be criticized and rejected for their lack of humanism. Thriving popular nostalgia for the revolution in the 1990s brought scholarly attention to studies of the Red Classics, particularly those produced in the first 17 years of the PRC. The most influential inquiry are the rereadings by mostly literary critics, which attempt to put literary work in a more complex historical context and cultural construction process.[32] The "rereading" method invigorates the approach to the study of the Red Classics by deconstructing various myths through close reading of the texts in the context of the period's political and ideological mood.

In comparison, the surge of interest in Red culture in the popular arena has been viewed with mixed feelings. The phenomenon was often seen as totalitarian nostalgia[33] or simply mummified relics and therefore a passing fad. The intellectuals' assessment of the resurgence of Red Classics has its basis in their critical introspective look at Mao's era. However, there is a need to recognize the complexity and the prevalence of this cultural revival, and further explore the complicated relationship between historical memory and commercial culture and between the texts of popular culture and their contexts of creation and reception. Zhong and Wang's anthology represents efforts to go beyond the "nostalgia" thesis to examine the lasting legacy of socialist culture in the age of capitalist globalization.[34] More recently, Roberts and Li's edited volume looks at the trajectory of Red Classics before and after reform.[35]

So far little of the available research on the Red Classics was done within the specific context of television drama.[36] Yet TV's refashioning of the Red Classics is probably the most fluid, encompassing and influential phenomenon in this cultural revival. Scholars largely reviewed these adaptations as a conscious act on the part of the market to cash in on the audience's nostalgia for a collective cultural memory. To fully explicate the tensions and complexities in the TV adaptation, one needs to examine a range of issues, including representational strategies, thematic devices, state control, funding, ownership, censorship, regulation and institutional restructuring, and post-Mao identity. Most importantly, these different dimensions are interconnected in dynamic and nonlinear ways. A full investigation of the phenomenon calls for a more systematic analysis of the whole process of cultural production and consumption, including the moments of regulation, consumption, and identity formation and how these discrete moments feed into each other. In particular, there is a need to establish a link between the research on the text and the cultural economy and identity formation.

Following the model of the "circuit of culture," this book attempts to analyze the Red Classics TV adaptations as a commodity, cultural artifact, and social practice. It studies the symbolic system of the TV adaptations, including the visual images TV employs to represent heroes or enemies. TV professionals create these representations so that viewers can identify with them. Identity is therefore closely linked with representation. The process of producing these TV drama adaptations, however, is subject to conditions of production in post-Mao China. Representation and identity are linked with the circulation of capital, media as an institutional practice, and political and social relations. Some of these conditions are unique to Chinese society. The cultural forms, production, and consumption processes are also subject to regulatory systems, which may come in the form of censorship, funding, or dominant discourse.

In adopting a holistic analytical framework that incorporates production, meaning, and consumption, this study also follows another thematic organization. It seeks to analyze the construction of identity through representations along the lines of class, gender, place, and faith. Since the mid-twentieth century, class, gender, race and faith have constituted the four most significant categories of social analysis in cultural studies, especially in feminist and postcolonial works. They function as the main categories through which people's identities are defined and as important markers of social differences. Although these organizing categories are neither objective nor exhaustive, they represent one possible and useful means to explore the transformation of Chinese society as manifested in the production and consumption of the Red Classics.

Another aim of the book is to explore the tensions and complexities thrown up in the adaptation process and the shifting cultural boundaries at the intersection of class, gender, and place. The adaptations of Red Classics are complex and often contradictory semiotic practices, but equally interesting is how these contradictory cultural practices and strategies interact with the political, social, and economic transformations as well as working class identities.

Class and gender constitute important forms of marking out personal identity in the reform era. Scholars from different fields have pointed out the contradictive practices of the Chinese state, which claims its adherence to the socialist legacy on the one hand, while embracing capitalist development paradigms on the other. This contradictory way of governance poses challenges to the principle of egalitarianism, the major socialist legacy. These challenges mainly revolve around the issues of class, ethnicity, locality, citizenship, and gender equality. This book traces how these social changes are producing new identities as well as transforming the old ones, as manifested in the TV version of the Red Classics. It aims to trace how the earlier, socialist subjectivities sewn in the original narratives of the Red Classics have been superseded by the new subjectivities commensurate with market systems in the TV adaptations. The new representations are not only subject to capitalist production imperatives but are also structured by the "existing rules of language and discourse," which are produced by capitalist and other social relations, the most representative examples are the class and gender-based struggles and their effects on different social symbols and signs.[37]

Class, gender, and place are not mechanically dissected categories. They exist in interrelated and complex relationships with each other. In her conceptualization of social changes in the UK, Doreen Massey[38] has made explicit the intricate interconnection between class, space/place, and gender. Class and class consciousness had been at the center of Chinese revolutionary discourse. Class forms the basis of one's subjectivity in Maoist society, and class struggle through mass movement is the central theme of the Red Classics. Women's emancipation was a major part of the agenda of the revolution. Even though women's causes constantly ran the risk of being subsumed in a general "class" discourse, as many Western scholars have argued, in reality they could not be achieved in isolation.[39] When reform started in the late 1970s, a new set of economic and social relations were formed. The old class and class-consciousness discourses were purposely abandoned. The state encouraged neoliberal ideas such as individualism, entrepreneurism, and self-improvement.[40] Old identities based on class divisions had to be reconstructed. The dismantling of the class hierarchy disrupted the gender relations formed during the socialist era. For example, during the socialist era, factory workers or manual laborers as the leading class were endowed with the attributes of masculinity and virility. A female hero in the original Red Classics is often shown, first of all, as a good worker who is competitive in the workplace's manual trade. The form of labor organization imposed by the market has seen manual laborers relegated to the unskilled, bottom echelon of the social ladder. This has engendered a feminization of the workers and manual laborers and given rise to a new masculinity characterized by neoliberal individualism, personal charisma, and entrepreneurism. Capitalism produces a new kind of femininity with which TV producers must contend in representing the revolutionary era.

Social relations invariably extend into space. Spatial relationships have undergone sea changes from the socialist revolutionary period to the current neoliberal free market era. State planning and the need for scale was emphasized in the first period, while the need for deregulation and privatization is called for in the latter. While both approaches are undergirded by a national modernization project, each calls for a different spatial makeup of the country. The examples include the heavy industry-based areas produced under the regional policy during the Mao era and the special economic zones created under Deng's economic reform policy. Each period has produced its own geographic inequality with its reorganization of national political and economic space. As Massey[41] rightly argues, the economic functions of regions and spatial division of labor are class relations "stretching out" over space. The decline in status of the old working class in the rust belt of northeast China is a direct result of the policy shift from heavy industries to service industries. An investigation of place-making strategies in a revolutionary base area such as Linyi must pay attention to the crucial issue of class. In the reform era, the position of the poor, agrarian population has been shifted from the center to the margin in the symbolic order of society and the government's push for economic expansion. Furthermore, gender also plays a role in the geographic constructions of space and place. Local authorities in Linyi, for example, coded the support for revolution in the area as female, or maternal, in an attempt to break the symbolic association of the place with poverty and backwardness, which incites revolution in the first place.

Apart from class, gender, and place, another concept that is most contested is Communist faith. Communist belief system is the cornerstone of the political identity and the theoretical foundation upon which the CCP draws its legitimacy to rule. It has enjoyed the status of religion at the rhetorical level and has been portrayed as the source of strength and truth for a revolutionary subject. In today's China where the Party's legitimacy has increasingly relied on its ability to manage the economy, the question of Communist faith become a vehemently contested area. It shares an intricately complex relations with traditional morality and ethics and has undoubtedly became the prism to examine the Chinese anxiety towards revolutionary history and its contemporary ramifications.

The above discussion indicates that each aspect of the Red Classics is necessarily related to, and intersects with, all other aspects.

## CHAPTER OUTLINES

This book follows two sets of organizing principles: thematically, the main goal of the three analytical chapters is to examine, through representation, the construction of subjectivity along the lines of class (chapter 3), gender (chapter 4), place (chapter 5), and belief (chapter 6). While each chapter is concerned with one theme, it also aims to illuminate how these four subjectivities interconnect. Applying the methodology of the "circuit of culture," each chapter was assigned a specific analytical task—media production in chapter 3, regulation (political intervention) in chapter 4, consumption in chapter 5, and representation in chapter 6. These analytical tasks aim to shed light on not only one single meaning-making process in the "circuit of culture" but also on how each moment articulates with other moments/processes.

Chapter 1 focuses on the TV industry and TV drama as a cultural form. It outlines the economic and political transitions that led to some relaxation and commercialization in the media sphere, particularly the television industry. This chapter aims to explicate the complex nature of the forces that drive change in the TV industry. On the one hand, the development and transformation of the industry is still controlled, regulated, and managed by the state; on the other, the industry is coming under the increasing sway of the market and rising consumerism. These two forces, however, should not be seen as simply oppositional. They accommodate each other, co-opt each other, and form new coalitions. The production and consumption of TV drama, the most popular TV genre, is also subject to the same dynamics. Chapter 1 argues that the dual role of TV and TV drama dictates that the recent TV adaptations of the Red Classics have to negotiate the tension between their own innovative thrust, global capitalism, and state control.

In chapter 2, I give a sweeping overview of the phenomenon of hybridizing the Red Classics through four different case studies. This chapter argues that as a result of both political and commercial pressures, the latest appropriation of the Red Classics is a compromised version that challenges a clear dichotomy between the official and the popular. It thus provides an overall background to the study of the TV adaptations. The four cases juxtapose how the revolutionary legacy is appropriated in three domains: the official, the popular realm of the Internet, and the avant-garde art circle. In each case, I attempt to show the contradiction and ambivalence manifested in the intention, the representations, and the production of the hybridized revolutionary legacy.

In chapter 3, I look at a key controversial issue in the TV adaptation of the Red Classics—the representational politics of heroes. Heroes and villains used to be portrayed as ideological opposites in terms of class struggle. With the deliberate suppression of class discourse in the neoliberal governance of the reform era, the black-and-white portrayal of heroes and villains could not find a niche in the market. TV adaptations of the Red Classics thus resort to vernacular and commercial cultures in their refashioning of heroes and villains to appeal to the increasingly sophisticated audiences. In the TV adaptations, the hero is no longer invincible or perfect because of his or her "proletariat" pedigree, but a self-made individual who earns respect through wisdom, unyielding spirit, and charisma. No longer a saintly figure, he/she invariably comes with a package of human failings. On the other hand, the enemies are also thoroughly remolded to take on a more humane face. The confrontation of the hero and the enemy has shifted away from the focus on justice and ideology to individual competence and integrity. The recasting of the boundary between the good and the bad thus serves as an example of discursive transition from the ideological to the technocratic and managerial.

Chapter 4 deals with gender and femininity, another key area in which the CCP took pride in effecting positive changes in the socialist era. The chapter investigates the contradictions and tensions surrounding the encoding and decoding femininity in two seminal television adaptations, *Shajiabang* and *The Red Detachment of Women*. It argues that the boundaries separating revolutionary women and femininity created in the Mao era have been significantly redrawn according to diverse political, economic, and cultural interests. This chapter stresses the dynamics between the key players involved in the production and reception of the TV adaptations—the TV network, the production company and production team, the television audience, the press, and various interest and pressure groups. This interplay of power produces a depoliticized neoliberal subjectivity for female revolutionary heroes—feminine, capable, entrepreneurial, independent, and sexual, yet within certain moral boundaries.

Chapter 5 uses Linyi, an old revolutionary base during the Anti-Japanese War (1937–1945) and Civil War (1945–1949), as an example to illuminate how consumption of the Red Classics is closely linked with the identity of local people and how locality plays a role in the production and consumption of the Red Classics. The chapter is concerned with unraveling how revolutionary culture continues to be an important resource for local identity production, and how, as the Party's authority and legitimacy become less self-evident, new strategies have been adopted to make the legacy more accessible to the public. Simultaneously, it also looks at how this discourse articulates with individuals' desire in negotiating their self-identity. It argues that the local government invokes ideas such as local traits (*min-feng*), locality (*diyuxing*), and human nature (*renxing*) to better enmesh official history with local memory as a discursive strategy for charting and understanding the revolutionary history that used to be narrated as a black-and-white ideological confrontation. The chapter sheds light on the intricate relationship and messy boundary between official culture and popular narrative. The reinvention of local identity and memory has everything to do with the local economy. The politics of inequality in place and space is played out around the binaries of rural-urban and inland-costal. As a revolutionary heartland, Linyi needs to overcome its spatial disadvantage in this new configuration of place production. The branding of the place as entrepreneurial, trustworthy, and humane represents the efforts to integrate Linyi into the global market. This discourse opens new subject positions that locals readily take on. This chapter also includes a part on Linyi locals' consumption of the Red Classics.

Chapter 6 looks at the spy genre, arguably most interesting and successful subgenre in the revolutionary, historical TV drama series, although not adaptions of Red Classics *per se*. I argue that programs in this genre do not focus on constructing a revolutionary subjectivity, but reference successful people who are calculating and good at scheming in today's workplace, and also speak to moral anxiety and mirror the precarious existence of the contemporary Chinese.[42]

This study represents the first large-scale systematic examination of the Red Classics TV adaptations by integrating several important processes—production, representation, consumption, identity formation, and regulation. In doing so, the project contributes to an emerging body of literature, which explores the important relationship between cultural productions, the formation of new social identities, and historical transformation in general. The Red Classics in their various forms span the socialist and post-socialist eras, and as such are both metaphoric and metonymic of social change in China in the era of reform. The research on the Red Classics adaptation phenomenon provides important empirical evidence to unravel the complex and intricate relationship between state power, consumerism, and cultural production.

## Chapter 1

# TV Dramas as Market Commodities, Cultural Artifacts, and Social Practices

The rise and popularity of the Red Classics genre have much to do with the structural changes to China's TV industry. In this chapter, I will discuss the broad context in which the production, regulation, and consumption of the Red Classics TV dramas take place. Modern Chinese TV is a product of the social changes of the reform era. Though still carrying the mandate of political indoctrination and public service, television has increasingly been reshaped as an advertiser-supported, consumer-targeted commercial enterprise in the emerging multichannel environment.[1] Therefore, the TV drama adaptation of the Red Classics needs to please several masters at the same time. What is regarded as acceptable, necessary, and normal by the state may not correspond with the requirements of the market or the intellectual elite. Under such circumstances, the transgression of boundaries is a perennial issue. The traditional binaries such as official/commercial, pedagogy/entertainment, and high/low are increasingly becoming blurred conceptually. For a subject such as Red Classics, the transgression of boundaries is especially pronounced and meaningful.

In the Introduction, I argued that a holistic methodology is needed to understand how the Red Classics genre is integrated into the cultural industry as a cultural product, and the complicated power struggles that are thrown up in this process. I proposed to use the "circuit of culture"[2] as the analytical framework to probe the crucial moments of production, consumption, and regulation of the TV adaptations. I take the "circuit of culture" to mean that TV dramas in China should be studied as market commodities, cultural artifacts, and social practices.

1

## TELEVISION DRAMA AS A MARKET COMMODITY

In the three decades since 1976, China has undergone a reform of market orientation that has profoundly transformed the communication and culture industry. Previously described as part of the propaganda state,[3] China's media were undisputedly the mouthpiece of the Party-state, taking as their major role the indoctrination of Party lines and propagation of state ideology. Market economics had little effect on the various media platforms, which were fully subsidized by the government. These party organs, however, have undergone significant changes in terms of institutional structure, funding model, social role, and content since China embarked on economic reform in the 1980s, particularly after Deng Xiaoping's call to further "socialist market reform" during his visit to the south coast cities in 1992.

Today's communication sector in China has been open to multiple purposes, forces, and editorial approaches. It must simultaneously seek to satisfy and appease the Party's direction and demands, provide information and entertainment to society and consumers, and pursue organizational survival, revenue, and power. The process of transformation has been "messy, protracted, confusing, and confused, littered with odd, even counterintuitive institutions, structures, and practices."[4]

The medium that best embodies the contradictions in this process is none other than the television industry. Television broadcasting started in China in 1958 and was initially introduced as a tool for political mobilization and social engineering.[5] During the subsequent twenty years, television remained a technology accessible only by a very privileged few and, consequently, had minimal influence. It did not constitute part of the popular culture, and even its capacity as a political propaganda tool was very limited.[6] The government alone funded TV stations. There was no relationship between the economy and television, and it could hardly be called an industry, with only one station, Beijing Television Station, running in the whole country for over twenty years. Programs were only transmitted sporadically in a handful of cities and very few people owned a television set.[7]

However, this tiny new technology has grown into a giant industry since China embarked on its modernization program in the late 1970s. Corresponding to the transition from a planned economy to a market economy and riding along with the massive changes in the media sector, China's television not only has undergone huge expansion but also currently operates under financial and policy structures different from before. By 2005, China had about 400 million television sets nationwide (about a third of the world total) and over 2,000 licensed TV stations.[8] In 2007, TV reached 96.58 percent of the total population.[9] These profound changes are the result of a series of government policies, funding model overhauls, institutional restructuring, and intensified competition.

## Funding Model Changes

From a political motivation tool to a popular commodity, TV drama has followed the same evolutionary trajectory as the TV industry more broadly. TV drama came into being in China in the late 1950s at the height of ideological contention between the socialist and capitalist camps, headed by the Soviet Union and United States, respectively. It took on its pedagogical role at its very birth. The first production, a one-episode drama entitled *A Mouthful of Vegetable Pancakes* [*Yikou caibingzi*], was aired in 1958 to promote the importance of thrift at a time when the country experienced severe food shortages. In the next two decades, the production of drama was minimal and nearly came to a halt during the Cultural Revolution, as most of the production units were engaged in intensive political campaigns. [10]

TV drama production was resumed in the late 1970s and quickly took on a new role, as watching television became a national pastime for hundreds of millions of Chinese viewers. This transformation process must be considered within the top-down economic and political context, as well as the bottom-up need for popular entertainment. Until 1979, China's television industry had depended completely on government funding. The government remained the only financial provider for the less than forty TV stations across the country, with each station broadcasting between three to five hours per day. Because of this financial straightjacket, there had been little incentive, much less the means, for the TV stations to produce dramas, except for some pedagogical single-episode programs required by the government.

By the mid-1980s, the government had introduced market mechanisms into the media sector, leading to the expansion of the press and broadcasting industries. The boom, however, was coupled with declining subsidies and provisions for financial incentives on the part of the state, due to reduced GDP revenue.[11] Left to sink or swim, the burgeoning television industry had to turn to other sources for income. Since 1978, television had gradually weaned itself from government subsidies and turned to commercial revenue, mainly advertising. The total turnover in TV advertising jumped from 15 million yuan ($US 2.3 million) in 1979 to 62.2 billion yuan ($US9.6 billion) in 1999, representing a phenomenal growth of 4,146 times.[12] This increase in advertising revenue was particularly spurred on by the "four-tier" policy implemented in 1983,[13] which localized the operation of TV stations and intensified the competition for alternative investment.[14]

Commercial funding profoundly changed the production and circulation of TV programs, including drama. On January 28, 1979, Shanghai TV station aired the first television advertisement ever in China for a tonic spirit. The ninety-second advertisement signaled that TV had started to acquire a new source of funding, and indeed, over the next two decades, advertisements became the largest source of revenue for TV.[15]

With the new revenue coming from the commercial sector in the form of sponsorship and advertisement, TV drama productions boomed. In the decade from 1978 to 1987, the total output of TV dramas amounted to 5,875 episodes, some thirty times the total amount produced in the first twenty years of television.[16] In 2005, the figure was a monstrous 15,000 episodes.[17] This growth emerged as a response to the strong demand from the market, particularly when the average Chinese household was able to afford a television set in the 1980s. Consequently, a good many more drama productions were needed to fill up the available time slots.

The diversified financing also means that "serving the Party" was no longer the sole agenda of TV dramas. The market had become another master, and TV dramas now had to establish themselves as a commodity, a marketable product sold to audiences through advertising. Over the next few decades, TV dramas had to continue negotiating the boundaries between the state and the market, while growing to become the most popular entertainment form for Chinese, second only to the news as the most watched genre.

From the mid-1980s, the original drama production units within TV stations were consolidated and expanded as drama production centers. This development contributed to the increase in drama output because of the increased production capacity. Investment in drama production was further commercialized and diversified. At the initial stage, drama production teams would solicit commercial sponsorship by selling advertising spots to businesses. The producers then traded the drama production, together with the advertisements, for program time with the TV station. Since 1995, TV producers have been able to secure bank loans, and financing through loans gradually became a standard practice in drama production. This diversification in funding gave a great boost to the production of TV drama. The number of production permits granted doubled from 1995 to 1999.[18] As the most preferred advertising medium, TV drama now attracted diverse sources of investment. The relaxed rules on ownership also contribute to the growth of a large sector of independent program-making companies of different sizes and production specialties. The production industry now comprises about 36 state-owned production companies, 300 independent and SARFT-registered companies, and 266 television stations with in-house production capacity.[19] Competition among these production units is fierce, with production costs escalating. Of the 10,000 episodes produced each year, only 20 percent make a profit.[20] While the production of TV drama is commercialized, the broadcasting is not. TV stations can rely on their monopoly over broadcasting to force the purchase price down. In 2002, the total advertising income for TV drama was 21.9 billion yuan ($2.73 billion), of which a meager 1.92 billion ($240 million) was spent on drama production.[21]

The provincial and local stations prefer to buy the rights to air less-expensive reruns from major TV networks, such as CCTV, after they are premiered by the bigger stations. The Red Classics TV drama series are often quite easily scheduled by major television networks not only because the theme has audience reach and appeal but also because it meets the political mandate.

Despite the commercializing trend in TV drama production, the Chinese government has not fully retreated from this cultural realm. In spite of reduced financial subsidies, the state is determined to keep a leash on the production and circulation of ideological work. In fact, after the June 4 incident in 1989, the power of the CCP's propaganda units has been strengthened.[22] The state has been maintaining control of this particular cultural product through various channels, including policy-making, legal regulations, and administrative intervention.

## Structural Overhaul

Chinese television has been a highly regulated sector. Channels of the national networks (CCTV and China Education Network) are broadcast throughout the country via satellite and microwave transmission. SARFT oversees the construction, form, and content of the networks, functioning as a regulatory body, a network builder and operator, and a propaganda organ.[23] At the local level, there are 27 provincial channels and about 300 regional city stations that both produce programs and transmit national network channels. These stations fall under the administrative umbrella of both the local SARFT bureau and local government. In addition to terrestrial stations, there are also over 1,200 cable stations built and run by various municipal and state enterprises.

The television industry experienced its first growth spurt in 1983 when the Party implemented the four-tier policy. This policy resulted in a glut of stations, with nearly 4,000 stations at the peak in 1997.[24] It simply became too cumbersome for the central administrative authority to manage the stations effectively. Self-funded, county-level stations saw no benefits in carrying CCTV's programs and started to barter for foreign programs and other mass appeal entertainment. The competition between the multiple stations for advertising money and programming was fierce, resulting in the decline of the advertising growth rate for the first time in 1998. The pressure to implement reforms was further intensified by other factors, including the entry of transnational media corporations after China's accession to the World Trade Organization (WTO) in 2001, and the possibility of losing territory in the cable market to the newly emerged telecommunications industry.[25] However, in this process, local stations have gained opportunities to try their hand in financing and developing their programs.[26]

The response to this multitude of challenges was a structural shakeup. In *Communication in China*, Zhao Yuezhi[27] describes this process and teases out the significant power dynamics. With a series of consolidation campaigns starting in 1996, the number of TV stations was reduced by half. The four-tier system was officially flattened to a two-tier system, with county-level stations and cable stations either dismantled or stripped of their programming capacity. In the meantime, under the slogan, "make it bigger and stronger," the state pushed for media conglomeration. The policy saw eighteen cross-media, cross-region broadcasting groups, such as Hunan Television, come into being. However, the mergers were resisted and curbed at key points by institutional barriers, vested bureaucratic interests, and central-local feuds. By 2003, the effort to nurture flagship conglomerations had lost much of its steam. To overcome the impasse, more radically revisionist commercialism was introduced. In the name of "cultural system reform," this project relegated media to a less politicized domain and opened up the market-oriented media sector to free capital investment. Television was now regarded more as an industry than a political and cultural agency. In an all-out effort to seek profit, Chinese TV focused on entertainment.[28]

**Programming Competition**

Commercialization produced fierce competition between various local stations and between national networks and local networks. The prime goal for channels has now become to fully exploit the advertising potential of television. This has a number of implications for TV programming. For example, to seek a larger audience share and to sustain its status as China's national broadcaster, CCTV, with its sixteen Chinese-language channels and three foreign-language channels, had to join the battle for ratings as the sector became more commercialized. This has had an impact on its institutional structure and social role, particularly in terms of staffing and programming. Over the last three decades, CCTV has undergone significant internationalization,[29] increased its news output, created a number of in-depth reporting programs and, when allowed, spoken for the public on social, economic, and political issues.[30] For example, in 1993, CCTV created the topical magazine, *Oriental Horizon*, followed by the highly popular in-depth investigative news program, *Focus*, in 1994. Local TV news was also transformed in terms of pace, incisiveness, and flamboyance.

Television stations have largely given up their role "as ideological brainwashers, but continue to be vital ideological managers on behalf of the Party-state."[31] CCTV serves as a very straightforward example. CCTV's prime time news would not reach 92 percent of the total Chinese population without the government's requirement that all local broadcasters carry the program.[32]

Here, CCTV's political capital is translated into economic capital in the form of lucrative advertising contracts.[33] In turn, CCTV carries the mandate to operate within a closer regulatory framework, carefully avoiding any offense to the Party. Indeed, this could be considered a classic example of dancing "because of the chains."[34]

While news and current affairs were under pressure to change, broadcasters gradually saw entertainment as holding the key to ratings success.[35] In the multichannel system, the calculation of costs-by-viewers-reached plays a big part in the head-to-head competition between stations. Schedulers are given more power and control, and their decisions are heavily skewed by audience research and other data. Audiences are grouped into niche markets based on their expectations and consumption power. One of the main measures to revamp the old system was the adaptation of the program commissioning strategy. The idea was introduced to China in the early 1990s. Traditionally, the broadcast networks were responsible for producing their own programs. Regardless of their quality, these programs had guaranteed scheduling spots. The new policy opened the networks to independent program-making companies for programs (excluding news) that were likely to achieve ratings success.

Given that drama series deliver more than 90 percent of all the advertising revenue for most provincial and local TV stations in 2002, for example,[36] it is no surprise that the reform started with this genre. Major television networks such as CCTV and BTV (Beijing Television Station) established their own TV drama production centers. TV drama production alone has grown into a large sector of over 1,000 companies. TV networks used program commissioning as a means to solve the problem of low-program quality and program duplication that had long plagued TV networks. By injecting elements of competition, such as price, into the selection of programs, it also helped to lower the cost. The outsourcing of production also enabled channel specialization, an initiative responding to the diversified consumer tastes and identities resulting from very diverse social values, expectations, and lifestyles in modern China. Narrowcasting, or *fen zhong* in Chinese, is a means for survival in the new multichannel environment. The prevalence of revolutionary nostalgia as a cultural phenomenon means that this topic would attract a high number of viewers, mainly the urban working class and peasants, particularly among the generation born during or before the 1960s. While many academics tend to focus on the urban, youth, and commercial productions, the practitioners within the TV industry have long taken note of the diverse nature of Chinese TV viewers and established the Red Classics adaptations as a market niche. These adaptations cater to the middle- to old-aged population born before the 1960s, who might harbor nostalgic feelings toward revolutionary culture, as well as middle to low-income urban working class and peasants.

The aggressive competitive scheduling on all channels provides a perfect example of how neoliberal market-based calculations have infiltrated the medium. Despite the fact that light entertainment has—to a certain extent—liberated itself from the socialist didactic approach and the elitism of the high culture movement in the 1980s, this turn to entertainment to compete for audiences has created new patterns of social inclusion and exclusion.[37]

Operating in these conditions, the Chinese TV system is indeed riding many horses at once. Various impulses—commercial, public service, and propagandist—are commingled in TV stations in various balances and gradations. The core editorial areas such as news and current affairs still carefully tread the Party line. However, even these editorial operations have upgraded their practices in many aspects to be more responsive to public needs and tastes. TV magazines and reality shows, with a strong emphasis on emotional tales, often help the viewers to deal with the harsh reality of contemporary neoliberal society.[38]

While tensions between government control and commercialization dominate the changes in the media industry, accommodations and compromises are increasingly recognized. The cultural environment in which media operate is indeed much more complex than many suggest. Jing Wang[39] articulates the convertibility of political, economic, and cultural capital in China:

> [N]ot only has the postsocialist state not fallen out of the picture, but it has rejuvenated its capacity, via the market, to affect the agenda of popular culture, especially at the discursive level. The state's rediscovery of culture as a site where new ruling technologies can be deployed and converted simultaneously into economic capital constitutes one of its most innovative strategies of statecraft since the founding of the People's Republic.

## Censorship Mechanisms

As discussed above, commercialization has reshaped the funding model, organizational structure, and programming practices of the TV industry. These changes, however, do not mean that the state has loosened its grip on the content of TV drama. The institutions that supervise the ideological functions of the media are still operating. For example, the production of TV drama is mainly supervised by SARFT. The other two state agencies responsible for cultural production censorship are the Central Propaganda Committee and the Ministry of Culture. From 1999, two censorship organs—the Television Drama Censorship Committee and the Television Drama Censorship Review Committee—were set up under SARFT to screen TV drama productions before their release. These two committees have provincial-level branches as gatekeepers.

In practice, government agencies such as SARFT exercise control over the production of TV drama through the means listed here:[40]

- Granting production licenses to the production unit: only production teams granted long-term or temporary production permits are entitled to make TV dramas. Most of the production units possessing long-term licenses are state-owned. They include national and provincial TV stations, film studios, and audio and video production companies.
- Subject matter planning as a whole: an annual TV drama subject-matter planning conference is held for all production licensees to identify contemporary popular topics and discuss their production plans in order to avoid repetition. This seemingly "market" practice, however, has a strong element of government control. Government agencies such as SARFT will often provide guidelines that outline the key topics anticipated by the government for the next year. Some of these key projects, usually in answer to a major ideological initiative or commemoration of an important Party event, will be designated to the state-owned production units as a political task. The implicit guarantees for the TV drama products to be broadcast on major networks are sufficient attractions for even many nonofficial production units to choose from these topics. This requirement was removed in May 2006.[41]
- Giving out permits for the production project: once a production company decides to commence a project, it has to submit an application to SARFT. In 2004, less than a third of the total submissions were rejected.
- Censoring before the broadcast and publication: the provincial broadcasting authority or SARFT must preview the completed TV drama productions before their formal release and broadcasting. Overt censorship of TV drama usually involves the removal of ideologically unacceptable content or editing and reworking certain parts of the episodes or series in order to satisfy the censors.

Case-by-case regulative measures—usually referred to as "notices" (*tongzhi*), "directives" (*zhishi*), or "decisions" (*jueding*)—are issued in an ad hoc manner to exercise control over specific genres.[42] In May 2004, when the readaptation craze was in its heyday, SARFT issued a notice to the administrative departments concerned, stipulating that all Red Classics TV dramas had to be submitted to SARFT's Censorship Committee for final approval after passing the initial censorship at the provincial level. The document stressed that current adaptations of the Red Classics invariably demonstrated a tendency toward "misreading of the original work," and were "based on a misinterpretation of the market," eventually "misleading the audiences."[43] According to the notice, the specific problems with the adaptations included imposing complicated love relationships on the main characters, representing the heroes and the villains with multiple personalities so that the ideological intention of the original work was distorted, and diluting content because of the length required for the TV format.

Apart from making the aforementioned regulations, the state also meddles in production matters and asserts its influence over content through participation sponsorship, setting up academic awards, and manipulating public opinion through the media. Nevertheless, this influence is only relative. First of all, censorship is never consistent. In fact, as James Lull[44] observes, television production censorship in the reform era can best be described as confusing. This is a result of two factors. First, even though government agencies provide general censorship guidelines, it is up to the censors to interpret how these apply to each individual TV drama. The arbiters of artistic standards, taste, and ideological correctness may vary to a great extent depending on who is doing the censoring. Second, the criteria for censorship constantly change to keep up with political and socioeconomic developments. Censorship tends to tighten during periods of unrest, particularly during a downturn in the economy. Political incidents such as the June 4 student protests resulted in the state tightening its censorship of TV drama production. At other times, however, TV dramas focusing on glitzy automobiles, cocktail bars, and businessmen dressed in sleek suits become the main attraction in keeping with the market economy ideology. With all the energy unleashed by reform, China's TV industry did not become an outright liberal commercial entity; rather, it now serves a dual purpose: providing entertainment for consumers and propagating the political agenda for the nation-state. This hybrid role can only be summarized as a media system with Chinese characteristics. The newly gained autonomy must be carefully exercised within the boundaries set out by the state. Balancing the two becomes a delicate business every TV station must deal with on a day-to-day basis. Indeed, the former leader Deng Xiaoping's metaphor, "crossing the river by feeling the stones," best describes the practices of professionals working in the TV industry.

## TV DRAMA AS A CULTURAL ARTIFACT

Having discussed TV dramas as market commodities in general, I now move on to discuss the content of these dramas. By the end of the 1990s, television drama had not only emerged as a full-fledged industry, but had also established itself as a significant entertainment form. TV drama is the major storytelling medium in China. Chinese audiences easily take up its dramatic narrative styles and structures, which are not so different from the traditional Chinese serial novel. TV drama enjoys much more popularity and has a much greater impact on society than film, theater, and novels. This is a result of several factors. The family-centered lifestyle, the limited choices in cultural consumption, the withering film market, and the relatively low cost per capita of television all contribute to the centrality of TV drama in the cultural and social life of ordinary Chinese. TV drama also provides daily entertainment that can be understood and enjoyed by the relatively large illiterate and semi-literate population, even though they are not the ideal consumers.

Like the TV industry in general, TV drama as a narrative form constitutes and is constituted by the rapid social changes that have taken place in the past few decades. Its episodic, serial format has been influenced by both international styles and native aesthetic traditions, and its production is driven by the need to reconcile a political mission with the dependence on advertising potential, all the while satisfying viewers.

## A Genre Beloved: The Development of TV Drama in China

With the dawn of the TV age in the 1950s, television drama has played an extremely important role in Chinese society. As a modern "bard," TV drama is the genre that reaches both the educated and the illiterate, the old and the young, the rich and the poor. Its unique position and impact results in heightened attention from both the intellectual elite and the Party's administrative and censorship bodies. It is unequivocally the most unique and effective form of mass media.

The curtain-raiser for TV drama was *A Mouthful of Vegetable Pancake*, a single-episode moral story about class struggle produced in 1958. Up to 1966, about two hundred TV dramas were broadcast by a handful of TV stations in big cities.[45] Most of the works carried the mission of promoting ideological and political education. TV drama did not become a powerful and popular medium until the early 1980s, when TV sets became a more common household item. The earliest production models for TV drama came from overseas. Since the late 1970s, and particularly during the early 1980s, the whole nation was mesmerized by long TV soap operas imported from Mexico and Brazil, as well as dramas from Taiwan and Hong Kong. The commercial imperative to gain audience approval was manifest in the nine-part *Eighteen years in the enemy camp (Diying shiba nian)*, the first TV drama serial launched by CCTV in 1980. A story about undercover communists working in the Kuomintang army force, the drama hardly distinguished itself in its characterization of model communist heroes or in its representations of ideological struggle. Rather, audiences were immediately drawn to its convoluted plot and thrilling action. This series, crude in its production, signaled the directions for the future development of Chinese TV drama. The serial form, similar to the Brazilian telenovela and congruent with Chinese narrative tradition,[46] would eventually become the formula for many dramas produced in the ensuing years. It was received with considerable criticism for catering to popular tastes and playing down the importance of politics, but it clearly demonstrated to both the audience and producers the entertainment value of TV drama.

Over the next few years, the genre became better resourced, with official support for the establishment of TV drama production centers, and official awards for outstanding TV drama. This effort led to a wider range of TV dramas in format, subject matter, and cultural level. The popular series included the drama adaptation of literary classics, such as *The Water Margin* [*Shuihu zhuan*] and *The Dream of the Red Chamber* [*Hongloumeng*], biopics about CCP leaders, and revolutionary epics. The most notable subgenre was realistic drama series dealing with significant social issues and moral dilemmas thrown up by economic reform, such as the 1986 sensational success, *New Star* [*Xin xing*], which was a series about a young, daring country magistrate battling bureaucracy and corruption in rural areas.

By the early 1990s, technological developments had paved the way for new program-delivery systems, multichannel expansion, and intensified competition for viewers' attention. The period was marked by a great innovative thrust in TV drama. A few young writers and TV production crews from Beijing Television Art Centre (BTAC), envious of the success of cheap imported productions, were eager to develop the new genre themselves.[47] Their first major hit, the fifty-part *Yearnings* [*Ke Wang*], immediately won over the entire population, achieving unprecedented ratings, and was repeatedly broadcast across the country after it was first aired in 1990. Despite the government's claim that it showcased good socialist artistic works, *Yearnings* was fundamentally a commercial attempt to sell an interesting story to the audience. There was a vague suggestion of political events such as the Cultural Revolution and subsequent economic reforms, but these served only as historical background to the main story. Otherwise, it was a typical TV series on family relationships cleverly grafted from international soap operas. It also adopted a number of techniques standard to international soap opera production, such as indoor blocking, multicamera shooting, simultaneous voice recording, and postproduction editing.

Snubbed by the elite for its vulgarity, *Yearnings* nevertheless represented the dawning of a new age of urban consumer culture in the 1990s. TV drama now not only advanced ideological agendas or promoted nation-building projects, but it could also be watched for its easy, entertaining style. The burgeoning trend was further developed in another BTAC production, *Stories from an Editorial Office* [*Bianjibu de gushi*], broadcast in 1991. The comedy provides a satirical account of how a group of editors struggles to run a tabloid magazine, ironically called *Guide for living*. Besides being the first situation comedy ever produced in China, *Stories from an editorial office* also drew business sponsorship by packing product placement advertising in the drama plot.

By the early 1990s, the two most important narrative formats—multiepisode series and situation comedies—had established themselves as the two main forms of TV drama and proved to be financially viable. Consumerism cultivated an audience that was more difficult to please than politically subjugated citizens, and producers were forced to consider more complex layers of social subgroups and identities, as well as divergent moral and political opinions. A variety of genres had established themselves to appeal to widely differentiated groups of viewers. These genres ranged from costume court series, military series, swordsmen series, and teenage idol series, to series focusing on personal and familial vicissitude. As the competition for ratings became ever fiercer, TV producers started to exhaust every available resource in order to maximize audience size.

## Major Forces Shaping TV Drama

As they are less politically sensitive than news, light entertainment and TV drama have the major responsibility to attract advertising revenue and maintain a high level of creativity. TV dramas largely fall into the two camps of "main melodies" (zhu xuanlü) and "diversity." The "mainstream melody" refers to the Party-ordained dramas or, more broadly, works that still carry on the socialist tradition and to some extent reflect contemporary social reality. TV stations and production companies regularly churn out biographies of national leaders and historical figures, stories of significant revolutionary events or compelling stories of reformists or contemporary moralists. The state continues to sponsor the production, circulation, and consumption of these works. A variety of themes, however, grow out of the rising plebeian culture *(shimen wenhua)*—the street-bred, mass culture[48]—and feed the consumer-oriented population with long martial arts series, personal stories of urban upward mobility, and tear-jerking melodramas of family relationships. Dramas of this type fall into the "diversity" category. However, the two types of drama never fit neatly into any discrete categories, but, rather, blend potentially opposed elements within them. One good example is the large number of revolutionary-themed dramas, which downplay class struggle while pursuing a nationalist discourse mixed with outrageous sensationalism and populism.

The fusion between state culture and mass culture is evident in quite a few recent TV drama series hits, such as *Sword show, Days of burning passion,* and *The sky of history* [Lishi de tiankong]. *Days of burning passion,* for example, is a twenty-two-part chronological tale about the life of a military leader, Shi Guangrong. Shi's identity as a devoted communist commanding officer sanctions the series as a revolutionary mainstream product. Nevertheless, the important historical events that made Shi a revolutionary leader only serve as a blurred background for his quibbling with his wife and three children. Shi is patriotic, idealistic, and brave, yet also domineering, rough, and patriarchal. Much of the characterization is done through the melodramatic dramatization of everyday events. It is perhaps not misleading to promote it as "revolutionary melodrama." Whether a revolutionary drama packaged in a commodity shell or the other way around, the formula of melding revolutionary icons with commercial gambits can be highly profitable. *Days of burning passion* was replayed five times on Beijing Television alone. The first run achieved a high rating of 12 percent.[49]

The dynamism between state control and media autonomy is not totally oppositional. Mainstream series with stories about good cadres or Party history have come a long way from the early, crude form found in *A mouthful of vegetable pancakes*. Now that the state lacks the ability to underwrite most of the drama productions and political indoctrination has lost its appeal, the official culture has to take on a "new face." This updated style borrows heavily from popular TV soaps in its characterization, sentimentalism, and plot formula. Geremie Barmé notes the infiltration of avant-garde art and commercial culture into state-sponsored cultural products, such as Party advertising, photography, and films.[50] However, one should not be too eager to embrace the thesis that consumerism now rules all. In fact, Chinese TV drama, although influenced by the market economy, western culture, and the logic of consumption, is still "largely mainstream in that it embodies political ideology, patriotism, collectivism, nationalism and heroism on the one hand, and the social ideology of the nuclear family and patriarchy on the other."[51]

In discussing the social conditions of TV drama, besides the state discourse and the rising market discourse, another important factor is elite culture (*jingying wenhua*).[52] After a pause in 1989, Deng Xiaoping endorsed further reform in 1992. In the face of accelerated commercialization, writers, scholars, and other intellectuals had to reorient themselves to avoid being sidelined by capitalism. Beginning in 1993, an emergent discourse on "humanistic spirit" took hold as a result of public discussions initiated by thinkers and writers. Intellectuals called for a revival of humanism to counter the vulgar commodification of popular art. Meanwhile, some careerists within the intellectual camps were making use of state funds and institutional structures to advance their own agenda.[53] The intellectual elite remain the third major force that TV drama must negotiate.

Because of these three different agendas, the production of TV dramas is very much a balancing act between *jiaohao* (critical acclaim) and *jiaozuo* (ratings). Before 1990, when ratings came to play a significant role in the success of a TV drama, the main concern of the production team was to seek official approval/sponsorship, as well as good critical acknowledgment, often in the form of a national artistic award and positive expert reviews. Some of the early major TV dramas were made with an aim only to achieve "state-of-the-art" status, with very little concern for production costs. For example, in response to the official call to promote the "national cultural essence" in 1984, CCTV commissioned the production of the thirty-six-episode TV drama remake of the classical novel, *Romance of the red chamber*. Not only did the shooting itself last for an exceedingly long three years, but the production process also reached new levels in terms of artistic standards: on-location shooting was done in major scenic spots across the country; actors for the main characters were selected from tens of thousands of candidates; experts on the novel were extensively consulted; and two lengthy workshops were organized to prepare the actors for their roles. However, this exclusive concern for artistic quality over profitability did not last long. When investment became increasingly diversified in the early 1990s, the struggle to win ratings started.

The race to secure high ratings forced TV producers and the networks to focus less on the state and the intellectual elite and more on ordinary viewers. Ironically, the start of the race for higher ratings marked the end of the golden days when one TV drama could receive remarkable audience ratings of 90 percent. While all TV production companies aim to maximize their audience, it was soon clear to the companies that their viewers did not comprise a monolithic whole. The economic reform launched in the late 1970s widened the rift between the urban and the rural, the east and the western hinterland, the upper class and the lower class, and between generations. It had become increasingly important for TV drama producers to target the right demographic, as advertisers reacted to the narrowing of their target audience. The need to identify a market niche for each consumer group was never so pressing.

As mentioned before, while the state has allowed commercial competition from time to time, it has maintained control over TV content through various means, such as policy, censorship, and production macromanagement. First, China's accession to the WTO did not bring overall content liberalization, as expected by many in the West. SARFT remains highly selective in admitting foreign media and incorporating foreign capital into content production and is quite adept at co-opting the influx of foreign capital.[54] Second, SARFT has developed a stock of censorship measures covering a wide range of matters to ensure compliance. Various administrative directives are applied on a case-by-case manner. For example, at the height of the anti-corruption drama craze in 2004, SARFT issued a ban on all features and documentaries with police and crime themes. In the same year, two notices were issued by SARFT to regulate TV drama adaptations of the Red Classics, with the implications discussed above.

The selective opening to commercialization, however, also ties the hands of the state in effecting changes in some areas. Despite the constant calls for more rural-themed production by the government, the area remains seriously underexplored, for the simple reason that dramas aimed at a rural audience do not appeal to middle-class urban audiences with purchasing power.[55] Production bases for genres with more limited advertising potential are under a degree of strain. With respect to rural themes, the state has so far failed to come up with a strategy to boost creativity in the industry. The business model dictates that quantity overrides quality when there are such low profit margins in TV drama production. Production units are more concerned about making a quick profit through appealing to a mass audience than pioneering new forms of television drama. Program cloning has also become rampant.[56]

## TV DRAMA AS A SOCIAL PRACTICE

TV drama reigns supreme as the preferred medium for advertising. Its appeal to advertisers and the saturation of the genre on various channels speaks eloquently of its popularity with Chinese viewers. TV researcher James Lull examined the urban household's fascination with a political soap opera, *New star*, broadcast in 1986, less than ten years after TV drama made its mass debut in China.[57] Every day in China, over 6,000 episodes of TV drama are broadcast to 100 million viewers. It is no exaggeration to say that the daily viewing of TV drama now constitutes an important part of everyday Chinese life. Yin and Yang[58] are right in arguing that TV drama in China is distinct from soap operas or situation comedies in the West. It does not merely provide fleeting entertainment; rather, it constitutes "nearly the only channel through which most Chinese read, enjoy and consume narratives."[59] In cities, lunch breaks are often dominated by discussions of characters or plot. In rural areas, watching village opera on special occasions or listening to storytellers in the market has largely given way to following a convoluted story line in the flickering light of the television screen.[60]

TV drama has not taken over as the "king of leisure" by a sheer stroke of luck. Technological, political, and social changes have enabled its rise. Its popularity also has roots in Chinese cultural traditions. Before the TV set became a household item, it was used as a cheap substitute for film technology. Chinese growing up in the 1970s to early 1980s still have memories of communal TV watching. At that time, only big state enterprises or work units could afford to purchase a TV set. It was put out in a public space, usually in the early evening, for their employees and their family members to watch together. Technological advances ensured that by 2005 urban households had an average of forty-two channels to choose from, while rural families could choose from thirty-three channels, with a national TV penetration rate of 98.2 percent.[61] Attempts by channels to gain market advantage often boil down to how successful their drama offerings are. This has led to the almost constant scheduling of TV dramas on Chinese TV, to the extent that TV drama has gradually merged with the fabric of everyday living. Its indispensable importance within the Chinese household is also buttressed by social and cultural factors, such as the family-oriented lifestyle of contemporary Chinese, the cultural and aesthetic affinity for linear, episodic narrative structures, and the limited repertoire of alternative social/cultural activities available to ordinary Chinese beyond home entertainment.[62]

## TV Drama's Inroad into Private Space

Politically, post-1989 cultural production has been marked by a shift away from socialist grand narratives. This is signified by the groundbreaking drama, *Yearnings*. Created shortly after the political debacle of June 4th, *Yearnings* deliberately departed from narratives that featured the state's intrusion into personal life. The individual's fate and feelings replace the life stories of role models embodying socialist morality or events illustrating the hard truth of class struggle. Even though the story was still political, its engagement with class, nation, and gender was allegorical. *Yearnings* pioneered a new form of narrative through which individuals construct their own identity.[63]

The significance of *Yearnings* is better understood in the historical context of public engagement with art and literature in Chinese society. The Party policy formed in the Yan'an years held that literature and art had instrumental functions, described metaphorically as either the "engineer of the soul," "cogs and screws" of the whole machine, or "weapons" on the literary "front."[64] Stringent Party policies and measures were in place to temper the cultural works that offered a model to civilian society. Heroic models were carefully formulated for the masses to emulate. Once a model work was created and perfected, often emerging out of a strenuous process, it was eagerly promulgated to the populace.[65] Millions of the Red Classics books, sometimes in the popularized form of comic strips, were printed for people to read. The private leisure of novel reading was made public through the organization of frequent group discussions where readers could share their reflections on the novels. Public life included the routinized group viewing of revolutionary movies and plays. Oral forms of storytelling were also utilized when people gathered together to discuss the bitter life in the old society and express their appreciation for their happy lives under socialism (*yi ku si tian*). During the Cultural Revolution period, the eight Model Plays (Yangbanxi) constituted the only cultural products available. Individuals were forced to conform to state ideology in part because there were no alternative cultural offerings provided. The heroes and the morals and ideologies expressed in *Yangbanxi* were drilled routinely into the public consciousness. Writer Chen Cun once described the experience of propaganda film viewing in the 1970s:

> I'm probably not wrong in saying that those films are of the most primitive kind. However, the problem is that they were once so popular that their box office was better than any movie blockbuster of today. At that time, there were hardly any urban residents who hadn't seen these films. They were no longer just a film, but the great victory of a certain political line and the liveliest lesson on class struggle.[66]

The cultural products created under the principle of socialist realism had the ultimate goal of interpellating individuals into "voluntary subjection to the socialist nation-state, in the name of which the CCP has legitimated its rule."[67] This was achieved by privileging the political and public over the private, domestic, and personal. The lofty meaning and purpose of everyday life was to embody the right class subjectivities prescribed by the Party, often embodied in the "typical characters" in model literary and artistic works. The socialist utopianism dictated that everyday life must be transcended and sublimated into a passionate experience, a higher-level existence for a political cause. This highly politicized life, although passionate and exciting, was at the expense of everyday life, as summarized by Tang Xiaobing: "With ideology or political identity as its sole content or depth, everyday life is organized, rendered meaningful and effectively reduced in form."[68] Each mundane moment in everyday living had to be imbued with political incentive and energy and linked with the collective, revolutionary cause of human emancipation.

The market economy has brought in a diverse means of cultural production, freed individuals from its total dependence and fixation on politics, and endowed people with more autonomy. The fashioning of a new post-Mao subject rests on overcoming the socialist past, setting free a human nature that was repressed and alienated by high moralism and over-politicization.[69] Public culture echoes as well as drives this reclamation of the private and personal from the public and political.

With literature and art withdrawing from their educational role by the 1990s, primetime television drama has since taken on the task of providing staple entertainment for Chinese. Although it never ceases to be a useful tool of indoctrination, it can never tout political idealism in the didactic way that the eight model operas once did. As the "cash cow" for nearly all the television stations, primetime's most important concern is ratings. Producers cannot afford to ignore the general dystopian mood with high official language and its content. It is no accident that *Yearnings*, a melodramatic tale about family, love, and individual destiny, enjoyed runaway success. Even though

*Yearnings* is still a deeply allegorical story of national identities, it signaled TV's turning away from "stories about workers *qua* workers" to "stories about domestic life and personal fates."[70] In spite of being criticized as corny and crude by some among the intellectual elite, *Yearnings'* popularity showed that popular tastes had shifted to the domestic, the personal, and the everyday.

From this moment onward, private lives were dramatized, and subject positions were developed and contested in a contingent manner within the course of daily life. The Chinese state broke away from the focus on class politics and adopted "a depoliticized neoliberal cultural politics of class and nation" in the reform era.[71] Television drama narratives are informed by this reorientation, reproducing the new configuration of social relations and in turn transforming social identities.

The evidence of this shift abounds. Ideologically, as a direct result of the state-sanctioned depoliticizing process, class-consciousness and class strug-gle have not only been phased out as primary concerns but also deliberately downplayed as viable themes. Instead, TV drama now promotes neoliberal characteristics, such as self-realization, self-development, entrepreneurial-ism, and Confucian virtues like filial piety. Workers, peasants, and soldiers are no longer the national icons, but have been replaced chiefly by the urban middle class.[72] Personal desires and individual fulfillment are the main thrusts, replacing concerns for collective interest and public welfare. Private, domestic space has become the preferred setting. Family, instead of any class-based community, is now taken as "a repository of affection, organic solidarity, and responsibility as cushion to ease the hardships of a market-oriented social transformation."[73]

Correspondingly, albeit in a very complex and contradictory way, today's TV viewers are not watching TV to take on the class-based subjectivities defined by the state or to learn how to become proper political subjects in the collective struggle for the emancipation of the proletariat. Instead, the alle-gorical modern citizen on the TV screen is often one who strives for excel-lence, wealth, personal pride, or even survival, through individual endeavors. This new subjectivity is cut from various characters of diverse social back-grounds including the urban underclass, and even revolutionary figures in drama series with historical or military themes, which I will discuss in detail in chapters 3, 4, 5, and 6.

## THE QUOTIDIAN NATURE OF TELEVISION AS A TECHNOLOGY

The turn from the public to the private is closely linked with the very nature of TV as a technology and the specific viewing context of TV in China. The nature of television as an everyday medium presents problems for political indoctrination. Visual media such as film, theater, and even posters were designed to transmit political messages in public space to faceless spectators who had the political competence to understand the political meaning of these visual texts.[74] These assumptions can no longer be made easily in the case of TV. No doubt TV is incorporated into ordinary people's lives. Program schedules and content play a major role in structuring their everyday lives. However, TV's domesticity determines that it is less reliable in structuring and establishing ideological positions.[75] Compared with the publicness of other media, TV has been incorporated into our domestic space, time, and practices, while public space has been suburbanized. This has implications for the consumption of TV drama. As a technology, TV now competes with the Internet, videos, karaoke machines, stereo systems, and cell phones, which are common in urban households. And even if individuals do switch on the TV, their viewing is constantly interrupted by family members, phone calls, commercials, housework, and so on. All in all, it is a very complex viewing context. If the viewer is not riveted by the story, they will most certainly change to another channel.

Rofel observes that this longing is closely tied with the domesticity of TV:

> The relocation of television viewing into the home (from official and public spaces where the few sets previously existed) turned that longing toward material and affective self-interest rather than toward the politics of the state.[76]

Even though TV is still heavily censored by the state, its domesticity allows the audience to see it as representative of a more open, global culture compared with the print media.[77]

The quotidian nature of the consumption of televisual narratives, as captured in the above quotation, means that the public cannot be force-fed any more. In the face of audience weariness, the grand narratives of the nation, such as the Red Classics, have undergone serious changes. For once, stories and characters that resemble ordinary people's own experience constitute the mainstay of TV drama and soaps. The conventions of grand narratives—the politically delicate setting, larger-than-life lead heroes, and Manichean model of good versus evil—have been carefully revised in an effort to address the discursive shift away from the statist representations and gain the largest viewing audience.

*Chapter 2*

# Hybridizing the Red Classics in Post-Mao China

## *The Production and Consumption Context*

As discussed in the Introduction, the canonization of the revolutionary, historic genre was a deeply ideological process, backed by the aesthetic hegemony of socialist realism and the dominant interest groups of the time. As the social-economic power structure changed and new alliances were formed, the status and content of the Red Classics were naturally challenged and transformed. In this chapter, I outline the broad context of the production and consumption of revolutionary culture in China in the reform era. This entails an outline of the negation of the Red Classics in the public arena immediately after the Cultural Revolution and their resurgence, albeit in a very different form, since the mid-1980s. I do so through three examples that illustrate and showcase the complex dynamics between the various forces at play. I want to demonstrate through these examples that the latest appropriation of the Red Classics is the result of both the political and commercial pressures and the new hybrid challenges, and breaks down the clear dichotomy between official culture and popular culture.

### HISTORICAL CONTEXT: NOSTALGIA AND THE RED CLASSICS

During the late 1990s, the term "Red Classics" (*hongse jingdian*) began to appear with regularity in the Chinese media. The concept comes from an earlier age, an invention of Chinese Communist Party (CCP) historiography. It generally refers to a body of politicized artistic productions created in line with the famous talks by Mao Zedong in 1942. In response to what he saw as the irrelevance of earlier artistic works, Mao Zedong gave his landmark speech at the Symposium of Literary and Art Circles held in Yan'an, calling for literary and art workers to engage in creative work for the common people; this set the tone of cultural policy for the whole Mao era from the 1940s to the 1970s.[1] The post-1949 Chinese art works produced in accordance with the policy were characterized by overt politicization, and mainly focused on the theme of class and class struggle and the efforts and sacrifices made by the peasants, factory workers, and soldiers for the socialist cause. The result is a large number of literary, musical, and cinematic texts that provide a series of cultural imaginaries in keeping with the needs, ideals, and directives of the CCP.

The Red Classics genre has had an enormous influence on the Chinese national psyche. Most of the Red Classics works were literary productions. From the 1950s to the 1970s, when reading featured as the major activity in people's cultural life, the Red Classics provided the main leisure and entertainment. A huge number of books were published and consumed by the populace. For example, *The Red Crag* sold five million copies within a year or so after it was published in 1961, creating a publication record in the novel category.[2] After the Cultural Revolution, there was another surge of interest in the book, and it was reprinted and sold another three million copies.

The transformation of the Red Classics runs in tandem with the radical changes in the configuration of political, economic, and cultural capital in Chinese society. Soon after the Cultural Revolution, the principles of Maoism—class struggle and continuous revolution—lost their appeal with the public. The factional struggles and political persecutions had led many to view the excesses of the past decade as highly destructive, and there emerged a strong demand for a "total negation" of the policies and practices of the era. China has since been through a depoliticizing process that repudiated Mao's ideology.[3] The Red Classics, as a core component of the revolutionary culture, were mostly dismissed as ossified, anti-human propaganda works with little aesthetic or artistic value.

By the mid-1980s, the previously outmoded socialist icons started to come back again. Several factors contributed to this renewed interest in revolutionary culture. Since the late 1970s, the CCP had largely abandoned Mao's pursuit of revolutionary hegemony as an alternative modernity and adopted economic development as its main goal for modernization. The pragmatic approach of developmentalism left an ideological vacuum. The old ideological system that had stressed revolutionary consciousness and class struggle along with its manifestation in the symbolic order was deemed obsolete, but there were not many effective alternatives except vacuous materialism and hedonism. While the first few years of reform witnessed a surge of optimism in modernization projects, a series of setbacks soon reset the mood. By the late 1980s, the widespread belief in what economic reform could deliver was soon replaced with anger and

disillusionment in the face of growing social disparity, corruption, and rising living costs.[4] A public dissatisfied with harsh economic competition in
society looked back to the past with a sense of nostalgia and a longing for
strong leadership, idealism, and egalitarianism, all principles eulogized in
the Red Classics.

Second, revolutionary culture as a lived reality still had significant appeal
in ordinary people's lives, especially those who grew up during the socialist
era. This appeal often comes from an emotional attachment to revolutionary
culture or a longing for its collective form.[5] Scholars have begun to examine
the affective and emotional side of Maoist discourse[6] and have argued from
different angles that revolutionary public culture has helped to shape "the
structure of feeling"[7] for the generations of Chinese growing up from the
1950s to the 1970s. While the entertainment industry started to inundate the
general public with sensational and sentimental private narratives, for the
middle to old aged and people of low socioeconomic status, the Red Classics
were created with sincere emotions and expressed lofty moral ideas. As Liu
Kang summarizes: "The nostalgic indulgence and sentimentalism of the audience and popular media are indicative of a deep-seated popular sentiment for
the revolutionary past, however fictional and imaginary, accompanied by an
equally sentimental sense of loss of sincerity and innocence."[8]

Furthermore, with global capitalism influencing all aspects of Chinese
society, the need to look for local cultural resources and unique Chinese
experiences has gained urgency. In this sense, the Red Classics have been
recognized as a national cultural heritage as well as a popular commodity to
be exploited for commercial gain. The reproduction of the Red Classics was
a conscious act on the part of the market to cash in on audience nostalgia for
a collective cultural memory.[9]

Since the mid-1980s, revolutionary texts, signs, and objects shunned in
the 1970s have gradually regained popularity. The nostalgia peaked in a
"Mao Zedong fever" (*Mao Zedong re*), in which this godlike "savior" was
reimagined, repackaged, and narrated as a humanistic figure in numerous
popular novels, TV dramas, and film.[10] Revolutionary-themed blockbusters
and TV dramas were produced, backed by huge government investment;
dozens of biographies, as well as numerous audio and video productions,
enjoyed phenomenal success. In 1993, for instance, the government initiated
a series of large-scale events to commemorate the centenary birthday of Mao.
The Pacific Video and Audio Publishing Company, seeing the opportunity
to cash in on these events, came up with the idea to publish a cassette with
thirty revolutionary songs sung by popular singers with modern electronic
accompaniment. With a next-to-nothing production budget, the cassette sold
7.2 million copies. Many families, all by now equipped with hi-fi CD players,
bought cassette players just to listen to this tape. Since then, revolutionary

songs have been constantly reappropriated and have now formed a genre of pop songs known as Red Songs, or *hong ge*.

The sentiment behind the Mao fever articulates ordinary people's desire for moral leadership and authority in the face of the breakdown of socialist ideologies and moral values. However, one cannot overlook the state's role in this collective rewriting of Mao. Sensing an opportunity to reinstate its legitimacy, the government joined hands with the market in turning Mao, a godlike figure, into an ordinary man. As Dai Jinhua astutely pointed out, the Mao fever in the 1990s "constituted a successful ideological operation as well as an act to consume ideology."[11]

## CRITIQUING THE RED CLASSICS: THE 1980S

Following Wang Ban's[12] insightful analysis of practices of remembering socialist history in China, one can discern two phases—the 1980s and the 1990s—in the engagement of the revolutionary past. According to Wang, in the 1980s, memories of the utopian revolutionary period had a critical sense of history and recognized the relevance of the revolutionary past in the reality of the reform era. The socialist past was often invoked in criticisms of the dystopian 1980s, awash in the world of materialism, corruption, alienation, loss of community, and moral decadence. Consequently, the resurgence of socialist cultural symbols was not without controversy. One example is the fierce debate surrounding the restaging of *Yangbanxi* after it was banned from the public by the CCP after the Cultural Revolution. Because of its highly politicized content and close association with Jiang Qing, Mao's discredited wife and major political player during the era, *Yangbanxi* was taken as a symbol of earlier political traumas. As a result, any mention of the art form was politically taboo in the early reform days. "It makes me tingle with fear every time I hear the word *Yangbanxi*," Ba Jin, the famous writer who was tortured during the political purges of the Cultural Revolution, said after he heard of the reappearance of *Yangbanxi*.[13] His remark was widely echoed across society. The incident is indicative of the sensitive nature of the appropriation of the Red Classics genre in the 1980s.

A well-publicized example of the critical appropriation of revolutionary canonical works is China's rock father Cui Jian's rendition of *The Southern Muddy Bay* [*Nanniwan*]. Nanniwan is a desolate area near the former communist headquarters, Yan'an. In 1942, the 359th brigade of the Eighth Route Army was deployed to open up virgin land to help the revolutionary base area become self-sufficient. It was hailed as a great undertaking in communist history, and a song was commissioned in the traditional folk melody of northern Shaanxi in 1943. When Cui Jian was invited to perform for the annual official

TV gala in 1987, he sang the song in a way that was distinctively different from the celebratory tone of the original version. Not only did he leave out the stanza that hails the achievement of the brigade, but he also used a number of musical devices to make it sound sad, as if lamenting the changes made to Nanniwan by the Communist army.[14] The performance offended Wang Zhen, commander of the 359th brigade, and cost Cui Jian his job. However, Cui Jian made a decision to sing the song in nearly every important gig after the ban was imposed. Cui's *Nanniwan* has since become a symbol of defiance. The incident provides an example of how the appropriation of revolutionary canonical works could open up space for subversion of the official historiography in the 1980s. It also showcases how the meaning of place is contested in the postrevolutionary age.

In the first phase of the revival of revolutionary culture, there was a genuine analysis of how the socialist utopian project led to the impoverishment of everyday experience. The public, especially intellectuals, came to realize that the authoritarian political culture had deprived them of pleasure, emotions, and desires.[15] Cultural elites were engaged in heated debates on alienation, on humanism in Marx's earlier writings, and on the restoration of individual subjectivity.[16] In the realm of literature and art, the Maoist policies were seen as limiting creative expression by imposing narrowly defined aesthetic standards. The collective, uniform identity based on class collapsed in ruin, "with no reliable system of ideology to sustain a liveable existence and identity."[17] The society experienced a sense of "spiritual crisis."

## COMMERCIALIZING THE RED CLASSICS: THE 1990S

By the early 1990s, China underwent a series of further transformations. After the political upheaval in June 1989, the leftists blamed the reform policy for loosening up ideological control. Nevertheless, Deng Xiaoping quickly reaffirmed the CCP's determination to further China's reform and marketization. On an inspection tour of south China in 1992, Deng made a speech in which he criticized the conservatives for quibbling over political name-branding and called for the reformists to be "a bit bolder" and to move forward "a bit quicker." After that, the government seemed to fully embrace capitalism in everything but name. In line with Deng's policy of "no argument over ideology," the CCP began to place all its emphasis on economic development. This led to a cultural weariness about politics and ideology, and cultural formations quickly shifted ground.

The criticisms of Maoist culture had gone by now. Private experience and sensual pleasure were not taboo, but rather routine subjects. The catch phrase was, "Follow your feeling" (*genzhe ganjue zou*), as one of the most popular songs of the time preached. After the calls for democracy, anti-corruption, and political reform were crushed in the Tiananmen Square repression of June 4, 1989, politics was shunned as a subject in everyday life. Rofel observes that post-Mao culture is characterized by two interlinking processes: the purging of politics seen as repressing human nature; and the positive embracing of people's sexual, material, and affective self-interest, which help foster a cosmopolitan humanity.[18] The 1990s witnessed an intensification of the second process. By that time, China's cultural scene was no longer dominated by state-funded propaganda and entertainment promoting the Party's primacy in history and political doctrine. A consumer revolution had engulfed China, transforming urban life and marginalized writers and artists who searched for "pure literature and art."[19] There was a sense of loss among the intelligentsia in the early 1990s, as they were no longer entrusted with the mandate of social responsibility, idealism, and conscience. High cultural forms such as literature no longer shouldered the mission of "savior" of society. With dwindling government funding for serious literature and art, the intellectuals voiced their concern over total commercialization. In 1993, a public discussion on the "loss of humanistic spirit" was initiated by a group of Shanghai-based intellectuals. The debate lasted for two years, but by the end of the mid-1990s, most writers, artists, and intellectuals were forced the live with the commercialized reality and to give up their posturing as the guardians of social conscience, moral ideals, and aesthetic standards. Many eagerly joined in the battle to gain a foothold in the burgeoning popular art market.

In the meantime, the cultural industry gradually adopted the model of transnational production, marketing, and consumption.[20] Imports from Hong Kong, Taiwan, Japan, and the West swamped the cultural market. Popular culture encroached into official culture and transformed it into a kind of "politico-tainment."[21] Just as often, the Party repackaged its agenda in a glitzy, consumer-friendly form to better appeal to the masses, now more commonly known as customers. The boundary between official culture and nonofficial culture had been greatly eroded.

In the 1990s, the appropriation of revolutionary culture accelerated and became more acceptable. Following the Mao Zedong fever, an interest in "red" culture became a fad. The Red Classics, being an important component of the propaganda tools used to engineer socialist citizens' consciousness, were the target for commercial exploitation. The Party saw this populist take on socialist icons as an opportunity to reinforce political pedagogy and to reiterate its historical legitimacy, which had become more and more sidelined in a consumer society. For the commercial sectors, the revival of revolutionary culture offered a market opportunity. In the mid-to-late 1990s, the restaging of the ballet versions of *The White-haired Girl*, *The Red Detachment of Women* and the musical version of *The Long March Song Cycle* [*Changzheng zuge*] were sensational successes, attracting large audiences.[22] Sensing that it would please both the authorities and the market, in 1997, People's Literature Press re-published a number of revolutionary novels from the 1950s and 1960s under the title, "The Red Classics Series." This seemed to fan the "red craze" even further. The name Red Classics became more widely used in both official and commercial discourse.

It is not only the profit-driven commercial production units that were engaged in tapping into the revolutionary culture. Commercially oriented practices such as global advertising techniques and even elements of avant-garde art had been coopted to transform the style of the CCP's ideological promotion. Barmé has referred to this updated form of propaganda as "corporate communism."[23] Contrary to the popular belief that commodification of the socialist sign system would lead to the weakening or diversification of Party control, he argues that repackaging Party culture to compete in the marketplace has actually strengthened the Party's domination. Barmé backs up his claim with several astutely made observations. First, the Party's adoption of rhetorical and representational devices from popular culture, language, and images desensitizes the public to the power structure behind the propaganda. Second, the Party maintains strict control over the mass media and thus is able to patrol the boundaries of the commercial appropriation of its sign system to a large extent. Third, media workers growing up in the post-Mao era are well versed in both the Party culture and unofficial culture. Through their efforts, the Party's view of history, nationhood, and identity has been turned into a pool of signs that Party propagandists can draw on. Fourth, the state-funded arts and propaganda industry and the Chinese avant-garde have a symbiotic existence, each relying on the other for ideas and representational styles. The end product is commodified avant-garde art packaged in political cynicism aiming at the international market and propaganda that looks innovative and "modern."[24]

Scholars have described the revival of revolutionary culture in the second stage as a postmodern or late revolutionary phenomenon.[25] The coexistence of the precapitalist, the capitalist, and the postsocialist economic, political, and social conditions, however, makes it hard for any attempt at labeling. Tao states that, on the one hand, revolutionary culture in this period was not intended for campaign-style ideological mobilization or the promotion of socialist asceticism; on the other hand, this particular version of Party culture could not lead to critical subversion of the Party-sanctioned public truths, because the state system and the form of government have remained unchanged. The revival is the result of marketization, the secularization of social life, and the rise of the entertainment and cultural industries working in tandem. The revived revolutionary culture relies on rewriting and appropriation, while incorporating motifs, styles, icons, techniques, and practices from the thriving commercial culture. Therefore, the end product is "commercially enhanced and manufactured, not merely state-directed," as Barmé argues.[26]

The official promotion of revolutionary culture has continued since 1989, while at the same time appropriation of "red culture" in commercial spaces has been commonplace. These appropriations often resemble postmodern culture in that the old socialist icons are taken out of context and juxtaposed. Wedding companies provide ceremonies in the Cultural Revolution style, with couples dressing up in army soldier uniforms, performing the loyalty dance and bowing to the picture of Mao Zedong. These were daily political rituals during the heyday of the Cultural Revolution. Meanwhile, "red tours" have become a fashionable tourist trend. Guang'an, a small town in Sichuan Province where the late president Deng Xiaoping was born, created a travel route called "Deng Xiaoping Hometown Tour." The travel route drew 5.4 million travelers and earned a whopping 1.7 billion yuan ($US 263 million) in 2004. Although a place with nearly nothing else of interest except Deng's birthplace, Guang'an has become one of the three most toured sites in Sichuan, a province famous for its many beautiful scenic spots and historical sites.[27] Pilgrimage to revolutionary sites was a tradition in the Maoist era. However, in the case of "red tours," it is worth mentioning that many of these tours are organized and sponsored by CCP institutions at the local level, in order, for example, to pass on the revolutionary legacy to Youth League members or commemorate the founding of the Party. In such instances, even though the tourist is largely motivated by a free trip, the authorities are happy to foot the bill, as the act of participating in these events still validates the Party's existence, even just at a symbolic level. It is quite hard to say who is taking whom for a ride. The ambiguous aim of the revolutionary tours is very indicative of the compromise each party is pushed to make in the appropriation of the "red."

The popularity of the "red" element is not confined to the street. On the screen, television advertisements, as the best embodiment of commercial culture, frequently evoke powerful red symbols to sell products. In recent two decades, a great number of Red Classics novels, films, and plays have been adapted into television drama series. The first adaptation, *The Making of a Hero*, was quite well received. The popularity of *The Making of a Hero* signaled the beginning of the "adaptation craze." TV producers quickly jumped onto the Red Classics bandwagon. A niche market had quickly become the primary focus of many aspiring investors. Revolutionary and heroic stories were transformed into products for consumers. From 2002 to 2004, more than forty TV drama series with a total of 850 parts were produced. Nearly every single popular work in the genre now has a television version. Most of these reproductions were instant commercial successes, attracting a reasonably large audience, with a few achieving a viewing rate of about 10 percent.[28]

The reinvention of the Red Classics bears the marks of postmodernity—the flattening of historical depth and the decontextualization and displacement of the original images. However, as many scholars have reminded us, postmodernity exists in China in a different way than in the Western context.[29] On the one hand, modernity is still an unachieved project in China, and the intellectual elites are still calling for the renewal of the Enlightenment mission of the May 4th movement, calling for modernization and cultural criticism and cultural renaissance. On the other hand, socialist revolution as a large-scale modernity project has left a legacy that is more than just residual. Its appeal and relevance to the Chinese public, especially the middle-aged and low-income population, cannot be denied.[30] In recent years, the socialist legacy on the postsocialist cultural trend in the globalized capitalist economy became a hotly debated topic with the rise of the New Left.[31] This partly explains the success of several television drama adaptations of the Red Classics such as *The Red Crag* and the TV soap, *Days of Burning Passion*. It is also why rewriting the genre in powerful narrative forms like TV generates much anxiety, fear, hope, criticism, praise, and many mixed feelings among various sectors of Chinese society. It is oversimplistic to view the reinvention as political pop[32] (*zhengzhi bopu*) and to interpret the phenomenon as the complete triumph of global capitalism or the retreat of a bygone revolutionary discourse in the face of commercialization. The process whereby politics makes room for the market is replete with tensions and contradictions. The reinvention of the Red Classics has become a perfect example of the marriage of free capital and state power, and a focal point for ideological struggles among various interest groups. State ideology and the market coincide, contest, compromise, and intertwine, producing a complex cultural scene. The real issue is "to what ideological end such kinds of public sentiment serve to reinforce or to undermine and to what extent the revolutionary nostalgia is manipulated by different power blocs and interest groups."[33]

## THE SPECTRUM OF GRAY: THE CULTURAL POLITICS IN APPROPRIATING RED CULTURE

In the following section, I want to explore how red culture is creatively reinvented through media for official, elite, and popular amusement. Furthermore, I seek to demonstrate how various forces have come into play in the appropriation of red culture. The re-emergence of red culture is driven by a complex combination of factors, including the commercial need to tap into a rich cultural resource, the nostalgic desire to look into the past for a lost utopia, and the Communist Party's attempt to develop its ideology in a world awash with materialism. In detailing the process of reinventing the red, I want to demonstrate that the evocation of a revolutionary past entails highly complex articulations, cultural negotiations, and contention over meanings, beliefs, and values. These diverse cultural configurations and media appropriations defy the simple bifurcation of "red" versus "black" and come into view as a kind of "gray"[34] with many subtle shades, which I call the spectrum of gray.

The three events that I describe here provide us with a window into the issues involved in reinventing revolutionary culture.

## The First Red Classics Adaptation: The Making of a Hero

Revolutionary-themed TV drama series made up a high percentage of the total drama productions from the 1980s to the 1990s. However, the first TV reinvention of the original Red Classics genre is generally considered to be *The Making of a Hero*, because it was a direct adaptation of the literary, film, and theatrical works of the Red Classics genre.

*The Making of a Hero* provides an interesting case to examine in at least three respects. First, its ratings success inspired other TV production units to tap into the Red Classics for subject materials, thus setting the trend for the TV reproduction of the genre. When CCTV broadcast it in 1999, it scooped a sizable audience, with a peak viewing rate of about 12 percent.[35] Second, the airing of *The Making of a Hero* set off heated public debate on the ideological meaning and values of revolutionary culture in commercialized China. This debate, facilitated by the news media, ran throughout the course of the production over the next few years. Third, the process of its creation and the rendering of the text embody the complicated contradictions and co-optations between the state, the public, the domestic entertainment industries, and transnational corporations, a common feature characterizing productions of this genre in the years following. Given the significance of *The Making of a Hero* as an example of the dramatic adaptation of the Red Classics, it is worthwhile to take a close look at how the project was developed and the complexity of its production and representation.

The project to remake *The Making of a Hero* provides a good example of how a commercial venture to seek profit and social impact was co-opted by the state.[36] In early 1998, Vanke Film and Television[37] proposed a television drama to commemorate the fiftieth anniversary of the founding of the People's Republic and celebrate the new millennium. In choosing the topic, the investors put forward several criteria: they wanted to have a large-scale project of high artistic standard worthy of Vanke's status.[38] After much deliberation, the producer chose to adapt a novel penned by Nicholas Ostravski in 1929. *The Making of a Hero* was an autobiographical account of a legendary young communist, Pavel Korchagin, from his childhood in a working-class family to his role in the Russian Civil War (1918–1920) and in the subsequent reconstruction of the Soviet Union after the World War I. Even though he suffered from rheumatism and typhoid fever and became blind and bedridden later in his life, he managed to write his life story through dictation.

Choosing to develop this project satisfied several demands. First of all, as a successful enterprise in Shenzhen, the forefront of economic reform, Vanke needed the cultural capital to make it a brand name. This meant mining thematic material that was not only commercially viable but also socially respectable. In this regard, a well-scrubbed mainstream project dedicated to a significant social and political event like the anniversary of the nation was safer than a purely commercial, frivolously themed TV soap or controversial, "downbeat" social drama.[39]

Perhaps more importantly, Vanke as a business expected economic returns for its investment. Although the decision to make a TV drama was an avowedly commercial act, many of the producer's considerations reflected a desire for profit. Before shooting started, director Zheng Kainan and her crew were convinced that there was a market niche for *The Making of a Hero*, as the book remained a bestseller in the PRC over several decades.[40] It remained on the list of books recommended to youth by government ideological organizations after the Cultural Revolution. Furthermore, the targeted audience was people who had grown up with the influence of Soviet culture in the 1950s and 1960s.

Another reason behind the decision to adapt *The Making of a Hero* was Zheng's personal opinion that China was ready for a TV drama with an all-foreign cast. Zheng was conscious of the fact that it had been common practice for foreign companies to finance TV or film production with a Chinese cast for cheaper labor. Now backed by the capital accumulated through economic reform, Vanke had the capacity to do the reverse.[41] The idea was trumpeted across the media as a selling point, providing an example of how national sentiments are packaged for the market.

The potential for commercial benefit and social impact with *The Making of a Hero* was not missed by the state. According to Yu Hongmei, who conducted extensive research on the production process, it was the Shenzhen Municipal Publicity Department (SMPD) that gave the project a final push when Vanke was still weighing the pros and cons of taking up such a subject matter.[42] The department fully embraced the concept and even decided to cosponsor the shooting. In February 1999, SMPD reported to its superior, the Central Publicity Department (CPD), about the project. Officials from CPD gave detailed instructions on the appropriate focus of the drama and its rendering. The arrival of the state propaganda agency on the production scene contributed a measure of official flavor to the project. This official affiliation was further strengthened when CCTV joined in later on. Shortly after shooting started in Ukraine, the crew realized that additional funding was needed.

On the advice of SMPD, Zheng Kainan approached CCTV to negotiate a deal. As a result, CCTV and its affiliate, China International Television Company (CITC), became investors in the project. Under the new arrangement, Vanke withdrew from its role as producer and became the production undertaker.[43]

One thing worth pointing out is that CCTV's claim on ownership was not only based on the drama's potential social impact but also on its potential to reap economic benefits. In an interview with *Beijing Youth Gazette*, CCTV was confident about getting back its investment through primetime commercial tie-ins with the show. As the distributor, CITC expected to gain through VCD merchandising and selling reruns to provincial and local TV stations.[44] Thus, the change in ownership of *The Making of a Hero* should not be viewed as the hijacking of an independent, commercial production by a state agency and mainstream television for propaganda purposes. Rather, it should be viewed primarily as an attempt to achieve competitive advantage in the primetime marketplace.

In keeping with the prevailing distaste for ideological indoctrination, the final product made two major changes to the original novel. First, it discarded the original portrayal of Pavel Korchagin as a quintessentially positive hero, instead depicting him as an ordinary person who struggled hard against adversity. Second, the adaptation to a large degree "purged" the irreconcilable class rift between Pavel and his first love, Tonya Tumanova. The relationship was impossible in the novel because Pavel was a proletarian soldier, while Tonya was an untransformed bourgeois. Since the 1990s, class and class struggle were abandoned or shunned as a mainstream ideological discourse in favor of consumerist values in popular representation. The romance between the hero and heroine in this TV adaptation was thus rewritten according to the mainstream ideology to fall nicely within the traditional Hollywood formula of immortal love surpassing class and family background.[45]

An important observation can be made based on the account above. The production of *The Making of a Hero* was neither completely propaganda-driven nor completely market-oriented. While China's complicated cultural production environment dictates that there can be many noncommercial considerations in the production of TV dramas, the concern over ratings and thus advertising revenue is a salient factor even in bona fide state TV drama production units like CCTV.

*The Making of a Hero* embodies in many ways the state and market dynamics in the reproduction of the Red Classics. Private production units such as Vanke now constitute the mainstay of TV drama capacity. While private players such as Vanke may be proud of their newly achieved prowess, the state still pulls the strings in many respects. As discussed above, Vanke's choice of subject took into account the state's nominal support for "main melody" dramas.[46] Riding on the fanfare of an important official event, the project allowed Vanke to earn the social status it needed, and the subject matter made it easier to pass censorship. Vanke also intended to feed off the institutionalization of state culture. The state project of promoting the Red Classics over the decades could translate into viewers' interest, therefore ratings. CCTV's "hijacking" of the project provides a footnote on how the state broadcaster "serves as a secondary center of power in shaping private television drama production and distribution."[47] As the national broadcaster, CCTV's scheduling power dictates the terms and conditions of entry for private drama producers. For Vanke, co-production with CCTV guarantees the much-coveted primetime drama spot on the national broadcaster. For CCTV, the collaboration makes it possible to absorb private capital and production techniques in producing a drama series that might resonate with popular taste and public sensibility.

## From the Party's March to My March: The Transformation of the Spirit and Format of the Long March

The year 2006 marked the seventieth anniversary of the Long March, the communist's massive military retreat from Jiangxi Province to the northwest from 1934 to 1935. The journey, which traversed some 13,500 kilometers and lasted 370 days, represents a significant episode in the history of the Communist Party. After the Long March, Mao Zedong established his status as Party leader over the decades to come. To commemorate the event, CCTV organized a remarching of the Long March and shortly after ran a weekly fifty-two-part reality show documenting the new march on its news channel.

*My Long March* was promoted as the most important program in CCTV's News Department in 2006. A high-profile propaganda initiative, its official mission was to reinforce Party symbolism. However, in the age of television, when viewers can easily "kill" the image with a flick of the fingers, any ideological hard sell would prove to be self-defeating. Even if CCTV is a monopoly enjoying state financial support, it still must generate its primary financial income. Faced with the increasing pressure to bring in funding and sponsorship and to remain relevant in the cultural market, it has to join the battle for ratings as the sector becomes commercialized.

In the case of *My Long March*, the hunt for money was even more crucial. The program was the brainchild of Cui Yongyuan, a CCTV talk show host who enjoys fame in China similar to that of Oprah Winfrey in the United States. As proposed by Cui, and as the trial of a new production system, the program was going to be made in "commission" format (*zhi bo fen li*), which meant that the production of the program had to seek its own funds, while CCTV was only committed to the broadcasting rights. On top of the 30 million yuan (USD$4.4 million) production budget, the producer of the program also aimed to raise 16 million yuan (USD$2.3 million) to set up twenty-five hospitals and fifty primary schools along the route of the Long March. Producer Cui was well aware of the implications of this approach for the ratings of the program. In an interview with the *New Beijing Gazette*, Cui remarked, "If the program turns out to be crappy, then nobody would bother to invest money into it. Without funds, the quality of the program will slip further. Later on, you cannot stay in the trade."[48]

With Cui's reputation, and in conjunction with the status of CCTV's news channel and the social significance of the event, the crew encountered very few problems attracting the initial funds and financial sponsorship. However, the producers knew that a documentary done in the old buttoned-up style and preaching didactic Party lines would not appeal to the increasingly sophisticated needs of the consumers. In fact, *My Long March* is anything but crude Party propaganda. It is quite hard to categorize it into any prepackaged television format. In a way, this reality show is a strange variant of *Survivor*, with staid Party ideological elements interspersed here and there, and at times, it reminds people of the reality show, *Big Brother*. *My Long March*'s format innovation was also a result of the changes in the TV industry. Commercialization, structural changes, and technological advancement in the TV industry in the 1990s led to a proliferation of television stations and channels at different administrative levels. With multiple underfunded, small-scale television stations competing head-to-head with each other, TV producers turned to genre imitation and, later, format appropriation for a quick, low-cost fix.[49] Reality shows and lifestyle TV programs play a central role in TV stations' efforts to build their brand and viewership. For example, in 2005, Hunan satellite launched *Super Girl*, a talent show fashioned after the format of *American Idol*. This quickly became the most-watched TV show in China, bringing in huge financial gain and spawning a number of copycat spin-offs across the country. Driven by the ratings race, even CCTV was forced to create its own reality shows.

*My Long March* is organized around the concept of humanism instead of any overt political message. This is clearly evident in the mission statement of the program:

> The "Long March spirit" has become symbolic of the positive and enterprising spirit for individuals and even the Chinese nationality. Its significance has surpassed its time. Re-marching the route is not only a way to challenge personal limitations, but also a way to relive the unique historical event in an authentic way, enabling us to experience vividly the difficult yet great revolutionary course of our older generation.[50]

From this statement, one can see that the significance of the Long March is translated into a modernist/Enlightenment discourse. It is now valued from very different angles: an individual enterprising spirit, self-fulfillment, the challenging of physical and psychological limits, human experience, and achievement. None of these notions serves the official claim that "it is a response to the call of the central government to better pass on and spread the red culture."[51]

Starting from these concepts, the program is organized around an individual who remarches the route, interviewing old Long March soldiers and observing the changes in the regions along the route, while at the same time experiencing first-hand the hardships and heroism of the March. This individual follows ordinary people's living conditions and life experiences, the local customs, folk culture, local livelihoods, and social development. The purpose of the remarch is to reflect history, but it is also future-oriented. Except for the sporadic moments when the team members of the new march paid homage to the Red Army soldiers who died on the route, there is not much recounting of the experience of the previous Long March. The forty-five-minute program is divided into two parts. In the first twenty-five minutes, the audience- sees how the team members were challenged physically and psychologically by marching, and the interpersonal dynamics between the twenty-two team members selected from different socioeconomic and educational background in different age groups. In the second half, it focuses on activities for the public good. Here, the struggle between the Kuomintang and the Communists, which was essentially ideological and class-based, is supplanted by philanthropic activities, another example of the grafting of humanist discourse onto revolutionary themes.

*My Long March* transgresses the boundaries of the official revolutionary genre in at least three areas. First, the organization of the production incorporated market mechanisms, such as the commission strategy. Even though CCTV had largely turned into an advertising-financed system by then, it was still a remarkable experiment for the news channel to loosen its guard against commercial interests, especially when the program deals with the revolutionary legacy. To allow for maximum editorial control over the content, the government usually funds programs made to commemorate a revolutionary event with great symbolic impact. Second, the content of the show is a far cry from the usual reiteration of the spirit and significance of the Long March. The TV producers had tried to connect two diametrically opposed discourses, that of the Maoist revolutionary spirit and that of neoliberal individualism and humanity. In this grafting process, the ideas of collectivism, class struggle, and indomitable revolutionary spirit were largely reconceptualized as teamwork, perseverance in pursuing one's goal, the willingness to challenge oneself, and physical and psychological prowess, all of which are qualities necessary for survival in competitive capitalist society. Third, the format of the program is participatory and interactive. Instead of the documentary format which was usually adopted for such occasions, the reality show has a more informal, accessible presentation style. The spontaneity of the format has a less authoritative tone and the program's perspective on the contemporary relevance of the Long March may have provided some sanctuary from stringent censorship. It seems to represent a more populist attempt by CCTV to become more attuned to popular interests and tastes.

## Spoofing the Red Classics: When Revolutionaries Meet Netizens

Of all the tampering with red culture, the most controversial approach involves spoofing (*e'gao*) revolutionary figures on the Internet. Spoofing is a new cyber language, employed to deconstruct or parody certain serious discourses for the sake of popular entertainment. Growing in popularity in China, spoofing often takes big-budget films as its main target, but most notably the socialist revolutionary icons. As spoofing is a new and still evolving phenomenon, scholars are still grappling with its cultural meaning and significance. Researchers tend to agree that spoofing on the Internet represents a carnivalesque-style cultural form that transgresses the boundaries of official norms and values and provide catharsis for the emotions repressed by political or social control.[52] However, it is still debatable if this represents a subversive act against official ideology and how effective these activities are. So far, most of the spoofing practices are individual activities without a common agenda or coherent strategy,[53] and the access to new media that enables its production and distribution remains limited to only a few.[54] The spoofing of revolutionary culture online is often a product of the negotiations between the state's regulatory efforts, the individuals' subversive, commercial or playful impulses, and the openness of the net.

One of the most famous spoofs is a short video clip entitled *Shining Star Hero Pan Dongzi Enters Singing Competition.*[55] *The Shining Star* is a film made in 1974 during the Cultural Revolution. It tells the adventures of the ten-year-old son of the squad leader of the Red Army in Willow Brook during the Second Revolutionary Civil War (1927–1937). Both the mother and grandfather of Pan Dongzi, the little hero, are killed by the rich and the Kuomintang army. Dongzi's father retreats with the Red Army to another area. With his determination to obtain revenge and achieve wisdom, Dongzi manages to create a great deal of trouble for the Kuomintang army and eventually kills his personal enemy, the local tyrant Hu Hansan. In the video clip created by someone with the pseudonym *Hu Daoge* (literally "messing around"), Pan Dongzi becomes a daydreamer who yearns to become a super star and earn big bucks. His father is the property shark Pan Shiyi, and all his mother wants is to get into the show *Super 6 + 1,* as she secretly nurtures a crush on the program host.[56] The class struggle between Pan Dongzi and the tyrant Hu Hansan is reduced to just a vulgar exchange between the competitors and the judges of the song competition.

Pan Dongzi is one of the many revolutionary figures parodied on the Internet. Another one is the army soldier Lei Feng, the soldier who Chairman Mao asked the whole country to emulate after Lei died from an accident in the 1950s. In the next few decades, Lei Feng became a mythical figure, the embodiment of the communist values of self-sacrifice, austerity, asceticism, and the abstract icon of goodness. In 2006, a photo of a girl was published online and news spread fast that Lei Feng actually had a first love.[57] Later on, the girl was identified and interviewed. She denied any relationship with Lei Feng except comradeship. However, the private life of a saint was too sensational to be missed by those drawn to controversy. Deng Jianguo, a filmmaker famous for causing sensations among the public, decided to do a thirty-minute online film entitled *The Girl of Lei Feng's First Love*.[58] The project came to a halt when SARFT intervened.

Spoofs such as the two mentioned above have met with very diverse responses. The official rhetoric is that these historical figures are "sacred," as they represent the collective memory and spiritual wealth commonly owned by the public. Thus, spoofing is "disrespectful" to the historical "truth" and the sacred feelings people hold for the heroes in the original works. As Party ideology has weakened, regulation and control is often legitimized in terms of anti-pornography campaigns or copyright protection, a legal governance discourse favored by neoliberalism. Zhao Yuezhi has defined these practices as "new features in the party-state power".[59] For example, in April 2006, several campaigns held in the name of protecting minors from pornography successfully eradicated some subversive materials from the Internet and garnered public support.[60] Similarly, Hu Ge, the creator of *The Bloody Case over a Steamed Bun*, an Internet spoof on director Chen Kaige's blockbuster film *The Promise* [*Wu ji*], was taken to court over the infringement of copyright.[61]

Public debates are vigorous with regard to taboos or their abstinence in the treatment of the past and public morality in general. Cultural elites largely take a negative stance toward the spoofing of revolutionary culture, condemning the practice for blurring the boundary between good and evil. They also condemn the spoofs for the deconstruction of heroic images and the ideals of socialism and for showing disrespect to the authors of the original works, as well as their infringing of copyright.[62] In several cases, relatives of the revolutionaries or the authors of the original works threatened litigation. When CCTV aired the spoof of Pan Dongzi as a promotion piece at a party held for journalists covering the twelfth CCTV National Youth Singing Competition, Bayi (PLA) Film Studio, producer of *The Shining Red Star*, made a formal complaint to CCTV, claiming that the distortion of this classic not only hurt the feelings of the creators of the original film and the devoted fans, but also misled the youth. The creator, Hu Daoge, was forced to apologize publicly to the studio.[63] The response from ordinary netizens varied greatly. In the case of the Lei Feng spoof, some vehemently opposed the act, saying that it was a kind of blasphemy against the country's most respected man. Some, however, saw it as a way the younger generation could break the strict ideological type-casting. Still others believed there was nothing wrong if it could help flesh out and humanize a well-known hero. Most were aware of the commercial motive behind the spoof, but nevertheless found it entertaining.[64]

The arguments around spoofs exemplify conflicting attitudes of contemporary Chinese toward the socialist past, deriving from the changing value systems during a period of official corruption, widespread cynicism, and the degradation of ideology. The fact that CCTV, the de facto "mouthpiece" of the Party, actually aired a spoof of a revolutionary classic is not a quirky act of some media professionals. It is evidence that the "de-ideologized" attitude has become almost a new official discourse. However, the important question is whether spoofing has become just a new fashion, thereby losing its subversive potential, or if it expresses oppositional meaning and gestures toward social resistance? It would be hard to deny that parodying the revolutionary classics was driven by commercial desires for sensational value. However, as long as the Party still claims an authorial position and guardianship over red culture, lambasting those works does challenge the state's hegemony to interpret the past. While spoofing may be vulgar and demonstrate a disregard for history, its defiant posture nevertheless has the potential to expand the horizons for more diverse cultural productions in the future.

## SUMMARY: REMAKING THE PAST,
## MAKING RATINGS IN THE PRESENT

Each of the above examples captures the creative use of red culture by the state media, intellectual elite, and ordinary consumers. Several broad observations can be made from these cases. First of all, the study of red culture in its new form must be embedded in the broad context of the evolution of post–Cultural Revolution Chinese culture. What defines the new era is the blatant materialism and individualism supplanting the radical search for idealism and morality as the new cultural hegemony. The transmogrification of red culture is symbolic and metonymic of the changes taking place in China, from a single-ideology culture to a complex, consumer-driven culture. Second, integrating red culture into the bourgeoning cultural industry as a commercial product is a highly complicated process. Compatible with the ethos of the consumer society, the use of red culture has become highly commercialized, tapping into people's nostalgic sentiment. However, despite their fragmentation, the values the Red Classics genre promoted, such as patriotism, nationalism, and self-sacrifice, are still valued by society. Third, the double bind of the Party-state and the marketplace serves as the major influence on the configuration of the "red," the former through exercising censorship and the latter through financing the production. However, neither ideological control nor market manipulation is fully capable of defining the ways in which revolutionary culture is evoked in the 2000s. Different forces could coopt, contend, and cooperate in unexpected ways at times. Finally, yet equally worth noting, the three examples not only showcase different forms of hybridization between the popular/official and market/state, they also exemplify three media formats, or three modes of story-telling, that is, TV drama series, reality show, , and Internet video. The formats of the media have implications for production, representation, and consumption. The reality show format of *My Long March* effectively evacuates any potential risk of reconstructing the "real" historical event, as required by a documentary format. The added advantage of focusing on the stories and crises of individuals provides multiple positions for identification, which help garner a wider demographic. The fact that TV drama in China has the middle class as its ideal target audience[65] has no doubt led to the melodramatic treatment of Tonya and Pavel's love story in *The Making of a Hero*, displacing ideological factors such as class division, with dramatic events and personality differences. On the other hand, the relatively free online culture has made the spoofing of the Red Classics possible. The producers of spoofs exercise much greater creative liberty, while the spoof's mode of address invites audiences with fewer tendencies to politicize and moralize. This book will focus on the TV seria remakes of the Red Classics.

*Chapter 3*

# From Chief to Chef
## *Remolding the Heroes*

The withdrawal of class discourse marks the most notable transformation in public culture. Class and class struggle used to provide the main structure for social relations. However, Chinese society has experienced major political shifts from the class-based moral economy to one based upon neoliberal wealth accumulation.[1] The CCP has abandoned its class base and positioned itself as the representative of the advanced forces of production. In this process, peasants and workers have lost their subjectivity as the masters of society and have been perceived as a burden in China's march toward a more affluent society. Class struggle is shunned as a viable and legitimate theme.

Following the phenomenal success of "Yearning" [*Ke Wang*] in 1992, TV serial drama started to provide new subjectivities that resonate with consumer-based culture. This has proved a very difficult task for adapting Red Classics, which shouldered the main task of modeling class-based social ethics and morals. Class opposition in the Red Classics genre is often embodied in the binary relations between heroes and villains. I begin this chapter by discussing the concept of "socialist realism" and its importance in molding heroic characters to their larger-than-life images and in reducing villains to paper-thin demons in the Maoist era. I then explore strategies used by TV production units in fashioning a socialist genre to cater to the tastes of the masses in the current cultural configuration. I argue that, on the one hand, the disappearance of class discourse in contemporary political, social, and economic life has been the major contributor to changes in the representation of heroes and villains; on the other hand, the erasure of class in the cultural domain assists in reinforcing the impression of the absence of class in social life. This dialectical process has resulted in the media's reorientation of the cultural politics of class. Furthermore, the quest for a depoliticized subject among cultural elites has decanonized the Red Classics and intensified a sense of repulsion against revolutionary classics. Finally, the rise of popular culture and consumerism has helped dismantle the sublime aesthetics of socialist realism.

The above elements paved the way for the TV adaptation craze in the first half of the 2000s. The adaptation that attracted the most public fanfare was *Tracks in the Snowy Mountain* [Linhai xueyuan]. The show went on air in January 2004, during a period when both TV crews and the networks, convinced by the huge ratings success of revolutionary-themed TV dramas like *Days of Burning Passion*, believed that the remake would be a winning bet. The adaptations arose at the right moment: the public looked back to the past with a sense of nostalgia and a longing for the collective benefits of socialism; the state had been searching for new ways to enhance its representational pedagogy; popular media such as TV had become a symbolic resource for the general public to make sense of reality and history; and the "red" culture could now be more safely appropriated for commercial entertainment. The attention given to the major Red Classics adaptations only intensified the fierce negotiations and contestations surrounding the production and reception of the heroes and villains. The double bind of the Party-state and the marketplace serves as the major influence on the reconfiguration of the Red Classics. However, neither ideological control nor market manipulation is fully capable of defining the ways in which the revolutionary culture is evoked in the reproduction. The exchange between politics and money is exceedingly complex.

Using the reworking of *Tracks in the Snowy Mountain* as the main case, I describe various strategies adopted by the TV adaptations to reinject ambiguity into the black-and-white universe of the Red Classics: the sublime, God-like image of the hero was made human by emphasizing the emotional, personal, and domestic concerns of the character and by endowing him with human failings.Although the stereotype of the villain was also ruptured by giving the character emotional sophistication and more neutral, middle-of-the-road images and thus equally interesting to analyse, I will focus only on the hero in this chapter. In the adaptation, the opposition between heroes and villains, which was framed in terms of class conflict in the high socialist days, is largely displaced to the plane of personal frictions. Taken together, these practices almost constitute a reversal of the typification process of the Maoist era. Specifically, I want to deal with the following question: How and why was the class struggle discourse diluted through the transformation of heroes in the TV adaptations?

## THE MAKING OF A PERFECT SOCIALIST
## HERO: SOCIALIST REALISM AND THE
## BOUNDARIES OF CANONICAL TEXTS

The Red Classics were created from the 1940s to the 1970s with the aim to develop a historiography of the Communist Party and to articulate Party policies. Artists and writers narrated the origins of the revolution and how revolution achieved victory after an arduous journey. They also described the social transformation under the CCP leadership. At that time, the main form of literary discourse was socialist realism.[2] Beginning in the 1930s, socialist realism was promoted as the only legitimate form for art and literature in the Soviet Union. According to Williams,[3] the version of socialist realism developed by Soviet theorists has one element that is fundamentally different from earlier definitions of realism in the West. Extending Engels' definition of realism as "typical characters in typical situations," the Soviets took "truly typical" to mean "the most deeply characteristic human experience," rather than typical experiences encountered in everyday life.[4] Realism, thus understood, departs from a sense of the faithful depiction of experiential reality and moves toward a selection of experience based on the "comprehension of laws and perspectives of future social development."[5] In the Soviet Union and China, applying the theory of socialist realism meant creating literary and artistic works that reflect the struggle toward the collective goal of socialism. The defining feature of socialist realism is its strong ideological resonance.[6] Its ideological grounding is the conviction that literature and art are class-based and must serve the dictatorship of the proletariat. After the Congress of Soviet Writers officially approved it in 1934, socialist realism was strictly imposed on artistic output.

The Red Classics are the end product of dogmatic adherence to socialist realism, which later evolved into revolutionary realism and revolutionary romanticism in China. It is a body of literature and art that narrates truth with certain political and moral values, norms, and prohibitions. In his Yan'an talk at a symposium for artists and writers in 1942, Mao articulated the idea that artistic endeavors should serve socialist ideology.[7] In that symposium, Mao called for literary and artistic workers to engage in creative work for the common people—the workers, peasants, and soldiers. By aligning itself with the needs and tastes of the people, the new "people's art" gained ethical legitimacy.[8] The imagined alliance with the people underlined the passionate utopia for which Mao and many writers and artists yearned.

A set of new norms was set up to outline the nature, function, and use of literature and art, as well as their subject and audience. The main task of socialist realism in the Soviet Union and China was to reaffirm the positive socialist reality and transform the population into conforming and contributing socialist subjects. It was part of the Party machine with the mandate of engineering "the soul."[9] The key to completing this task was to create positive heroes with behaviors and thoughts for people to emulate. The instrumental nature of art and literature as a political tool required the depiction of heroes in an idealized state. Any artistic expressions not in this vein would be criticized as a distortion of reality. Art works were required to deal with important subjects, mainly comprised of revolutionary struggle or rural life. In terms of aesthetic style, sublimity[10] was what every artist aspired to achieve.[11]

The new hero should be a socialist subject and epitomize the "prescribed political identity."[12] How the heroes should actually be depicted, however, was a topic constantly under debate during the seventeenth years after the founding of the new People's Republic. In May 1952, *Art and Literature Gazette* (*Wenyi bao*), the official newspaper of the United Association of Chinese Literature and the Arts, opened a column called "Discussions on creating new heroic characters." In the second Congress of the Writers and Artists Federation in 1953, Zhou Yang, the paramount literary arbiter in socialist China, made a keynote speech on producing "typical" characters (*dianxing renwu*).[13] A typical character was believed to represent the essence of a social group or stratum.[14] Creating typical proletariat characters was considered the same as creating a positive, heroic character.[15] The "ideal figure" consistently called for by Zhou Yang in the three congresses of the Writers and Artists Federation predated the formula for the "perfect hero" prevalent in the cultural products of the Cultural Revolution period. His core view rested on two premises: First, in terms of character development, the backward-to-advanced narrative pattern should not be regarded as typical for heroic figures. In other words, heroes are born perfect and should not go through a "growth" stage.[16] Second, the weaknesses of the heroes can and should be left out in the literary representations. This second rule denied the possibility of a rounded characterization.[17]

Even though the debate would last another two decades, the principle of constructing the perfect hero was established and strengthened. It was a "sweeping clean" process targeting the traditional literature stocks "possessing ontological significance—writing about reality, about humanity, about subjective feelings, writing about both heroes and small figures; castigating evil (exposing darkness) and praising good (extolling light); and so on"[18] This process saw the state machinery force writers and art workers to acquire the new revolutionary language and discourse in their creative endeavors. Individuals who did not play by the rules were relentlessly criticized and punished.

Applying Foucault's concept of the "episteme," which is a system of rules that enables the production of a discourse and governs its formation, literary critic Li Yuchun examines the transformation from the May 4th Enlightenment literature to the Red Classics. He identifies three major changes in the production of literary discourse: First, a shift from modern individual values to the collective values of the worker-peasant-soldier; second, a methodological shift from "experiences" and "facts" to "standpoints" or "world outlook"; third, a shift in principle from "literature of the man" to "literature of the class."[19]

The Red Classics consist of a didactic mapping of ideology onto cultural products. As literary historian Hong Zicheng describes, these works were created "within the confines of the established ideology, narrating established historical themes to achieve established ideological purposes."[20] The addition of the latter meant that heroes needed to be elevated to an even greater level of perfection.[21] The most important guiding principle for literary and artistic creation was the "three prominences" (san tuchu) theory, formulated in November 1969 by Yao Wenyuan, the chief propagandist and a member of the notorious Gang of Four during the Cultural Revolution.

Hailed as a major contribution to socialist artistic theory, this principle was applied to a number of theatrical works that later served as the model for artistic works of all different genres.[22] Following this principle, the central heroic characters in these works all possess "loftiness, greatness and perfection" (*gao, da, quan*). Analyses of the characterization of heroes in novels created during the Cultural Revolution show that the heroic characters normally possess a number of preferred qualities: in terms of personal background, heroes tend to be young, single, of heroic descent or orphaned, and have military experience; in terms of physical qualities, heroes are normally of "strong constitution," with "big and bright piercing eyes, a vigorous air and an unaffected expression"[23]; in terms of ideological qualities, they are conscious of class line struggles between socialist roaders and capitalist roaders and display altruism and collectivism; in terms of temperamental and behavioral qualities, they show kindness and magnanimity, honesty, politeness, and rebelliousness. An example of this formula being carried to the extreme is Hao Ran's novel, *Golden Road* [*Jin guang da dao*], which depicts a protagonist that is modeled so didactically on the formula that even his name, Gao Daquan, literally means "loftiness, greatness, and perfection."

## REMAKING THE HEROES

The previous section describes the discursive environment in which the transformation of the Red Classics into TV format was undertaken. In post-Mao China, it proved challenging to find new ways to present revolutionary works created with narrow views of politics and high official language. In the 1980s, the film realm had a trial run of reinventing Party history in the popular imagination. Subjects such as the Anti-Japanese War and the Yan'an legacy were recast within experimental films, such as Zhang Yimou's *Red Sorghum* [*Hong gaoliang*, 1988], Wu Ziniu's *One and Eight* [*Yige he bage*, 1983], and Chen Kaige's *Yellow Earth* [*Huang tudi*, 1984].[24] These films addressed the issues of nationhood and heroes with enough ambiguity to allow them to fall within the state discourse on Party history, while at the same time pushing the detailed historical events into the background and adopting a personal viewpoint.[25] Unlike these films, the TV adaptations of the Red Classics must honor a number of preexisting productions in other formats, as well as a much more prescribed storyline. The difficulty is obvious: On the one hand, presenting stereotypical characters in a formulaic plot is unlikely to engage audiences in the depoliticized popular discourse and is ill-suited for a medium such as TV, which favors a naturalistic approach to representation and allows greater intimacy with an audience. On the other hand, the original works are still part of the revolutionary heritage to which the Party claims ownership, and it cannot be denied that these stories once offered certain pleasures to their viewers at an earlier time. Both old ideological strictures and new commercial concerns help outline the boundaries the TV adaptations must negotiate.

One example that encapsulates the complexity of adapting the Red Classics to new cultural expectations is related to the presentation of heroes and villains. The opposition between the hero/chief protagonist and the villain/class enemy forms the main theme and the drama that propels the story development in most Red Classics. As I discussed earlier, class struggle is regarded as anti-modern and outmoded, a political excess to overcome in the current popular discourse. While the heroes lose their "typical" features as portrayed in the original version of the Red Classics, the class discourse is simultaneously dismantled and written off. Understanding how the language and theme of class struggle were obliterated in the TV adaptations provides insights into the logic of cultural practice in post-Mao China. In the following section, I will focus on the evolving heroic characters in *Tracks in the Snowy Mountain* to discuss tensions and negotiations in appropriating the iconographic characters in the Red Classics, a process that has proven to be very contentious.

*Tracks in the Snowy Mountain* is one of the most popular Red Classics; its popularity partly derived from its legendary-tale type of narration. It focuses on an adventurous small brigade within the CCP army, rather than a panoramic recounting of historical and social events. Written by Qu Bo in the 1950s, it is a story about the eradication of defeated Nationalist bandits who had joined professional brigands and landlord tyrants in Northeast China's Manchuria in 1946. The bandits were trying to locate a large amount of crude opium left by the Japanese army to finance their offensives against the Communists. Meanwhile, both the Communists and the bandits are searching for a map marked with liaison stations for Kuomintang spies. The hero, Yang Zirong, who is modeled after a real soldier, slips into the bandits' stronghold and wins the trust of the enemy leader. Based on the intelligence Yang provides, the Communist army is able to eliminate the bandit den.

Some literary critics tend to classify *Tracks in the Snowy Mountain* under the "revolutionary popular novel genre," together with *Railroad Guerrilla* [*Tiedao youjidui*], *Struggles in the Old City* [*Yehuo chunfeng dou gucheng*], and *Armed Squad behind the Enemy Line* [*Dihou wugongdui*]. Written in the 1950s, these novels, although invariably engaged in representing revolutionary heroes as their subjects, distinguish themselves from others in that they are more deeply rooted in the Chinese vernacular fictional tradition.[26]

Critics have offered detailed evidence for this close relationship between revolutionary popular fiction and vernacular culture. Even though writer Qu Bo tried very hard to follow the stripped-down formula of "making the good better, making the bad worse," his characterization was nevertheless criticized because his heroes and villains were modeled on the archetypes of vernacular classics. Although Qu Bo may have been profoundly influenced by the vernacular novels,[27] his struggle to stamp out the "invisible folk culture structure" from his work is beyond dispute.

Like many other Red Classics, *Tracks* went through an ideological "purifying" process after it was written, and the novel was revised several times by Qu Bo. A major publishing success, the novel caught the interest of several drama companies. In 1958, an opera version with the title, *Taking Tiger Mountain by Strategy* [*Zhiqu Weihushan*], was created based upon the episode depicting Yang Zirong's battle of wits with the bandits. In June 1964, *Tiger Mountain* was performed in the national Peking Opera convention and was watched and approved by the top leaders of the country. It was then refined into one of the eight Model Revolutionary Works widely performed during the Cultural Revolution.[28] Yang Zirong became a household name. Nearly everybody growing up in that era could sing the famous aria sung by Yang Zirong during his first encounter with the bandit leader. In this theatrical work, all the distracting traditional motifs were sanitized. The love stories between Shao Jianbo and army nurse Bai Ru were removed from the story. Shao Jianbo's revenge plot was also removed. Yang Zirong had morphed into an icon of socialist realism—lofty, great, perfect. Paul Clark's study of model operas found that heroes in *Yangbanxi* possess a mythical quality; "they start the drama fully in command of the ideological resources and emotional discipline to tackle the challenges ahead."[29] The idealization of heroes, and the demonization of the enemy on the other side, was a practice based on the concept of "typification" (*dianxinghua*) in socialist realism. Guided by this principle, Yang Zirong, as the central hero of *Tiger Mountain*, embodies the essence of the proletarian class and therefore must be distinguished by wisdom, bravery, uprightness, and strength.

More than thirty years later, TV producers face an audience no longer accustomed to crude ideological indoctrination or didactic recounting of historical events. Additionally, as Rofel[30] has argued, urban residents embrace consumerism as an identity that is constructed on the structural dichotomy between the past and the present. The present is marked by consumerism and the search for wealth, while the past is associated only with politics. This results in a construction of the socialist past as a time to be transcended and forgotten. TV's commercial nature dictates that it must anticipate the fidgety public mood.

How to concoct a mix that satisfies all the vested interests remains a challenge. For the production team[31] of *Tracks in the Snowy Mountain*, the strategy was to restore the invisible vernacular elements in the original novel and flesh out heroes like Yang Zirong with humor, toughness, and a small dose of anti-establishment sentiment, while not threatening the legitimacy of the war. The basic storytelling rules were set: heroes are fighting for a just cause, and bandits deserve to be eradicated. But within these rules, there is plenty of room for presenting heroes as human beings with "warts and pimples."

One strategy the TV adaptation adopted is to play up the legendary elements of the location—the vast, sparsely populated land of Manchuria covered with snow, the pine forests, a steam-engine train snaking through the ice, and a hostel built with wood in the middle of nowhere. These elements work as a backdrop for the squad soldiers gliding gracefully in skis, with their white camouflage cloaks flying in the snowflakes, or for the bandits, all clad in self-made wolf-skin hats and coats, looming here and there in the mythical woods. The cast speaks northeast dialect, which further enhanced the exotic flavor of the show. The northeast dialect, similar to Mandarin in pronunciation and thus accessible to a majority of audiences, is very rich in idioms and colloquial expressions. This constitutes a small transgression, considering that fictional heroes in the Red Classics all speak with a pretentious clear and rich tone (*zi zheng qiang yuan*).

What draws the most criticism in the new adaptation are the significant alterations to Yang Zirong's character. Instead of a born hero, naturally brave and wise, he is now a chef in the army. This is considered a trivial position in the Chinese army not only because chefs are not entitled to the heroism that goes with participation in battle but also because their work is concerned with the "material bodily lower stratum," as Bakhtin put it.[32]

In the opening scene, Yang Zirong makes his first entrance riding on horse-drawn skis and chanting an erotic local tune. A moment later, he is bargaining with a local grain vendor, warning him to only sell the best cornmeal to the Communist army he is serving. On his way back to the base camp, he rescues female soldier Bai Ru, who faints and falls off her horse due to fatigue. When younger soldiers inadvertently call him "chief," he is embarrassed and irritated and says, "Listen, I'm not a chief, nothing but a chef."

Indeed, Old Yang is not a particularly disciplined person. In fact, he is quite foul-mouthed. He once made a living wandering around in the underworld among the bandits. When the commander encourages him to join the special squad for wiping out the bandits, Shao Jianbo, the squad leader, firmly declines. Shao voices his concern to the commander:

> We all know what sort of person Old Yang is: His background is very complicated. He was once a security guard for the wealthy. He can make conversation with any sort of person. The chap is just too tricky. No wonder he can speak bandit slang. He is not like Gao Bo or Luan Chaojia, who each suffered bitterly in the old society and have deep class hatred and who therefore joined the revolutionary army in their youth. Neither is he like Sun Dade, who was an innocent student before joining the army. Take a look at the members of our squad—they are all members of the Communist Party or Youth League. But Old Yang did not even write a single application letter to join the Party. He certainly enjoys a drink or two as well. As soon as he drinks, he will start singing those obscene tunes, sweetheart this or sweetheart that.

At the same time, Old Yang himself does not fancy joining the squad too much either. He only becomes a scout squad member because the chief taunts him. His reputation being such, when he reports to the squad reluctantly, the squad soldiers confront him with the question: "So, apart from being able to speak slang, what else can you do?" When Yang answers sulkily, "I can cook," they jeer in response: "Oh, so it all has something to do with the mouth."[33]

His ruffian style causes him further trouble when the squad moves into the village. Shao tells him off when he starts his obscene songs during a joint celebration with a squad of Soviet soldiers. Unable to stand the Russian skiing coach Sasha's advances on army nurse Bai Ru, Yang buries four sharp-pointed sticks in the snow, causing Sasha to fall badly on the ice when demonstrating flying techniques to the squad. This leads to a good scolding from Shao. He also privately arranges for a captive bandit to meet his wife. Not only that, this bandit's wife was once Yang's fiancée, a woman who had married a bandit due to a bizarre combination of circumstances. Part of the story revolves around the ambiguous feelings that Yang and his former lover have for each other when they meet each other again after living a world apart. His fiancée's son was abducted by the villain, Vulture (*Zuoshandiao*), and it seems Yang's decision to penetrate Vulture's den was partly fueled by the desire to look for the son for his fiancée. In the last scene, Yang is killed when chasing after the son.

To a certain extent, Old Yang's exploits diminish the serious overtones of the Red Classics. His behavior may not seem that bad, but as a heroic character, he certainly exceeds the limits established in the heyday of the Red Classics. The embellishment of his character has been stripped to a considerable extent. He is now human, full of little flaws just like us, and his heroism is somehow inadvertent. To many, his brave actions constitute a trivialization of the war because they are motivated partly by personal revenge.

The emphasis on kinship relations is not accidental but critical to the rewriting. Li Yang[34] points out that in the socialist genealogy of knowledge, identification with a class was achieved through transcendence of one's kinship. Li's study demonstrates how the identification with kinship was overcome and sublimated to that of class in *The Red Lantern* (1970), another key work of the Red Classics genre. In *The Red Lantern*, "ties of blood" are considered a barrier to the real bond formed on the basis of class. As a conspicuous narrative device, the three main characters in the story are not related to each other: Li Yuhe, a railroad worker who engages in underground work for the Communists in the Anti-Japanese War, adopts Li Tiemei, whose parents died as revolutionary martyrs. After his comrade-in-arms sacrificed his life for the revolutionary cause, Li looked after his comrade's mother and took her as his own mother. When Li's real identity is exposed and Japanese special agents take him away, Grandma Li reveals this special family relationship to Tiemei. This greatly inspires Tiemei to follow the example of her father and carry the revolution through to the end. *The Red Lantern* transformed the traditional human relations based on Confucian ethics, replacing them with a brand-new class-consciousness and class relationships. Partly due to its archetypal characterization of Li's class background, *The Red Lantern* was considered the "model" of the eight Model Revolutionary ModeWorks.[35] Similar devices became the normative practice and can be found in a number of other artistic creations made during this time.

As Li Yang [36] observes, the subordination of kinship to class was a process that, in the case of *The Red Lantern*, involved several rounds of revisions. In the earlier film version of *The Red Lantern*, there were still displays of affection between the three family members. These details were eliminated from the Huju opera version, which came out later, but traces of a kinship bond were still kept in the parting scene when the three generations of the Li family pour out their grief before Li Yuhe's execution. At this stage, kinship was still regarded as being consistent with the class bond. However, this narrative mode was completely changed in the Peking Opera version, where kinship became a negative relationship in need of transcendence. This is encapsulated in the last few words that Li Yuhe says to Tiemei before his death: "It is said that nothing is deeper than the kindred feeling; to me, class love is weightier than Mount Tai."

Acknowledging and exploring the emotions of Yang Zirong and other protagonists in the Red Classics is part and parcel of a grand project in post-Mao cultural production. This project involves endowing the protagonists with newly embraced humanism and individualism, in an attempt to reject the political passions of socialism. In a way, the project represents almost the reversal of the process whereby revolutionaries were made saintly in the socialist era. Heroes are depicted as ordinary individuals struggling with common problems in human relations. Almost all the TV adaptations promoted their works with a claim that they would craft a more realistic and natural image of the protagonists as compared with the original version. How to take iconic heroes down from the altar is the selling point for these reproductions.

Common humanity comes packaged with sensationalism in the new formula. A more "humane" hero provides a mass audience with their daily after-work excitement. The extreme form of heroic character based on this formula is the "villainous hero" of the revolutionary historical genre. As mentioned above, this formula was developed by writers like Mo Yan in his *Red Sorghum*, brought to the screen by big names like Zhang Yimou, and then replicated in primetime TV drama. Two smash hits produced with this type of character are *The Sky of History* and *Sword Show*.

In these bloody primetime series dealing with the Anti-Japanese War, the main heroic characters are almost all villains to the bone. Unlike the Red Classics written before the Cultural Revolution, which employ the hero's residual "slipperiness" as a device to emphasize their heroic spirit, in the new TV versions, the heroes are like China's Rambo or James Bond.[37] They no longer epitomize the essence of the oppressed class, but are presented as individual war machines. They struggle not out of concern for social order or justice, but as a result of their innate untameable nature.

The reinvention of revolutionary mass culture for popular entertainment has generated much anxiety, fear, hope, criticism, praise, and mixed feelings among various sectors in Chinese society. Unfavorable comments on the representations of heroes appeared after the first run of *Tracks in the Snowy Mountain* on Beijing Television (BTV) in March 2004. Citing public anger as a reason, SARFT (2004) issued a circular regulating the TV reproduction of Red Classics. The official sanction was followed by a wide variety of articles and viewer letters in mainstream newspapers highlighting audience dissatisfaction—even indignation—over the "unfaithful" revisions of the original work. Celebrity figures, such as the CCTV program host Cui Yongyuan, made comments in public that they dare not watch the adaptation for fear that the familiar images in their minds would be changed beyond recognition.[38]

Most controversies over the TV dramatized version dwell on the representation of Yang Zirong, as the following review makes clear:

> The new version is a collection of clichés. Adding those so-called emotional
> entanglements is what the production crew was pleased about. They seemed
> to believe that these changes enriched the original novel and made it more
> compelling. But this kind of emotional spice is the easiest to add . . . At the end
> of the series, when Yang Zirong runs up and down the mountain searching for
> his lover's son, we could not help but wonder: Is this still *Tracks in the Snowy
> Mountain*? If they have such a rich imagination, why cash in on the fame of
> *Tracks in the Snowy Mountain?* They could as well do a totally new one on
> suppressing bandits in Northeast China.[39]

Some of the reviews ridiculed the adaptation by renaming it *Love Affair in the
Snowy Mountain.* Liu Bo, the author's wife, was interviewed and claimed that
the rendering of Yang Zirong was not "proper": "In this show, Yang Zirong
is depicted as a glib, grumpy man, playing all sorts of little tricks, and even
having some romantic relationships with a fictional bandit's wife. I think this
is totally unnecessary. I believe this type of character needs to be dealt with
more discreetly and seriously."[40] Interestingly, nearly every negative review
qualified its comments by stating that the stereotyped, flattened images of
heroes and villains must be changed somewhat. But nobody offered any solution for how to expand and renew the representation.

The ideology of class and class struggle is now so obsolete in the public
discourse, it hardly surfaced in the media discussions on the audience's
response. Some tend to explain viewers' responses in terms of generational
differences. For example, the *Beijing Evening News*[41] conducted interviews
and grouped the viewers' responses according to their age. In its final report,
the paper concluded that revolutionary-themed TV dramas would never
please everybody. According to the report, the sixty-year-old cohort was
deeply troubled by the new elements added in the series. This group of viewers experienced the war and tends to take the TV's reinvention of heroes as
blasphemy against the sacred revolutionary images. In the report, sixty-five-
year-old Mrs. Liu is quoted as saying: "I was very angry after I saw the first
few episodes. Yang Zirong was portrayed as a wise, brave, and charismatic
hero in the novel, film, and *Yangbanxi*. How come he is now a cook?" The
fifty-year-olds were very familiar with the original text and identified strongly
with the original story. But they showed little interest in the TV adaptation.
According to fifty-six-year-old Mr. Lin:

> Our generation all read the novel and watched the *Yangbanxi* and film version
> . . . Many people can easily recite the original script. I watched some of the
> drama series. I don't feel it offers anything interesting.

Those viewers in their forties were disappointed that, contrary to the publicity hype, the TV version provided no real interesting breakthroughs. Mr. Li, a TV editor, was quoted as saying: "This work influenced three generations, but it was too bland and too ordinary. Commercial elements are not just confined to love entanglements. The script should be better done, more fast-paced and absorbing, more suspense and more interesting plots." Those viewers in their thirties only had vague memories of the original story and thus made few comparisons with the earlier version, but they presented themselves as media-savvy. Some were critical of the mise-en-scène and factual mistakes. For example, one interviewee, Mr. He, told the reporter: "I've only watched a few episodes, but they happened to be full of slips and holes." Younger people in their twenties have showed little interest in the Red Classics TV version.

Applying Althusser's concept of "interpellation," critics such as Zhao Yong[42] argue that the viewers' critiques of the TV adaptations were motivated by genuine discontent. Some of the strong feelings invested in the criticisms of the adaptations certainly point to the normalizing effects of the Red Classics. Socialist narratives commanded broad followings in the formative years of the now old and middle-aged. The hegemony of these narratives had made it impossible for people to exercise their agency. As a result, these generations eventually embraced the subjectivity prescribed by dominant ideology. However, Althusser's thesis suggests a subjectivity always predetermined by the ruling ideology. Such a position overlooks two important factors in the construction of subjectivity: First, there might be a number of discursive practices at play at the same time, including everyday practices. Second, the process is ongoing—subjectivity is constantly renewing itself and antagonism to a collective subjectivity is possible when a collective subject "finds its subjectivity negated by other discourse or practices."[43] Recent studies of the genre have shown that, even in highly politicized eras such as the Cultural Revolution, negotiated or subversive readings of the Red Classics were still possible.[44]

The very heated public debate over the TV adaptations may suggest that the ideological over-determination argument is only partially tenable. But this leads to another interesting question: If a large part of the audience is made up of socialist subjects shaped by the revolutionary discourse, why do so few of them use class discourse to frame their objections in the staged polls or debate in the media? In condemning the commercial rendering of heroes and villains, most people only resort to the idea of "authenticity" by declaring these representations as "untrue" and contrary to their own experience of history. The glaring absence of class suggests that it is no longer a viable trope in the public space provided by the media. Even a state agency such as SARFT did not dwell on the question of who can be considered a national icon and the legitimacy of class struggle. Instead, the original Red Classics texts were recast as a kind of cultural heritage that needed to be defended.

## CONCLUSION

As one of the earliest TV adaptations, *Tracks in the Snowy Mountain* foreshadowed the strategies used in a large number of other adaptations in the ensuing period. The formula applied by the TV remakes exemplifies the typical complexity in turning a genre for political indoctrination into a cultural product for consumers. The proletarian nobility of the heroes and the dramatization of life and death conflicts between different classes could not be sustained in the TV adaptations when viewers are no longer hailed as political subjects.

The revisions to the representations of the heroes and villains in the Red Classics adaptations should be considered in the context of the disappearance of class discourse in contemporary Chinese society. Despite, and perhaps because of, the mounting social conflicts, there has been little incentive to reinscribe the concept of class back into the popular discourse. From the CCP to the media, and from academia to the much-hyped emerging "middle class," social polarization is conceived in terms of different social "stratum" existing in economic interdependence instead of class opposition, signaling a drastic shift away from the Marxist conception of social relations. The state's emphasis on a "harmonious society" represents an effort to paper over the drastically denigrated social status of peasants and workers, formerly the much-respected heroes of society. In the meantime, the former social enemies—the landlords and the bourgeoisie—can now be incorporated as the aspiration of the middle reaches of society.[45] The adaptation of the Red Classics reflects and is shaped by this change.

The attempt to erase class discourse from the TV adaptations remains a highly sensitive matter, despite the fact that consumerism and commercialization are now readily embraced as a global ethos. The responses to the adaptations seem to suggest that despite the shifting public mores, central figures in national narratives such as the Red Classics still carry their historical baggage. Changes made to the adaptations must honor the taboos defined by chief stakeholders. Emotional entanglement may prove to be incompatible for these heroes. Even small-scale tinkering with the personalities of the heroes or villains is fiercely contested and negotiated. As Chinese culture struggled to remake its notions of legitimate authority, TV adaptations of the Red Classics have not come up with an updated hero with enough moral and political complexity to rival its black-and-white predecessors. The formula of the "unholy trinity of sex, violence and profanity," which worked well in some of the more recent revolutionary TV shows and literary works, could not be applied to the Red Classics without some serious problems. In this sense, TV drama, as the main conveyor of a mass culture, indeed specifies the limits of legitimate thought in contemporary China.

Furthermore, it is widely recognized that the Red Classics once provided the pleasure of familiar faces, good music,[46] aesthetic models, and sublime sensations.[47] The treatment of the Red Classics is also tied up with fundamental questions about how to view the revolutionary legacy and national icons. As long as the Party-state still maintains its rhetorical endorsement of the legitimacy of the socialist revolution, some of the institutionalized aspects of the national narrative must be preserved. In the meantime, the economic reform the state instigated has changed social relations in post-Mao society. In the commercialized symbolic order, the heroic workers, peasants, and soldiers have been seriously marginalized in the media. TV adaptations of the Red Classics provide the rare few chances for these figures to re-enter the representational world. However, the production of the TV adaptations is implicated in the fundamental contradiction of the continuity of the political system and the state's radical promotion of marketization and privatization.[48]

The TV adaptations provide textual evidence of how the meaning and theme of class is reconfigured and negotiated. The viewing of the Red Classics adaptations is motivated by very complex incentives. To better understand, how the meaning of the adaptations is interpreted and negotiated, one needs to carry out more detailed audience research.

*Chapter 4*

# Getting the Right Mix

*Revolutionary Women and
Contemporary Femininity*

This chapter looks at the issue of gender and how gender and class intertwine in the TV adaptations of the Red Classics. The adaptations of three seminal Red Classics—*The Red Detachment of Women, Shajiabang*, and *Struggles in the Old City*—have attracted one common criticism from audiences: the female revolutionaries in these primetime TV dramas are too feminine and too beautiful. Given that attractive female characters have become a staple ingredient of primetime TV drama and generally considered appropriate within this genre, the audiences' critique points to the contested nature of women's representation within the Red Classics adaptation. The debate over what a revolutionary woman should or should not look like, both in the production process and in terms of audience reception, indicates that women's bodies are a crucial site of political-economic exchange and ideological contestation.

In this chapter, I will closely examine how the boundaries of concepts such as femininity, gender, and familial relations are constructed, maintained, transgressed, and repaired, by analyzing the female characters in one TV adaptation of the Red Classics. By comparing the current version and its relevant predecessors, I draw out the historical process of cultural production and regulation in the definition of boundaries. I argue that the dissonance manifested in the production and reception of the Red Classics reflects the inherent tension between television's commercial thrust for good ratings, the artistic impulse for innovation, and the state's desire for social control. The transgression must define itself against the norms and authority of the state. The TV adaptations of the Red Classics thus enunciate the redrawn parameters of the uses of the socialist legacy in a drastically transforming society. They demonstrate how each era produces its own political, economic, and ideological forces, which interact to shape the ways femininity, women, and gender are portrayed.

## WOMEN AND FEMININITY IN THE SOCIALIST ERA: THE REPRESENTATIONAL CONTEXT

Women's emancipation was always high on the CCP's agenda. Women were encouraged to cut their hair short and to free their bound feet, thus liberating women's bodies from oppressive traditions, and to seek marriage partners based on their own choice. This occurred in the Chinese Soviet Area established by the Communists from 1927 to 1937.[1] Soon after the People's Republic was established, the first regulation published by the government was the *Marriage Law of the People's Republic of China* (1950), which made companionate marriage the only legitimate form of marriage as opposed to the arranged marriage.[2] Throughout the 1950s and 1960s, equality between women and men remained an important grand narrative of socialist modernity. Women, as Mao Zedong once claimed, could hold up half of the sky.

However, the alliance between the state and women was never as straightforward as it seemed. Scholars argued that in granting women equal rights in politics, economics, education, and marriage, the state exploited women by subsuming them under the nationalist agenda and denying them their differences.[3] For example, Zhu Xiaodong[4] points out that liberating women from their tight corsets and bound feet in the 1930s was largely driven by the need to mobilize women for field labor while men were serving the army in the Communist-controlled area. More importantly, reducing the bond between the woman and her family was a way to break the confines of a closely knit household, making it easier for the revolutionary elite to harness individuals to the cause of revolution.[5]

Evans's 1997 study shows that from 1949 to the 1980s the hegemonic discourse on women and sexuality was marked by women's self-denial of their sexuality and individualized self.[6] Women were expected to take responsibility for maintaining social and sexual morality. In addition, love and marriage were defined as moral and social obligations to the collective and the state rather than the individual. As "empty signifiers" of class, the gender specificity of this category of women was neutralized, de-emphasized, and masculinized.[7] Femininity and sexuality were purged from the representational context. Anything related to an individual's private life and personal feelings was regarded as irrelevant and deleted wherever possible. Humanitarianism and human nature were condemned as "honey words" of the ruling class to rub out the division between classes and to hide the nature of class struggle during the Cultural Revolution. What is normal and natural in human relationships, or *renzhichangqing*, was especially harshly criticized in literary creations.[8]

With the end of the Cultural Revolution, post-Mao China saw multiple attempts to repudiate the radical leftists and their political excess. Part of the "thoughts liberation" movement involved the call to release repressed human nature. Women and femininity were no longer conceived solely in terms of class and other political attributes. A more tolerant, open public ethos emerged toward the subjects of sex, sexuality, love, and marriage. The discourse of the elimination of sex differences was gradually losing ground. However, as Harriet Evans[9] argues, the reassertion of a natural femininity in the narratives of the 1980s is based on a naturalized and essential sex difference and has in a way contributed to the perpetuation of gender hierarchy. As economic reform deepened in the 1980s, competition for employment intensified. Some male intellectuals blamed the equal entry of women into the labor force for intensifying social problems by forcing men to return home to take up domestic work. The decline of the master narrative of women, which portrayed them as the absolute equal of men, gave rise to the call for the return of some women to the home[10] and the re-emergence of discourse about the "essential role" of women.[11]

The overt backlash against the women's movement was fueled by the dawn of the consumerist era in the 1990s, when the commercial drive and the patriarchal male gaze increasingly demanded an explicit sexual dimension to women. The discursive construction of women's thoughts and behavior were extremely complex at this stage. On the one hand, the commercial discourse required women to be beautiful and feminine and to be seen as attractive by males. On the other hand, Maoist discourse that promoted equality and new social and political roles for women has left a complex and multidimensional legacy, which, combined with the ethos of capitalist modernity, requires women to be competent and independent in the job market. Therefore, the ideal woman in the reform era is simultaneously "young, beautiful, fashionable, sensual, gentle, virtuous and dutiful, considerate, strong and independent. At home, she should be able to run the automatic washing machine and microwave; outside, she should be a skilled independent woman, who drives a car and competes hard in the workplace."[12]

On the cultural production scene, women as a sexless class symbol tapered off by the end of the 1970s. However, the economic and political changes brought on by reform are having both positive and negative effects on women. Cara Wallis's[13] analysis of Chinese women in the official Chinese press elucidates the contradictory nature of official discourse on gender roles in the reform era. Wallis found that while the government press stresses the equality of Chinese women rhetorically, they nevertheless position women as inferior to men. When TV drama established its standing as the most important everyday entertainment in the average Chinese home by the mid-1980s, a greater variety of women appeared on the screen. The divergent roles of skilled working woman, traditional domesticated mother and wife, tough lady boss, and teenage girl idol were all explored to capture the varied interests of a more fragmented audience. Generally speaking, TV primetime drama affirms the normative gender system, portraying women as docile and domesticated, with motherhood as the essence of femininity.[14] A more explicit sexual aspect of female bodies is noticeable in the representations, but overall, images of women on TV were more conservative compared with cinema images, which are much more sexually charged.[15]

The intricate relationships between gender, the nation-state, and dominant social discourse provide a window through which I examine the changing boundaries of gender and sexuality in the process of cultural production and consumption. In reviewing the construction of gender, femininity, and sexuality in different adaptations of *Shajiabang*, I raise two questions: How does the construction of revolutionary heroines change in response to the commercialized cultural reality of post-Mao China, and how far can this transgression of gender norms established in the socialist era go in today's environment?

## NEGOTIATING BOUNDARIES: GENDER, FEMININITY, AND SEXUALITY IN SHAJIABANG

The changing discourses on women and femininity in the past few decades present a paradoxical task for television drama producers in adapting the Red Classics. On the one hand, androgynous female heroes in the socialist imagination are destined to be unattractive to modern audiences, as there has been "a general abhorrence of the state-imposed masculinization of the female"[16] as portrayed during the Maoist period. On the other hand, making the original depictions over with the commercially sexualized discourse would probably be a thankless task, for the Red Classics genre is not the usual domain for eroticism.[17]

In the following section, I will analyze how this paradox is played out in the depiction of women, femininity, and love in TV adaptations of *Shajiabang*, with a brief discussion of *The Red Detachment of Women*. I want to demonstrate that the contradictions and tensions exposed in the production and consumption of the heroine's images reflect inherent contradictions in post-Mao ideology. The market, concerned with producing, first and foremost, an entertaining show, often resorts to portraying women as sex objects, but in doing so, it has to negotiate the boundary not only with a rhetorically socialist state but also the socialist legacy as a lived experience for many viewers. Even though "the market, unlike the communist state, does not police the boundaries of ideological correctness so much as constantly expand them in whatever direction sales are to be made,"[18] it must be careful not to stretch the limits too far beyond the boundaries of the permissible zone when it comes to the representation of women in the Red Classics.

*Shajiabang* was a model work promoted during the Cultural Revolution and was well received by audiences.[19] It was first performed in 1960 as a Shanghai opera (*Huju*) under the title, *Emerald Water and Red Flags* [*Bishui hongqi*], in the 1960. After a few major revisions, the new version, now entitled *Sparks amid the Reeds* [*Ludang huozhong*], was performed in 1963 to a wide audience and caught the attention of top leaders. It was then recommended to be transformed into a Peking Opera version to appeal to audiences in different regions. A writing group, led by the well-known writer Wang Zengqi, polished the script. The efforts to improve the lyrics, music, and acrobatics lasted over a decade. The experimentations in *Shajiabang* expanded the conventions of the national theater and turned it into a popular repertoire even in the years after the Cultural Revolution.[20] Its protagonist, Sister A Qing, remains one of the best-loved popular characters in the *Yangbanxi*. The publicity in the lead-up to the TV adaptation centered on the choice of actor for Sister A Qing and the possible new interpretations of the heroine.

The story unfolds during the Anti-Japanese War (1937–1945) in the prosperous country town of Shajiabang, in Jiangsu Province, along the Yangtze River. Shajiabang was a battleground for competing guerrilla branches, including local bandits, the New Fourth Army led by the Communists, the Nationalists, and the Japanese. New Fourth Army commander Guo Jianguang and seventeen other sick and wounded soldiers are recuperating from their wounds in the town. When the Japanese become aware of the Communist presence, they move to mop up all the New Fourth Army soldiers in the area. Guo and his men are forced to take refuge in the nearby reed marshes. In the meantime, the Nationalist Party, the alleged ally of the Communists, sends their spy, Diao Deyi, to recruit local armed forces and keep watch on the movements of the wounded Communist soldiers. Sister A Qing (the leading female role) is the leader of the underground Communist cell, and she runs the teahouse as a cover for a liaison station. With incredible intelligence and steadfastness, Sister A Qing artfully dismantles the different factions within the enemy camp by her worldly wisdom and social skill. With the information and help provided by Sister A Qing, Guo and his troupe rout the enemy in a single battle.

For several reasons, the story presents an extremely interesting case for analysis. First, it features a woman hero, Sister A Qing, as its protagonist. Second, it shares many common features of the TV adaptations of the Red Classics, such as humanizing the hero and enemy and romanticizing the relationships between the male and female characters. Third, it is unique in its negotiation of gender boundaries in that it is one of the TV industry's latest reproductions[21] of the Red Classics and thus able to adjust its strategy based on lessons learned from earlier adaptations. Analysis of *Shajiabang* sheds light on the discursive strategy employed in producing the TV adaptations. The characterization of Sister A Qing is central to the TV drama, the *Yangbanxi* version, and its humbler precedent, the local opera *Sparks amid the Reeds*. The image of Sister A Qing was revised in each version in keeping with the prevalent ideology and discourse of the time. Specifically, this process involves the establishment and consolidation of the normalizing power of the revolutionary discourse, its gradual decline, and the rise of consumerism.[22] It is thus worthwhile to examine how these changes were made.

The central narrative device in the Huju opera, *Sparks amid the Reeds*, is the dual identity of Sister A Qing as both an undercover Communist agent and a teahouse owner. According to Wen Mu, the script writer of *Sparks amid the Reeds*, the original role of the teahouse owner was played by a male actor, but was later changed. The role keeps alive the link between this local opera and the popular legend genre, which often features a disguised hero or demon. In both the Huju version and the Peking Opera version of *Sparks amid the Reeds,* Sister A Qing was the bridesmaid of the wife of local military troupe commander, Hu Chuankui, and was able to manipulate the situation to her advantage. It was Sister A Qing who smuggled the New Fourth Army soldiers disguised as an opera troupe into Hu's wedding banquet. Sister A Qing thus plays a pivotal role in the victory in the final scene.

The important works of *Yangbanxi* usually bear the imprimatur of individual political leaders' direct interventions. *Shajiabang* was no exception. Jiang Qing, Mao Zedong's wife, and her allies actively involved themselves in the revision of *Shajiabang*. In 1964, Mao Zedong and Jiang Qing watched the Peking Opera version of the play and gave a number of instructions for revision, which aimed at reducing elements of the popular legend genre and the prominence of Sister A Qing. Mao described the wedding scene as "farcical," and suggested the Communist soldiers launch a surprise attack in a heroic manner from outside and annihilate the enemy en masse.[23] Jiang Qing went further in stating that the decision as to whether to give more prominence to Guo Jianguang, the commando platoon leader, or to Sister A Qing, was a matter concerning which line (the bourgeois or the proletarian) the play emphasized.[24] The extensive revision in 1965 pruned the wedding scene and downplayed the centrality of Sister A Qing. Both the wedding scene and the identity of Sister A Qing as an undercover agent have a strong folklore flavor, potentially distracting from or even competing with the authority of the established revolutionary discourse in the 1960s.

Along with the loss of folklore plot elements, the *Yangbanxi* version that came out of the major revision was stripped of any private discourse associated with love and kinship. As Sister A Qing is addressed as *"sao,"* literally sister-in-law, which signifies her marriage status, we know Sister A Qing is married. This is apparently a deliberate device. A young pretty unmarried woman running a public teahouse would inspire too much erotic speculation about sexual relationships. Sister A Qing's husband, however, never appears in the show. There is just one line in the opera that vaguely suggests he is elsewhere doing business. But the protagonist is never allowed to harbor any personal feeling toward him. Her relationship with the leading male role, Guo Jianguang, is strictly one of revolutionary comrade-in-arms.

However, even though Sister A Qing's personal life and feelings were stripped to the bone, there remained one element in the play that still had an element of folklore. The change to the ending of the *Yangbanxi* version did not alter the relationship structure between the roles.[25] It is still "one women versus three men," namely Sister A Qing versus political instructor Guo Jianguang, secret society Chief Hu Chuankui, and Kuomintang agent Diao Deyi. In the heyday of class struggle, this structure left room in the imagination for a forbidden love affair.[26] Chen Sihe[27] astutely observes that this narrative structure provides a chance for folklore ideology to compete with state ideology. Sure enough, this "one woman versus three men" structure has proved to be a Pandora's box, raising the issue of private sexual desires, which greatly complicates the plot.

This "one woman versus three men" gender dynamic was the reason behind another version of *Shajiabang*. In 2003, a novelette with the same name was published in the literary magazine *Jiangnan*. Its author, Xue Rong, explained his motive in rewriting the story as such:

> I'm very familiar with Peking Opera version of *Shajiabang*. For as long as I remember, this story is about the relationship between a woman and three men. This relationship was depicted as very serious in the earlier versions. It is not normal for the characters to have only such [serious] relationships. There should be relationships between spouses and other humanized relationships. [I wondered] if it is possible to create a new work by making up the relationship between these roles. I believe I'm allowed such freedom in novel writing. Therefore, I wrote this novelette. [28]

Based on this urge to debunk the political encoding of the saintly Sister A Qing and to restore her original state of being, the novelette explores her libidinal possibilities to the full. The once "chaste" Sister A Qing is now a licentious woman, sexually involved with Guo Jianguan and Hu Chuankuai at the same time, while her incompetent and chicken-hearted husband secretly provides for a woman who bears his child in the countryside. She is not, however, a liberated woman who uses sex to challenge traditional patriarchy.

Sister A Qing's extramarital affair is not so much a release of passion but a choice she is forced to make for survival. As a consequence, her sexual agency is seriously compromised. She is also pejoratively described as barren. Considering that China's traditional ideology defined womanhood by its reproductive role, Sister A Qing's subjectivity becomes flawed. Constructed largely by subverting the original portrayal, and lacking inherent narrative logic, the novelette version proves less than convincing.

Xue Rong's paraphrasing of *Shajiabang* can be described as "a plebeian cultural adventure," characterized by its anti-establishment sentiment, its tendency to desecrate the saintly, and its commercial thrust. While the novelette could be read as a nuanced cultural text, I will focus on one dimension: the responses that it generated, which turned the novelette into an attention-grabbing media event. The critique of the novel underscores the specific dimensions of Chinese society's anxiety about women, femininity, love, and sexuality.

The novelette caused much agitation soon after it was published in February 2003. A violent attack was launched immediately by the Municipal Propaganda Department of Changshu, which has jurisdiction over the town of Shajiabang, the setting for the story. In the typical manner in which official responses are solicited to attack an artistic work that the state finds distasteful, the Municipal Propaganda Department organized a forum attended by literary organizations, such as a writers' associations from the provincial and municipal level. The result was an article published in provincial party organ *Zhejiang Daily*, stating that "the novelette is a serious insult to feelings of the people," as it "represents a slander to the heroic images in people's mind," and consequently, it "has serious political mistakes."[29]

The highly politically charged terms in which the article casts its judgment were glaring at a time when the official attitude toward popular culture was more freewheeling. However, the article was widely republished in the press, and similar antagonistic comments appeared in major newspapers and literary magazines. Many criticized the novelette for its "distorted, insulting representations of heroic figures," or for being "unrealistic" historically or artistically. Some saw it as morally degrading and obscene, posing a threat to "public order and good morals" (*gongxu liangsu*).[30]Shajiabang local authorities expressed their indignation on the grounds that the novelette seriously damaged the reputation of their town and was bad publicity that would affect their economic activities. The response was overwhelmingly negative. The only exception was a few literary critics who came out to defend Xue's right to deconstruct the original work, even though they did not necessarily think it was a good literary piece. In March 2003, the Shajiabang Town Council, in the name of "one million Shajiabang residents," and the Shanghai New Fourth Army History Research Association jointly submitted a written protest to the publisher, *Jiangnan* magazine. At the same time, the relatives of Wen Mu, the scriptwriter of *Sparks amid the Reeds*, threatened to take the writer and the magazine to court. *Jiangnan* magazine's editor-in-chief at first refused to back down but was forced to write a self-criticism letter which was rejected when delivered in person to the representatives of the New Fourth Army. Mounting pressures in the ensuing months forced the magazine to publish a written apology and the editor-in-chief to resign. By this time, the incident had evolved into a sensational media drama that involved possible lawsuits, personal attacks, renowned scholars, and local authorities.

Amid this public fury regarding the "blasphemy" toward the heroine, one thing is worth noting. The outcry against the disturbance of "public order and good morals" is particularly tied to the infidelity of Sister A Qing. What the public or the state find irritating is not the commercial appropriation of a hero's image. In fact, if one does an online search of Sister A Qing, one can easily find a series of restaurants, hotels, snack food chains, and holiday resorts with the brand name of Sister A Qing. But so far, these have not caused much concern. This indicates that the real issue is not about Sister A Qing's persona being sacrosanct, but about what has become acceptable and what remains untouchable in the commercial present.

In fact, the revolutionary narratives and images constitute important symbolic and emotional capital for "place branding" in locations such as Shajiabang. Scholars have defined "place branding" as attempts to harness the distinctive features of a location to allow people to maintain an imaginary relationship with the place.[31] This crafting of space relies heavily on images of the place in published narratives and popular culture such as film, TV, and literature. It often aims to present the city as a tourist spot or a location for business investment. Therefore, how to construct a revolutionary location has not only political stakes but also economic ones. The latter is probably more important to the local government. The Shajiabang local authorities protested so strongly about the novelette depiction not least because a morally sound Sister A Qing and profit hang together. Zhu Yahui, the town head, told reporters that the novelette would result in his town suffering from "immense economic losses."[32] Shajiabang is now a tourist destination, with the reed marsh as its main attraction. Scenery spots modeled on Peking Opera sets are everywhere. Most of the hostels have names such as Sister A Qing, as do the boats that take the tourists around the marsh.[33] One reason for disciplining the representation of Sister A Qing is precisely because it interferes with the normal course of appropriating her image as a commercial brand name.

Ironically, money is probably the main factor that drove *Jiangnan* magazine to publish the novelette in the first place. As literature gradually makes way for other forms of popular entertainment, literary magazines are forced to battle for money to survive. *Jiangnan* magazine's circulation has dropped from 100,000 copies to a mere 2,000 in the past few years. Zhang Xiaoming admitted that he spent most of his time looking for financial support after he was appointed as the editor-in-chief. The publishing of the *Shajiabang* novelette created a cultural event that drew consistent attention for several months. However, it did not boost the magazine's circulation, as might have been expected.[34]

I argue that the novelette touched a raw nerve because gender and sexuality are marked out as sites of symbolic struggle in the ideological field as class is suppressed as a relevant category. This is manifested in the way that the sexual aspect of the novelette had been constantly singled out in the media for the purposes of audience attraction. Most of the reports on the event have headlines such as "Yangbanxi Shajiabang Updated with A Licentious Version: Cultural Circle Shocked"; "Sister A Qing Turned into A Licentious Women: What is the Use of Literary Works"; "Sister A Qing Depicted as a Loose Woman, the Wind of Parody Swept Shajiabang"; or "Sister A Qing Turned into Pan Jinlian, *Jiangnan Magazine* Apologising."[35] Whatever stance their news stories adopted toward the event, the media in general identified Sister A Qing as a newsworthy "selling point" (*mai dian*). This serves as an indicator that Sister A Qing's sexuality is at the center of this debate.

In his close reading of films dealing with marital infidelity and its threat, McGrath[36] makes an insightful observation that infidelity is metonymical of the desires awakened by the new imaginary of global capitalism in the reform era. Furthermore, this body of films articulates "the individual anxieties aroused by private desire as well as collective anxieties over the very privatisation and commodification of desire and fantasy."[37] He points out that "the trope of infidelity, with its inherent aspect of ethical transgression, manifests a broader anxiety over the ethical consequences of the privatisation of desire, and in particular over the accompanying divestment of commitment to the good of a larger collective, whether it be the nation, the commune, or the family."[38]

Following McGrath's argument, I want to further argue that this anxiety is particularly salient in the TV adaptations of the Red Classics genre, not least because this genre is a product of the collective utopian vision articulated in the Mao era. In the following section, I will delineate how the female heroes in the television remake of *Shajiabang* were rendered in response to institutional regulations, audience and critics' feedback, and ratings pressure. In order to appease these various forces, the television adaptation became watered down in both its revolutionary idealism and commercial thrust. It showcased how television prime time has adapted to the profoundly changed environment during the age of cultural marketization.

## THE TV ADAPTATION: GETTING THE RIGHT MIX

As described above, the television adaptation of *Shajiabang* shoulders a lot of baggage. A few earlier television adaptations of the Red Classics genre attempted to stretch the limits by eroticizing the main characters, but this failed to boost their ratings. Instead, these shows generated heated debate in the press, with many viewers expressing their discomfort with either the characters' feminization or the amorous relationships between the heroes and the heroines. On top of these shows' ratings failures, SARFT was irritated by the defiling of the official canon, and, as mentioned in chapter 1, issued a notice, which in effect forewarned the TV production teams of a possible ban.

One example is the TV adaptation of *The Red Detachment of Women*, which was a popular film in 1961 and was later adapted into a model ballet during the Cultural Revolution. The heroine, Wu Qionghua, is the daughter of a poor peasant who suffers as the slave girl of Nan Batian, a landlord despot in a village on south China's Hainan Island. Hong Changqing, the Communist Party representative, rescues her from a water dungeon where Nan Batian has incarcerated her. Wu then joins the revolutionary corps to seek personal revenge, and, under the influence and education of Hong Changqing, she gradually becomes a conscientious revolutionary fighter. Wu Qionghua is portrayed with a fiery temper in the film, and there are many close-up shots of her eyes burning with indignation.

However, in the TV drama, Wu Qionghua's feisty personality is downplayed. During a press conference before the start of shooting, Yuan Jun, the director of the television version, claimed that the new Qionghua "should outgrow the old one. She should above all be cute, delicate, and charming, so that everybody has the urge to help and protect her. This will make it easier for the audience to relate to her."[39] The TV version of the drama was refashioned into a "teenage idol" type of show, a melodramatic genre portraying glamorous teens as protagonists, set in urban locations. The delicate "feminine" actress Yin Tao plays Qionghua. In the TV version, the women soldiers wear neat clothes, change their hairstyles at will, and invariably seem to have a crush on Hong Changqing, the male Party representative.

The TV version downplays the didactic content of class struggle, represented by the feud between Wu Qionghua and Nan Bantian in both the feature film and ballet. According to interviews with the film director, Xie Jin, love scenes between Wu Qionghua and Hong Changqing were shot but later censored.[40] As planned, the TV version turns out to be a teenage idol show. However, the producer's experiment failed: teenagers did not identify with the kittenish women soldiers fighting in the jungle several decades ago. Middle-aged to older viewers found the reinvention of femininity and sexuality squarely at odds with their own values and were enraged by it.

SARFT's criticism represented the official disapproval of this show. In April 2004, SARFT made clear that it would not put up with excessive modification of the Red Classics by issuing two special administrative orders. One stipulated that production companies dealing with such topics must seek approval from national-level agencies rather than the local level. The other criticized several recent TV adaptations for tarnishing the Party's revolutionary legacy by presenting the heroes in a way distinct from the original portrayal. The reinvention of the heroes' sexuality and romantic life was particularly singled out as the worst offense. These orders served as a warning to production units, particularly those remaking the Red Classics. Because the official criticism could result in a postproduction revision or even a total ban, it could be translated into financial loss. The dominant viewer reaction and official attitude toward these earlier adaptations served as a yardstick for the production team of *Shajiabang* on how free their reinterpretation could be.

The second element that the television adaptations must take into account is the struggle over the novelette's characterization of the main characters. The novelette caused such a fury that the TV production crew had to be extremely careful to tread the line prescribed by the public discourse and to present "appropriate" characterizations.

## She Is Strong, But Not Always: Sister A Qing's Sexuality

Considering the above factors, the challenge TV producers face is to provide a story with moral clarity and enough drama to sustain the interest of the audience. The intention to capture the widest possible audience was made clear in director Shen Xinghao's statements that the show will "provoke the older people's memory and introduce [the story] to the younger ones."[41] The production team's solution was threefold: first, eliminate romantic relationships for the main positive characters, such as Sister A Qing and Guo Jianguang; second, hire big names for the main roles; and third, inflate the interplay between visual and verbal elements. Here, for the purpose of my argument, I will only focus on the first two points.

The removal of Sister A Qing's romantic entanglement is an exercise in self-censorship. This is apparent in the director's comment in a press interview:

> We believe that the viewers would find it hard to accept transforming Sister A Qing from the shrewd and capable Communist in the Peking Opera to a licentious lady boss. Seeing that many people have complained about the portrayal in the TV adaptations, we finally decided to delete the part about Sister A Qing's love affairs.[42]

The ultimate decision on Sister A Qing was that the series should be revised to emphasize her shrewdness and competency, while adding in an element of sensuality. She now devoted her energy wholly to the battle of wits with the enemy and remained in only "working relationships" with the male leading role, Guo Jianguang. But, as a new selling point, both Sister A Qing and Guo now have good-looking assistants as their sidekicks, who are with them constantly, but their relationships never go beyond camaraderie.

Sister A Qing's de facto single life and her sexuality were, however, continually troubling to the producers and scriptwriters. Indeed, the actress in the role looks so young and beautiful that her ability to maintain her honor among a group of powerful men needs to be explained. In one scene, a few customers chatting in her teahouse raise the issue of why no man has yet laid his hand on Sister A Qing. One of them offers an explanation: "Sister A Qing's popularity comes from her ability. She is the type of woman that men respect and women warm to." The scene and the line are obviously intended to contain the danger of Sister A Qing's sex appeal.

Throughout the series, the ambiguous attitude of the producers toward Sister A Qing's sexuality is ubiquitous, emphasizing her attractiveness while defending her purity. The script has cut out the romantic relationships between Sister A Qing and her Communist comrade, but she is depicted as the object of sexual desire for the Japanese Army officer who follows and harasses her. But this transgressive desire, coming from a villain, is rightfully thwarted and punished. In doing so, the moral integrity of Sister A Qing is protected, but the gender norm that a beautiful female body will eventually end up serving as a male fantasy is addressed. What is more interesting is the scene that occurs straight after the harassment incident. Sister A Qing comes home and sits motionless in the backyard of the teahouse, enraged, exhausted, and lost in contemplation. Her adopted son, A Fu, notices her unusual look, and asks her what has happened, to which she sighs and deliberately replies: "It is at time like this that I terribly miss your Uncle A Qing. Women after all, are still women."

This is a significant statement in that it is purposely construed to transcend the socialist discourse of gender neutrality and reclaims a specific gender identity for Sister A Qing by emphasizing her desire for protection from a strong man. It partly squelches the doubt that many may have secretly harbored long before: How did this woman, beautiful and living by herself, deal with the three men without feeling threatened? Here the "one woman versus three men" formula creeps up again stubbornly. In the *Yangbanxi* era, this question could not be dealt with openly, as heroes were larger than life without the complexities and demands of sexual desire. But in the commercial environment of contemporary China, it has become a matter of urgency for this anxiety to be addressed and, more importantly, addressed within the changed gender norm to hold the audience. Sister A Qing's statement transgresses the socialist norms in two ways: First, she is a hero made human in that she feels vulnerable and frustrated at times. Second, in spite of her competence and worldliness, Sister A Qing was portrayed as having an Achilles heel: when her sexual purity was under threat, she felt her inability to defend herself and hence needed her husband, a male figure, to protect her. The postsocialist discourse, while exposing the heroine to sexual violence and ethical dangers, did not endow her with the agency to get out of her predicament. The tensions engendered by the adaptation's departure from traditional norms in the original work are thus addressed by coming back to the traditional notion of a "helpless" and "vulnerable" woman.

## Can Sister A Qing Be Beautiful? Femininity Rearticulated

As discussed above, the preproduction publicity trumpeted the hiring of actress Xu Qing as a tactic to attract viewers. The actress was typecast as sweet and sensual, and most of her previous roles as an urban, modern, sexy girl did not prepare audiences for her leading role in *Shajiabang*. In explaining why Xu was cast for Sister A Qing, director Shen Xinghao explained that she impressed him as one who has the ability to take on a huge variety of roles.[43] However, I argue that casting a sex symbol in the role of Sister A Qing is a deliberate strategy on the part of the production team in its efforts to attract younger audiences. This tactic did not proceed without negotiation and contestation. According to media reports, the television crew drafted a line-up of possible actresses in order to survey potential viewer reactions. When the actor Chen Daoming recommended Xu Qing to the crew, it did not appear immediately to the executives that she was "the one." But Chen believed Sister A Qing's role should be positioned as "an attractive young *qingyi*" (a female role in traditional Chinese opera). His interpretation convinced the crew that the kittenish Xu Qing could be cast as Sister A Qing.[44]

Chen's interpretation of Sister A Qing is not so different from Xue Rong's depiction in the novelette. In defending his portrayal of Sister A Qing, Xue said:

> This story happened in the Jiangsu and Zhejiang region. I know this area, particular the small towns in this area, very well, because I grew up in this milieu. In our neighbourhood, nearly every town has a woman that either runs a tofu store or a teahouse. They are the type that is good at juggling various involvements and they naturally have more stories than most of the ordinary women.[45]

Judging from audience feedback, Xu's casting and her performance generated most of the controversy, mostly related to notions of femininity. Most

viewers compared Xu Qing with the actresses in previous theatrical productions, and many criticized her acting as too coy. There was a general
sentiment that her modern and girlish character was poles apart from the ste-
reotypically capable and steady Sister A Qing.[46] Some wrote to say that Xu's
glamorous looks and sweet manner cry out for attention, and it was too hard
to believe that she could carry on her business as if this counted for nothing.[47]

The comments on Xu Qing's looks and mannerisms were standard in many
press reviews of the series, and questions about her looks were posed to her
constantly during interviews with the press. To these comments, the director
said he valued Xu's personal charm. "Sister A Qing is a smooth and slick
teahouse boss who is good at manipulating social relations. It does not bother
me if she was a bit attractive."[48] Xu reversed the question and asked: "Why
can't Sister A Qing be pretty?"[49] Xu admitted she had not seen the previous
productions before she was chosen for the role, but in her imagination, Sister
A Qing would be terribly pretty and so were the actresses playing her role in
the past. Xu said:

> Sister A Qing was the idol of that [socialist] era. But my Sister A Qing is more
> in keeping with contemporary aesthetic standards. I'm not afraid of being
> compared [with actresses starring in the role previously]. Sister A Qing is a
> strong woman. She has two sides: as an underground Communist agent, she is
> righteous; but as a teahouse boss, she is tactful in currying favors from all her
> clients.[50]

## THE PREDICAMENT OF WORKING WITHIN THE
## CONFINES OF POLITICS AND THE MARKET

In the talks given on the image of Sister A Qing by the production crew, she
is constantly described as a Janus-faced woman. The intention of the production crew was to endow Sister A Qing with enough depth in her character
to appeal to today's audience within the permissible zone. To achieve this
means transgressing the settled boundaries of what a revolutionary heroine
should be. However, how far this transgression can go, and in what area, still
needs to be mapped out carefully. Here I identify three strategies the production side adopted.

First, knowing that a revolutionary heroine is a hard sell in society and
that overt political indoctrination is shunned by the public, Sister A Qing's
political and class identity was downplayed and kept to a minimum. Instead,
her wit and business competence were emphasized in order to establish her
authority, now that her ideological stance no longer naturally generates symbolic power. However, she still has to be patriotic. Nationalism being the

predominant master narrative in post-Mao China, even Xue Rong's commercial rewriting had to honor this boundary. In defending the editorial decision
to publish Xue Rong's rewriting of *Shajiabang*, Xie Lubo, deputy editor-in-
chief of *Jiangnan* magazine, told the press that the main focus of the story is
the Anti-Japanese War because A Qing, even though depicted as a coward,
makes a suicidal attempt to bomb the blockhouse of the Japanese troupe
and dies in the operation.[51] The political markers of Sister A Qing were still
inserted in the production of TV drama here and there, not only to appease the
state but also as a tactic to speak to the memory of the older audiences who
have watched the Peking Opera version. For this purpose, these intertextual
political markers were made to resemble the original scene on a superficial
level, but they generally do not mix well with the overall de-ideologized tone
of the series. One example is the final scene, where Sister A Qing reveals
her real identity to the enemy, stating loudly: "I'm a Communist." The scene
was transplanted wholesale from the Peking Opera, but one viewer told me
that the scene looks so odd and out of place that he nearly burst out laughing.

The second strategy involves the treatment of Sister A Qing's sexuality.
Although the TV production intended to reverse the denial of sexuality from
the beginning and to add sexual elements to the new image, the strong disapproval surrounding her out-of-control sexuality in the novelette, both official
and unofficial, set the limit for the TV production. After deliberation, the
producer opted to not deal with the matter. However, there was a need for
room to maneuver. The repressed sexual relationships found their way into
other characters: the supporting characters from the revolutionary camp and
the main characters in the enemy camp. In the TV series, a love triangle was
arranged among New Fourth Army soldiers Da Gang, Xiao Wang and nurse
Xiao Ling. In addition, there were dating scenes with the rebellious village
lad Sha Silong and his fiancée, Xiuzi, who was constantly harassed by the
spoilt nephew of the local rich landlord. More importantly, this dangerous
and destructive sexual desire was embodied in local thug Hu Chuankui, who
carries on a clandestine love affair with a widow and, later on, is seduced by
a sexy Nationalist spy. Similar plot elements fulfilled the formula for pulp
fiction. The TV series thus still offers voyeuristic pleasure for the audiences
while seeking to satisfy political orthodoxy.

Third, compared with taboo-laden sexuality, nonsexual femininity is
marked as a safe terrain and constitutes the major efforts of the TV adaptation
to restore the human sensibility of Sister A Qing. The casting of Xu Qing as
the leading role, the character's clothing, makeup, gestures, and mannerisms,
as well as a number of plot elements, all contribute to this characterization. I
have already discussed the implications of casting Xu Qing as Sister A Qing.
In the series, Xu is shown as a conventionally beautiful woman, with perfect
accessories and glossy hair neatly tied up. She is shown in traditional clothes,

resembling the costume in the Peking Opera version, but hanging and fitting perfectly onto her slim body and made of beautiful material and tastefully color coordinated. She moves gracefully and throws alluring glances.

Sister A Qing's other feminine qualities include being caring and sympathetic, which were promoted in the press as a defining feature of the TV series. Caring for self and others was defined as a feminine responsibility in Chinese society in this era.[52] Sister A Qing's respectability and authority were earned through her ability to care and help. Indeed, Sister A Qing uses her respectability (*mian zi*) many times in the series to defuse tensions. She provides timely comfort to Hu Chuanqui's father when the old man is distraught at his son's unruly behavior. She offers her shoulder to Hu Chuankui's widow to cry on. She organizes the wedding for Hu Chuankui. To her shop assistant, she is humorous and considerate. Furthermore, her role as a mother, which is left out in the opera and valorized in the novelette, is restored in the series. Sister A Qing's new role as a mother for A Gui is a deliberate design to restore Sister A Qing's respectability in the traditional patriarchal sense. To maintain consistency with her childless status in the Peking Opera version, the TV series added A Gui as Sister A Qing's adopted child. This way, she assumes maternal responsibility and conforms to the status quo without directing too much attention to her feminine body. This narrative strategy thus reproduces the traditional way of assessing the value of women and serves to contain and domesticate the difference set into play by socialist discourse.

## THE GENRE MISMATCH: WHEN THE GRAND EPICS MEET THE EVERYDAY SOAP OPERA

While the narrative strategies used in the TV adaptation could be taken as economically and ideologically motivated, genre change is another factor to which few scholars have paid much attention so far. Most of the Red Classics were created as novels, or plays in the case of *Shajiabang*. What characterizes this body of literature is a national epic style, grand in time-space structure and heroic in spirit. Literary critic Zhang Zhizhong[53] suggests that the grand narratives and epic style demand that the conflicts in the Red Classics be based on politics and ideological struggles, while personal relationships can only play a supplemental role. The Red Classics tend to focus on moments of national crisis, landmark historical events, and life-and-death battles and wars—the occasions when individual fate, personal love, and kinship, seem to be trivial.[54] Zhang argues that this is why TV viewers have found unpalatable the adaptations spiced up with love and kinship relationships. Zhang further points out that some of the Red Classics works, while realistic or even at times very close to a kind of pure recording, nevertheless bear strong links

to the classical *chuanqi* (stories of marvels) genre. This narrative literary tradition, dating back to the fifth century, normally records "human events that
give rise to feelings of wonder or marvel."[55] This generic affinity to *chuanqi*
often endows the characters and the narrative in the Red Classics with a sense
of "unusualness." These unusual qualities were deliberately played down
in the adaptations and submerged within the depiction of everyday local
customs.

Zhang's approach draws attention to the significance of format in the adaptations. However, what Zhang does not touch on is the artistic specificity of
the TV drama genre. That is, to account for the reasons why the adaptations
take on a specific form, one must understand the genre requirements of TV
drama. First, the domestic nature of TV drama [56] dictates that the experience
of watching TV at home is completely different from watching films or seeing an opera in the theater. Film and opera are watched in a dark space, with
large audiences seated in front of a large screen. The striking visual and sound
effects often demand the full attention of the viewers. TV drama, on the
other hand, is watched in an everyday setting on a much smaller screen with
images and sound of relatively inferior quality. The TV viewing experience is
often interrupted by day-to-day house chores and interactions among family
members. Television drama thus does not resort to spectacle as its aesthetic
goal, but instead demands realism. This inherent approximation to the "real"
is summarized succinctly by Thornham and Purvis:

> "Reality," then, in all its rawness, disorderliness and excess, is a quality which
> characterises television in a way that simply does not apply to film, whose more
> focused narratives concern events which are assumed to have been already
> completed before the film begins.[57]

The nature of TV drama as a story-telling machine thus favors the dramatization of everyday life,[58] where personal relationships, love, and everyday
routines play a big part. As such, while the grand battle scenes in some Red
Classics works provide fodder for the film to play up the visual and acoustic
spectacle, they are not the ideal subject matter for TV drama in terms of the
mode of representation and consumption. Therefore, in nearly all the TV
adaptations, the role of spectacle has been reduced and the focus has shifted
to the subjectivity of individuals, with their depth and complexity, and their
everyday lives. This characteristics of TV drama does not respond to the
demands of the sublime aesthetics in the Red Classics, but is the inherent
principle of the medium that carries the story.

The criticism of Zhang and others can also be understood in terms of
the gendered nature of cultural forms. While the Red Classics can be characterized as masculine, with their realistic style, rounded psychological

characterization, and severity, the world of the TV drama adaptations is feminine, in that it emphasizes glamour, emotions, feelings, and private domesticity.[59] This is one of the reasons why critics such as Zhang Fa[60] and Zhang Zhizhong,[61] find the two genres incompatible. Beyond these criticisms lies the wider problem of principle—the hierarchy of cultural forms, which regards TV drama as inferior to literature.

## CONCLUSION: DEFINING FEMALE HEROINES IN POST-SOCIALIST CHINA

The transformation of *Shajiabang* offers an excellent example of cultural production and reception under both socialist and post-socialist conditions. Two opposite processes can be identified in this transformation.

First, in the heyday of socialist cultural experiments, female heroines in the Red Classics were denied their gender, sexuality, and femininity under a "class inscription" in the name of gender equality. The female body and sexuality, kinship, and familial relations were displaced by the political code of class struggle. However, this political gender identity has a connection with the traditional Confucian view of women as guardians of sexual morality.[62]

The growth of consumer society since the late 1970s has redefined gender distinctions and created a proliferation of market-driven representations of femininity.[63] The normalizing standards of good and evil based on class have largely ceased to operate, and the female body and sexuality have been reinstalled in the revolutionary figure. Femininity and sexuality have become the subject of contentious public debate and women's essential characteristics, suppressed during the Maoist years, have started to remerge in public. Simultaneously, women's ability to compete in the private market has become the new defining feature of female modernity in the reform era.[64] Representing the female revolutionary hero now entails reinscribing the differences between the sexes[65] and representing the female revolutionary in the spirit of the market economy, with its pursuit of individuality, wealth, social mobility, and success.

However, the transgression of the official gender norms must honor boundaries defined by the post-socialist cultural production conditions. Conspicuous in this boundary is the continuation of Confucian puritanical ethics of sexual morality. Traditional values of female chastity were maintained for revolutionary heroes in the revolutionary texts. Sex and sexuality have continued to be highly sensitive issues in post-Mao popular discourse. Sexuality is still kept in the private sphere, and the state vigilantly patrols the representations of sex and sexuality in the public sphere.[66] The unconventional representations of revolutionary women can get mired down in controversy and invite public criticism or an official ban. Therefore, there is no commercial incentive to push the boundary on this issue. Eventually, the state and the market comply in the denunciation of this radical transformation of sexuality.

By comparison, the television adaptation of *Shajiabang* represents an interesting experiment in integrating political interest and commercial feasibility. Drawing lessons from the previously failed attempts at reinventing the genre, the TV adaptation deliberately maintains a certain degree of ideological continuity with the socialist era in its portrayal of the heroines. It does not critique the relationship between women and the nation, and its depiction of the heroine's sexuality remains within the parameters of the gender norms implicit in Maoist communism. But the adaptation also provides a dose of viewing pleasure by presenting a glamorous, feminine, yet competent heroine in keeping with the new imagination of women in the post-Deng era. Sister A Qing's manifestation of sexuality is confined within the "superficial"—the makeup, hairstyle and clothing that bring out her naturalized feminine attributes. Her characterization as a capable woman in the revolutionary text is enhanced in the adaptation. The state participates actively in limiting erotic characterizations of revolutionary women, as in Xue Rong's novelette, but acquiesces to the representation of these figures as visually appealing and sexually attractive and capable. The negotiations surrounding the construction of revolutionary women and femininity has taken place with considerable conflict. TV has actively participated in negotiating, repairing, and maintaining the boundaries of gender norms.

# Chapter 5

# Living Red

## Production, Consumption, and Local Memory of Revolutionary Culture in Linyi

Linyi, a medium-size city in East China's Shandong Peninsula, presents itself as a good case to explicate the complex relationships between place, locality, and local memories. As a revolutionary heartland, the place once enjoyed political and cultural centrality in the Maoist days. However, the stigma that Linyi carries now puts the place on the periphery in the shift toward the market. In response to the changing political and cultural circumstances, both the local state and ordinary people see the need to repackage Linyi's revolutionary cultural heritage with different meanings and values.

In chapters 3 and 4, I have looked at the construction of subjectivity along the axes of class and gender. In this chapter, I will shift the focus to place. In the same way that I have examined how class and gender interact to produce social subjects, I will look at how place, as a social marker, interacts with class and gender in constituting subjectivities. The analytical focus of this chapter is consumption. Specifically, this chapter examines how viewers respond to the state's place-making strategies through consumption of the Red Classics.

Scholars have demonstrated how television successfully appropriates the socialist ethos and communication styles to translate neoliberalism into an effective moral economy and to facilitate neoliberal subject making.[1] With a similar purpose but a different focus, this chapter examines the cultural politics of propagating the nation's revolutionary legacy, at a time when the Party's authority and legitimacy have become increasingly less self-evident. More specifically, this chapter looks at how the "Yimeng Spirit," a new conception of locality in Linyi, is propagated through media production and representation, and how the resulting media texts are taken up in the reinvention of local identities. In this way, the chapter seeks to delineate the media's role in the production and consumption of local identities. Using Linyi as an example, this chapter illuminates how the revolutionary legacy was repackaged through media production in a depoliticized discourse of human love and compassion. In the case of Linyi, the local government invokes ideas such as "local traits" (*minfeng*), "locality" (*diyuxing*), and "human nature" (*renxing*) to better enmesh official history with local memory. Meanwhile, the locals invoke unofficial histories, myths, and local memory in their quest for a different social imaginary. This act of humanizing and localizing represents a new possibility for engaging with homogenous official history.

The chapter is divided into three sections: The first section deals with the complex way Linyi locals appropriated the Red Classics for their identity formation. It looks at how the key concepts of realism and class struggle were negotiated and contested in the everyday consumption of the Red Classics. The second section examines how "Yimeng Spirit" was promoted as the core of place-specific subjectivity for Linyi through media and how the locals respond to and negotiate with this place-making strategy. Place-based identity is shown as intricately linked with class and gender. The third section describes how the essentialized place identity is appropriated by market innovations to forge productive new subject positions.

## LIVING RED: THE EVERYDAY CONSUMPTION
## OF THE RED CLASSICS IN LINYI

Linyi presents itself as a good case study to explore the complex relationships between place, locality, and local memories. It once served as a revolutionary base and played a pivotal role in the success of the Communists in the Civil War. Several large campaigns were fought in the area, and the heroic deeds of the locals during the war were textbook propaganda pieces for the Party and staples of popular cultural entertainment. In the market atmosphere, pursuit of consumption and moneyed success are gradually replacing the public enthusiasm for collective political activity, as well as being staples of popular cultural entertainment. However, the revolutionary mark that once distinguished Linyi now puts it on the periphery in the shift toward the market. In response to changing political and cultural circumstances, both local and state authorities and ordinary people see the need to repackage Linyi's revolutionary cultural heritage with different meanings and values.

Linyi has been branded in different historical periods as a result of the state's place-making agenda. Linyi was represented first as a Confucian stronghold, then as a sacrificing mother who nurtured a revolutionary army, and more recently, as a commercial hub. The discursive shift reflects the changing trajectory in state governmentality, narrative, and vocabulary, from a socialist moral economy that stresses collectivity, egalitarianism, class struggle, and revolutionary idealism, to a neoliberal rationality that puts commercial success, self-improvement, and an individualized enterprising spirit at the center of its paradigm.

Another source for constructing the local identity for Linyi is Confucian ethics. The revival of Confucianism increased in the 1990s as a result of a "return to conservatism" after the political upheaval of 1989 produced a backlash against "radicalism."[2] The state-led campaign to institutionalize Confucianism was a conscious act of the CCP designed to consolidate its leadership and ideological control.[3] With the loss of faith in Maoism, the revival of Confucianism also filled the moral vacuum created by three decades of unchecked economic and social changes.

In post-Mao China, the revival of Confucianism as both an official endeavor and a populist interest encountered few obstacles. The popular scholar Yu Dan became a nationwide celebrity with her contemporary interpretations of *The Analects* on TV, while in arenas such as the TV drama, Confucian values such as fate, faith, favor, face, filial piety, patriarchy, and frugality have underpinned the themes of various subgenres, replacing or even subverting the revolutionary or socialist values that previously dominated cultural products.[4]

In fact, the discourse itself is extremely complex and charged with high tension. Different government policies call for different subjectivities, as realized in the Red Classics that were produced throughout different eras. Lisa Hoffman[5] vividly articulates the re-spatialization of Dalian from an industrial city to a commercial center in the north, as well as the corresponding subjectivity this change has introduced, and how these new positions have forged neoliberal subjects in the post-reform era. Echoing her arguments but taking them in a different direction, my discussion of the transformation of Linyi stresses the tensions and contradictions in the competing discourses. These tensions manifest themselves in media productions. Meanwhile, the everyday consumption of these media products further compounds the complexity. My inquiries in this section thus focus on a set of core questions: How do viewers experience the Red Classics? How do they see changes that have been made in the TV version of the Red Classics? Do the viewers respond to the place-making practices of the state through media? What is the nature of this response?

The research findings derived from my fieldwork[6] indicate that the Red Classics are still highly relevant in contemporary Chinese life. All of the respondents to the survey and interviewees confirmed that they had some exposure to the Red Classics. Film still remains the major medium in propagating the Red legacy. About half the respondents prioritize film viewing as the major channel through which they experience the Red Classics. Television re-runs of old films account for the next most significant medium through which viewers are exposed to the Red Classics. Less than one-third of the responses mention Model Opera, picture-story books (*lianhuanhua*) and literature. While television viewing is a voluntary choice, many respondents first encountered the Red Classics through organized collective viewing. Sometimes respondents watched the Red Classics through the *dianying xiaxing*, a term referring to a government endeavor in the Maoist era that used mobile projection teams to visit rural areas and show the Red Classics films to villagers or urban poor. Sometimes the film viewings were organized by schools or work units. Some respondents had an ambivalent attitude toward this viewing, often forced upon individuals as political education, but quite a few recalled the experience with fond memories.

One survey respondent described the experience emotionally:

> [My experience with the Red Classics] began with the open-air film show when I was little. The mobile projection team set up the screen and they usually aired two movies of different subjects every time. The children would come out early with their folding stools to grab the best spots. That is one of my most wonderful memories of childhood.

These accounts suggest that the propagation of the revolutionary legacy from the 1960s to the 1980s had been consistent and effective in the revolutionary base area. The Red Classics, nowadays believed to be a crude form of propaganda, first came to ordinary Chinese in various modern media such as film, ballet, and opera, which are metonymic of modernity to the locals. They offered a different form of entertainment—fresh, easily accessible, and widely different from the traditional story telling or local opera, which constituted a major source of entertainment for a closed, economically backward area such as Linyi. Even though there was a strong tendency in the 1990s to repudiate the role of revolution in the Maoist era as a form of political radicalism,[7] the pleasurable experience, the sense of exoticism and excitement the Red Classics provided to the generations growing up with them cannot be simply dismissed as brain-washing. The Party-state's claim to the socialist legacy is not only much needed for its own legitimacy, but it also provides coherence for generations of Chinese in making sense of their feelings and past experience.

The Linyi locals' accounts indicate that cinema was not always an expensive production relying on spectacular visual and acoustic effects. In fact, it once served as an important tool in narrating the nation's origin and destiny, which was then actively and commonly affirmed in the communal watching. Today, the commercialized pursuits of mainstream Chinese cinema have introduced a disconnection with peasants, the marginalized, and the urban poor. TV drama now shoulders the task of providing popular entertainment, as well as imageries that reflect the collective fear and aspirations of the masses, consumed free of charge and at the convenience of the viewers.

## OWNERSHIP OF HISTORY, REALISM, AND COUNTER MEMORY

In the focus group discussions, interviews, and surveys, realism seemed to be a major evaluative criterion for judging the Red Classics and the TV versions. This concern is closely associated with locality; the respondents tended to make comments on films and TV dramas that dealt with local events. For example, thirty-one of the seventy-one survey respondents in Linyi mentioned *The Red Sun* [*Hong Ri*][8] when they were asked to list the Red Classics they know. The discussions I had with the interviewees tended to revolve around subjects that feature the Yimeng Mountain area, such as the TV dramas *Yimeng*[9] and *The Red Sun*. The respondents' perception of authenticity was based on a number of factors, including the narrative of historical events, the acting, the props, the costumes, and even the location of the shooting. In commenting on the realistic aspects of the Red Classics, locals feel strongly that they "own" the history and that they have the credentials to present a true version of the past.

Opinions tended to diverge greatly regarding which version is more authentic: the original revolutionary-themed works made in the Maoist era or the TV adaptations made in the 2000s. In the intervening period, a neoliberal discourse has largely superseded the class-based ideology. A humanistic, charismatic, individualistic, and entrepreneurial type of subjectivity has overcome the self-sacrificing, morally perfect Party martyrs. In a focus group meeting at Linyi Normal Institute, participants argued heatedly over which versions were more realistic. Two camps formed mainly according to age. The more senior participants pointed out that they could not easily identify with the television adaptations of the Red Classics works because these commercial cultural products "are not true to history." Lao Huang, the television director, believed nearly all of the commercial reproductions failed, as they completely "changed the flavor" of the original works. For the older interviewees, what cannot be changed includes not only the historical facts but also the representation of the heroes and enemies in the original work. For example, Lao Huang commented that he simply could not take a liking to the current revamped image of the central character in *Little Soldier Zhang Ga* [*Xiao bing Zhang Ga*],[10] since the little soldier's image in the original film is strongly rooted in the hearts of people. The new "Gazi" (the nickname for Zhang Ga), far better dressed and full of urban street smarts, conflicts too much with memory. Huang said:

It is all right [for the TV adaptation] to depict the innocence of boyhood. But the story happened during the cruel conditions of war, after all. Too much of the cuteness and pranks is just not realistic.

Lao Lu, the dean of the School of Social Development in his late fifties, criticized the TV drama representation of Sister A Qing, the Communist undercover agent in *Shajiabang*, as improperly rendered:

It is true that some facts were covered up due to political needs in the model opera version, but it is more realistic than the TV representation. She [Sister A Qing] might as well be a singing-girl [in this drama series].

More strident criticism centered on *The Red Sun*. Lao Huang believed the film version of *The Red Sun*, produced in 1963, is far more realistic and better produced than the thirty-six-part TV drama series made in 2008. To Huang, *The Red Sun* is based on real historical events and the main heroes all have prototypes, thus leaving little room for a more daring, creative interpretation. Huang was backed by Lu, who stressed that the film version of *The Red Sun* more faithfully depicted the historical Menglianggu Campaign and the main figures involved the battle. "The film was already accepted as truthful by people, since it spoke to the memory of many witnesses of the war," said Lu.

Lao Huang's and Lao Lu's comments are representative of their generation's interpretation of revolutionary media products, and they echo responses I received in 2006 when I conducted interviews among the diasporic Chinese community in Australia.[11] This generation still bears residual memories of the war and childhood media practices. Earlier research carried out in the Australian Chinese community found that there is a "crossover from memory to nostalgia"[12]in the consumption of revolutionary media products among adults. Back in Linyi, the older generation demonstrated a stronger tendency to assert their historical and cultural competence, embedding it in memory. This flagging of first-hand experience and memory is exacerbated by the increasing commercialization of revolutionary media products.

In Beijing, I interviewed eighty-four-year-old Mao FY. After joining the New Fourth Route Army in 1943 as a health worker, Mao took part in the famous "Menglianggu Campaign" depicted in *The Red Sun*. In general, Mao said he preferred documentary rather than feature films or TV dramas on revolutionary history. Speaking with the authority of first-hand experience, Mao told me he found the new TV reproduction of *The Red Sun* untrue to reality, and thus hard to accept. The representation of the hero, Shen Zhenxin, a fictional divisional commander in the TV drama version of *The Red Sun*, failed to fully impress Mao. The whole effort to "humanize" Shen irritated Mao in one way or another. Shen not only spent most of his time pursuing a female junior officer but also set up blind dates for his guard. Mao also found his constant swearing and petty rages unappealing.

Mao commented:

> Where did this "human element" come from? At that time, most soldiers didn't have time or opportunity to start relationships. Only those who were over 28 years old were eligible for marriage, and getting married needed to be approved by different levels of leadership. You could not simply add all these tricks from the Reform era into [the media products of] that age.

However, the older generation's memories and interpretations were challenged by the younger generation, which has developed a more globalized media competence and has a less affective affinity with revolutionary cultural heritage. In the above focus group discussion, the two younger participants, Xiao Wei and Xiao Zhang, both interrupted when Lao Huang and Lao Lu made the comment that new TV adaptations were not faithful to historical truth. "I think it is a misconception to take the old Red Classics as the truth," Xiao Wei said to Lao Lu. "There is no so-called 'historical truth.' The truth you talk about is only the truth in your head," Xiao Zhang said to Lao Huang. "I believe the TV adaptation is more realistic compared with the earlier versions," said Xiao Zhang. Finally, Xiao Wei asked, "In the original Red Classics, the Eighth Route Army soldiers nearly never die. Can you call this realistic?"

The above comments made by the younger people show that the interpretation of events by the older generation is not observed or respected by the younger generation. In fact, the younger participants were quite eager to present themselves as cosmopolitan, global viewers. The ideological, moral, and aesthetic preferences of the younger viewers are symptomatic of a shift in attitude toward the past, which destabilizes the narration of revolution. However, it is important to understand that the discursive change is not linear, coherent, or one-directional. As a result, the viewers manifested complex and contradictory behavior and perception in their media consumption. This is showcased in the response of Xiao Li, a forty-year-old journalist with Linyi Television. Li said she harbored the same type of doubt over the new TV release of *Little Soldier Zhang Ga*. However, she changed her mind several episodes into the TV show:

> My son made me watch with him, and at first, I just did it as a duty. But as I watched more, I began to see things from my son's point of view. It is true that this "Gazi" has a more contemporary feel, but for children, a TV show has to be fun, more than anything. The Gazi in the TV version has a strong personality and the acting is good. His worldview came from his experience in life, which

is convincing enough. While the old film version had a propaganda purpose, the new one can appeal to the younger ones too, even if they are further away from the War period. For example, my son is very close to his grandma. When Gazi's grandmother was killed by the Japanese Army, my son could easily relate to Gazi, because familial love is universal, regardless of time.

Even for the older generation with their stronger sense of morality, national sentiment, and firmer commitment to revolutionary memory, the contradiction is still clear. It is particularly salient in their perception of Zhang Lingfu in *The Red Sun*. Zhang is a paramount figure in modern Chinese history. Strikingly handsome and extremely talented, he was one of the most well-known and highest-ranking generals of the Nationalist army. Zhang led a legendary life. Early on in school, he had already made a name as a fine calligrapher. In 1924, he abandoned his study at Beijing University to follow Chiang Kai-shek in the Nationalists' advances against other warlords in the North. In 1936, in a moment of rage, he shot his wife and was sentenced to ten years in jail. However, his immense military talents earned him a second chance. He was soon released to serve as a regiment commander to fight the Sino-Japanese War (1937–1945). Zhang successfully led a number of campaigns against the Japanese and his courage and military tactics earned him both fame and jealousy among his peers. In 1945, Zhang was promoted as commander of 74th Corps, an elite Nationalist military unit. Despite his huge reputation fighting against the Japanese, Zhang remained a prime foe of the Communists. Zhang's troops inflicted heavy losses on the Communists in the Lianshui Battle in northern Jiangsu Province. In early 1947, the 74th Corps was again at the forefront of Chiang Kai-shek's series of attacks against the Communists in Shandong Province. A number of factors worked against Zhang's army. Eventually, he was trapped in the mountainous terrain of Mengliyanggu, in Linyi, where he fought to the end and was killed in action by the Communists in a cave hideout.

Zhang's life presents a thorny case for media representation. While the Communists took great pride in defeating him and his army, his unmatched courage, tactics, and victory in the decisive battles against the Japanese are undeniable. The contradiction needs to be reconciled in the viewers' minds. The official historiography was reconfigured and challenged in the form of myth and hearsay. Myths and hearsay are a collective strategy of memory to counter the state's selective rendering of historical figures such as Zhang. This is similar to how Yi villagers use exorcisms and ghost stories to deal with the trauma caused by the Great Leap Forward famine.[13]

For example, after hearing about my research interests, Lao Yu, a retired cadre who once served as head of the Propaganda Department of Mengyin County, where Mengliyanggu Campaign was fought, volunteered to talk to me about an "unofficial truth" regarding Zhang's death. As far as Yu knew,

Zhang was not killed by the Communists, but committed suicide. He was prepared for his death and that is why he left a letter stating his determination to kill himself in order to "return the favor to the Party." After his death, his head was cut off and thrown into the river. However, myth has it that somehow, miraculously, the head and body joined together and floated to Nanjing, then the capital of the Nationalist government. Chiang Kai-shek held a grand state funeral for Zhang. In addition to Yu's serious story of Zhang's death, there are other stories about the mysterious happenings surrounding Zhang's death. One goes that the moment before Zhang's death, a dark cloud flew over a hill where Zhang stood. It was a strange thing because for days there had been a cloudless sky, causing a serious shortage of water supply for Zhang's army. As soon as Zhang saw the cloud, he sighed and said to his subordinate: "It is my fate to die here."

All these narrations paint an image of a tragic hero who must eventually die when the time comes. These comments refuse to conform to the official version of historiography, but rather stubbornly call for sympathy for a hero in dire straits. The contradictions in the official narrations of national history, such as the film version of *The Red Sun*, leave gaps that can be filled by the imagination of ordinary viewers. Hearsay and mythical stories form one strategy to counter official historiography. This strategy is needed in Linyi on a daily basis. In the Menglianggu Memorial Museum, my friends and I discussed Zhang Lingfu and Su Yu, the Communist commander who was responsible for the decisive victory of the major campaign. When I probed a little further on how my friends perceive the battle, which wiped out not only the ablest enemy of the Communist New Fourth Army but also the army that distinguished itself in action against the Japanese invaders, most of my friends failed to give an answer. Indeed without the class discourse in place, and with the improved relationship between the Nationalist Party in Taiwan and the CCP in mainland China, the significance of Menglianggu could not be easily justified and Zhang's fall can only be explained in terms of bad fortune, strong personality (his arrogance), and the internal power struggle within the Nationalist army. In fact, this is exactly the narrative strategy adopted by the TV drama adaptations.

## THE GOOD OLD LOCALS OF LINYI

The above discussion shows that the locals in the Old Base area of Linyi still identify strongly with their revolutionary heritage, as many feel they have complex stakes in the specific narratives of the nation. However, there has been a deep sense of ambivalence among this community regarding how to interpret heroic socialist stories such as the Red Classics. This ambivalence mainly results from the discursive shift in the revolutionary legacy. As discussed by scholars such as Wang Hui,[14] Arif Dirlik,[15] Zhao Yuezhi,[16] and more recently, Zhong Xueping and Wang Ban,[17] the CCP has been pursuing a contradictory policy that both confirms the socialist legacy for its own legitimacy and, at the same time, repudiates it as political radicalism opposed to modernity.

The change in the "hierarchy of identity" caused by shifts in the political, economic, and social environment is happening in a wide range of places, such as Jiangxi[18] and Dalian.[19] Under such circumstances, seeking ways of smoothing out the disjuncture in transforming ideology is both high on the agenda of the local government and a daily need for ordinary people. In the case of Linyi, there is a concerted enthusiasm for reviving an authentic core of values for the construction of a local identity type. This identity is closely linked to the state place-making project in the reform era. The project hinges on the conception and propagation of the "Yimeng Spirit."

Linyi's *laoqu* identity has been contested in the last three decades. The improvised practice at local official level to make the revolutionary past more accessible, relevant and effective is most clearly demonstrated in the conception and propagation of the "Yimeng Spirit" in Linyi. From 1990, the Propaganda Department of Shandong Provincial Party Committee waged four large-scale campaigns to promote and research on "Yimeng Spirit." This is what they call "political brand making (*dazao zhengzhi pinpai*)." Compared with other types of revolutionary spirit, Yimeng Spirit is celebrated for its grassroots nature. It combines Yimeng people's fine character and advanced revolutionary thoughts.

The above discussion demonstrates a significant shift in defining Yimeng revolutionary history: the focus on locality and local identity as a means of branding revolutionary history. In the case of Yimeng Spirit, I would argue that the Party's propaganda apparatus invokes the locality and local characters as a strategy to narrate the revolution in a paradigm different from class struggle. There are several advantages in doing so. First, it allows the Party to get around the issue of class conflict, which is no longer politically convenient in the current environment. Second, the notions of "local traits," "locality," and "local characters" speak well to local longings for reshaping the past in a way that is less loaded with ideological meanings. Third, representing the locals as historically and traditionally trustworthy, responsible citizens open up new subjectivities commensurate with the current ideology of entrepreneurial spirit. These notions are useful in producing new subject positions fit for neoliberal governance in the context of China's economic reform. They will also help facilitate the commercial use of the imagery of the revolution, reinforced in propaganda as well as within literary and artistic representations.

The development of Yimeng Spirit is a conscious act of the Party at different levels. It emerges from the urgent need to reconcile a contradiction: Linyi is a revolutionary heartland because its rural poverty had incited revolution in the first place; at the same time, Linyi is not part of the rural interior, the poor cousin of the coastal cities that have already successfully embraced global capitalism. Linyi, thus, serves as a painful reminder of the inability of socialism to provide for the very people that made the revolution possible. Together with various poverty alleviation programs designed to boost Linyi's economy, the Shandong provincial government and the Linyi municipal government have sought to achieve a rhetorical makeover—to transform the image of Linyi as an economic backwater into the image of Linyi as a vital link in the national economy. This requires the suturing of two narratives: the old narrative of Linyiers as the sacrificing sons of the Party and nation, and the new narrative of Linyiers as pioneers in the national drive for economic development. The meeting ground of these two narratives, as the propagandists discovered, is the locality and the special traits of local people. David Goodman's research on translocal identity in Shanxi Province argues persuasively that the Party-state can effectively project a translocal identity with which the locals seek to identify.[20] The case of Yimeng Spirit confirms this argument, although in the case of Shanxi, it is a provincial identity that the Party-state helped to breed, while Yimeng Spirit is linked to identity at the more local, prefecture level.

The idea of Yimeng Spirit was conceived by the political elite in the state propaganda organs, and this was followed by all-out efforts to delineate, develop, and promote the idea. In November 1990, the Propaganda Department of the Shandong Provincial Party Committee and the Shandong Social Sciences Association commissioned research on Yimeng revolutionary culture. The research team, comprising scholars from the disciplines of philosophy, economics, sociology, and ethics, made a submission on promoting Yimeng Spirit as a cultural vision. From 2004, the local Party organized a series of thirteen events aiming at selling the idea to the general public. These included workshops and seminars, the publication of books theorizing the Yimeng Spirit, revisiting and revamping revolutionary-themed artistic productions, and campaigns to promote moral role models embodying Yimeng Spirit.

A number of artistic works featuring local revolutionary history have been remade. The major work commissioned to further the image of the 'Yimeng" brand is a TV series entitled "Yimeng." The forty-two-episode serial was commissioned by the Linyi Propaganda Department to narrate the locals' contribution to the founding of the nation in the Anti-Japanese War (1937–1945) and the Civil War (1946–1949) in a popular dramatic form. Although the series is not a Red Classics adaptation per se, it nevertheless incorporates into its plot a few stock stories and characters from the Red Classics that the region is known for, including the story of Hong Sao. The story of Hong Sao (literally Red Sister) is nationally known and serves as a metonym of Yimeng Spirit. The tale goes that in one of the "mopping up" (looting) operations by the Japanese army in the winter of 1941 in the Yimeng area, a soldier of the Communist Eighth Route Army went into a coma due to the excessive loss of blood in a battle. When a local woman found him in a backyard, she realized that he was seriously dehydrated. Unable to find any fluid, the woman, who happened to have recently given birth, fed the soldier her milk. In *Yimeng*, this story was incorporated into the female characters of a Yu family, in which mother, daughters, and daughter-in-laws are imbued with the "local characters" based on Confucian ethics, such as benevolence and compassion, gratitude and return of favor, and filial piety and chastity.[21]

## LOCAL RESPONSES TO MEDIA'S PLACE-MAKING: TRANSGRESSING THE REVOLUTION-BOUND LOCALITY

My analysis so far has outlined the media's discursive shift in delineating revolutionary modern history from a class-based, black-and-white ideological confrontation to a rather ambivalent, locally centered cultural approach of appealing to emotions. This is encoded in the imaginary about the place of Linyi and has complex implications for local identity formation. In fact, the success of this discursive shift will hinge on whether local people embrace the idea of reconstructed history based on an essentialized local identity. In this section, I want to explore further the interplay between the national narrative, personal experiences, and identity formation in Linyi.

The in-depth interviews and focus group discussions I conducted in Linyi have revealed that there is a collective social desire to discard official historiography and reclaim local memory. This attempt to disrupt the reified, black-and-white official narrative is manifested in various myths and superstitions the locals resort to when talking about the revolutionary past. These were rooted in individual memories, which are often lived, personal, incoherent, irrational, and anti-modern. In his book on trauma, history, and memory in modern China, Wang Ban[22] sees history as having a paradoxical relationship with memory. On the one hand, official history selectively uses and invents collective memory to make a coherent narrative about the past which serves the nationalist or socialist construction agenda. On the other hand, this history is hostile and suspicious toward memory, because memory encompasses meanings and values that connect individuals within society in ways that conflict with the orthodox administrative, economic, or exchange processes prescribed by history. Individual anecdotes, speculations, and remembrances are suppressed in official representations, but they surfaced in my interviews with informants. Sometimes recounted in an offhand manner, these narratives nevertheless call into question the authority of the historical narrative and give it an ambiguous look.

The Social Development Institute of Linyi Normal College has several research projects on Yimeng Red Culture.[23] In a focus group discussion which I organized in their research center, a group of teaching staff and postgraduates from the Institute together with a visiting television drama director had a heated discussion on what was unique about the revolutionary legacy in the Yimeng area. Professor Ji, the director of the Institute, explained that the uniqueness of Yimeng Red Culture lies in its long time span and the human compassion it manifested.[24] Linyi is the country's oldest revolutionary base, embodying the CCP's development from its early days until the founding of the PRC. At the same time, the tradition-bound Linyi people have shown extraordinary sincerity and a primal kind of love toward their fellow human beings. This compassion is believed to cross class boundaries at times. Ji said:

> Our region is strongly influenced by Confucian culture. Local people are kind and follow traditional ethics. When life and morality come into conflict, life prevails. Certainly in the case of Hong Sao [Red Sister-in-law], the class antagonism is not really obvious. She just did what she could to save a man from dying, and that was the important thing. I believe she would save a Japanese soldier if he were dying. The Americans say we do not value life. This is so untrue. We are the ones who value life most.

Ji gave me several examples to illustrate the 'unsophisticated' nature of the locals. The first example is from the period of the Western colonisation expedition to China in the 1870s, when a German naval vessel approached the coastal area of Rizhao City, then a county, in the region, but was too large to pull into the shore. Locals were watching but apparently failed to understand that there was a war going on. According to this story, the German Navy asked a missionary to pass on the message to the locals that they would be rewarded with a silver coin for each German soldier they helped to come ashore. The locals enthusiastically took on the lucrative business. As a result, it only took about two hours for the Germans to take over Rizhao County.

This outrageous behavior of the locals could be treated as a case of high treason when nationalist and anti-imperialist sentiments run high. It contrasts sharply with literary and filmic images of villagers tortured to death because they refuse to give essential information regarding the plans of the Communist underground organization, or heroic household stories such as that of cowherd Wang Erxiao.[25] More importantly, the reason for this wrongdoing, in Ji's account, is the locals' "simplicity, to the point of foolish-ness" *(chunpu dao youdian sha)*. This lack of sophistication and trust in oth-ers may lead to foolish acts, but it is understandable and can be forgiven. This suppressed stratum of memory unearthed by Ji bluntly dismisses the category of nation and class as an encoding ideological assumption and foregrounds a cultural explanation instead.

Memories and personal stories related to me by my informants also dis-rupt the national and class boundaries between the oppressed and the enemy that are prescribed in the official narrative. The relationships between the Nationalist army and peasants were always full of antagonism and tension in the mainstream narratives.[26] However, Lao Huang,[27] a television director, said that the locals had fond memories of the Nationalist Fifty-Seventh Army when it fought in the area. The soldiers, like the Communist-led Eighth Route Army soldiers, were highly disciplined. Huang also told me that local ban-dits once looted his uncle's house and nearly cut one of his ears off. It was Japanese army medical staff that treated his uncle. Ji also provided another anecdote: during the Anti-Japanese War, Japanese soldiers could venture into the village shops at night to buy wine and then wander back drunk without worrying about their safety.

## GENDERED WRITING OF PLACE: FEMININE AND MATERNAL LOVE AS SIGNIFIERS OF SACRIFICE AND HUMANITY

To reinscribe Linyi as a place full of a "humanistic spirit" instead of a revolu-tionary heartland dominated by poverty-incited class conflicts, cultural works such as the TV drama *Yimeng* rely on fashioning subjects who are "good old locals." The construction of this humane subjectivity is best realized by depicting the Old Base area and its support for the revolutionary cause as distinctively feminine.

Such stories as "Red Sister-in-Law" for which Linyi is known from, have been eulogized in various artistic creations, including musicals, ballets, local operas, and films. They are taken as highly symbolic in the revolutionary narrative. The fact that a mother's milk, meant for her baby, was given to an army soldier signifies the locals' all-out efforts in support of the Communists' war efforts. But one issue has become unclear in the market era: What is the political agency underlining the act of giving to others? In the Party's dis-course about class struggle, the answer is self-explanatory: Yimeng women's sacrifice comes from their affinity with the proletariat and hatred toward the oppressors, be they landlords or the Japanese invaders. However, in the cur-rent ideological shift from the revolutionary to the market, the CCP-sanctioned class consciousness must be replaced with more contemporary credibility if people are still to identify with the heroes and their revolutionary spirit. I argue that the Hong Sao-type of stories is codified with a certain ideological ambivalence so that they can also be read in humanistic terms.

*Yimeng*'s newly forged subjectivity for Hong Sao—that of a loving, humane older sister—no doubt departs from the canonical texts. The official record has it that Hong Sao's prototype was a mute peasant woman named Ming Deying. The fact that decades later, she was found and reunited with the injured soldier Zhuang Xinmin whose life she had saved completed the revolutionary legend and gave emotional closure to the story. Political exhibitions, such as the Yimeng Spirit Exhibition,[28] invariably display photos of Ming and Zhuang together. Ming's wrinkled face and a grateful Zhuang almost metonymically stand for the relationship between the revolutionary base and the Communist army—that of a self-sacrificing mother and her son. It symbolized the class-based solidarity between the proletariat and the Party that represents its interest.

But after seeing these photos in various revolutionary sites in Linyi, I was told by my interviewee, Lao Huang, that this Ming was not the real Ming and that soldier Zhuang was not the one actually saved. Not that Hong Sao was a total fabrication. The man who is credited with bringing the story to light, a propaganda cadre, told Huang that everything was true except that the real Hong Sao never wanted to be known. When the soldier started to recover in hospital and news of his fortuitous rescue started to spread, the woman told him to be quiet about the whole thing because she felt really embarrassed and did not want to enrage her husband and thus risk a divorce. Nobody came forward when the CCP tried to identify the real Hong Sao. The event was thrust on Ming Deying because she was mute and could not object, and Zhuang was obliged to submit in the end. This speaks volumes about how women are not only useful to the revolution corporeally but also discursively. The real Hong Sao offered her milk and had to offer her story as well, despite her desire not to publicize it.

Lao Huang's intimate knowledge of the Hong Sao event largely concurs with the official narrative, but differs as to whether Hong Sao has political agency. In his account, Hong Sao is a woman who steps outside the bounds of traditional ethics to rescue a man by feeding him her milk, yet she does not pride herself on this act by embracing the moral legitimacy granted to her by the Party. According to Lao Huang, her extraordinariness lies in her ability to let compassion overrule the traditional ethical implications her actions might have. It is not about her obligations to a fellow member of the same class. This revision of the story stubbornly puts Hong Sao's struggle into the realm of moral economy, but this is not a class struggle. It lays bare the constructedness of the official narrative about Hong Sao. The fact that Ming was mute is a metaphor of the voiceless female subject in the nationalist discourse. Spivak's famous article, "Can the subaltern speak," most clearly identifies the historically muted subject of subaltern women in the Third World.[29] Working mostly within a postcolonial deconstructive framework, Spivak stresses that women lost their subjectivity/voice under the dual suppression of patriarchy and imperialism, both during and after the national independence struggle in India and other colonial countries.[30] Here we see a double process of speaking for women: in the revolutionary era, Hong Sao's act was usurped by the state ideological apparatus to promote class consciousness; and today, cultural elites are trying to speak for women again in the humanist discourse. The subaltern women still cannot speak for themselves.

Lao Huang's depiction of the iconic Hong Sao departs from class-based socialist discourse, but fits in the essentialized "good local" narrative promoted by TV drama. In Huang's voluntarily searching for an alternative account of the Hong Sao story and offering it eagerly as the "truer" version, one can indeed detect a desire to transcend the revolutionary-bound Old Base identity. What drives the locals to stipulate a cultural essence of the locality? Here I suggest that one of the main reasons for this emerging recourse to traditional order and cultural essence is the contradictory state discourses on history. In three decades since the reform, state historiography is "schizoid": on the one hand, it avows revolutionary history for its own legitimacy, while on the other hand, it promotes a counter discourse to repudiate the Maoist past in order to justify the neoliberal economic order pursued in the new era. This contradiction, in the context of Linyi, has created an anxiety in local identity.

Another reason for the return to tradition and culture is that the commercialization and mockery of revolutionary culture has been so prevalent that self-righteous Party propaganda risks "malfunctioning," or even inviting ridicule. This ideological detour, made in the face of other competing discourses, is nowhere clearer than in the making of the Hong Sao sculpture for the Yimeng Exhibition. Initially, the Linyi Chinese Communist Party (CCP) Propaganda Department commissioned the Academy of Fine Arts of Qinghua University to design and make a sculpture of Hong Sao as part of the project. However, after researching the history of the event, Professor Hong Mai'en, the exhibition's chief designer, at first refused to include the sculpture section in the exhibition. Hong told the Propaganda Department that he doubted whether the story was true and was worried that it would be received with cynicism. First, Hong was disturbed by a fake photo event during the Sino-Vietnamese war in the late 1970s. Dubbed "Hong Sao in a new era," the photo, depicting a woman feeding a People's Liberation Army soldier with breast milk, was widely published by the media, and only later disclosed as a fake. The subjects of the photo were merely posing. The story caused widespread disgust about the manipulative nature of propaganda. Second, artist Liu Gang created a series of artistic works in which he mocked various revolutionary characters, including Hong Sao. In his controversial parodic installation, a man in PLA uniform was shown sucking on the breast of a woman dressed up in the traditional attire of the Yimeng Mountainous Area. Because of these competing discourses at work, Professor Hong Mai'en expressed his concern over technical difficulties in rendering such a subject as Hong Sao. In this case, the revolutionary body, which was sublime and asexual and accepted as a popular icon, is now open to erotic association.

Professor Hong was eventually convinced of the legitimacy of Hong Sao's sacrificial spirit, after exploring revolutionary heritage in the region and encountering locals personally. Interestingly, his belief was not only pre-mised on historical "facts" but also on a naturalized local identity—that the "good old Linyi locals" were capable of such good, selfless conduct because of their cultural heritage. Lao Li,[31] a local official in charge of the exhibi-tion, told me that Hong Sao's devotion should be understood as maternal: "It's the natural feeling a *lao sao* [the local term for older, married women] would have for an adolescent soldier her son's age. Some soldiers were as young as 12 or 13. Surely one could understand motherly love." To contain the possible indecent associations with the sexual body of Hong Sao, the "negotiated" version of the sculpture depicts an older woman baring her breasts, looking ahead, while a teenage boy lies unconscious on her lap. In a way, this sculpture is representative of the awkward position of the revo-lutionary heritage in post-Mao China. Hong Sao's body, once claimed by the Party, is now turned into a contested site where contradictory discursive forces operate.

The recuperation of the traditional and the local are thus attempts to get around difficulties and contradictions in replacing the old revolutionary iden-tity with a new, neoliberal one in this new context. It affirms the revolutionary past but remains ambivalent toward the class subject position prescribed by the state. As the socialist revolution is regarded as a disruption to the ultimate success of capitalism in China, deploying concepts of local cultural essence instead of class agency to narrate the local past constitutes a conscious reac-tion to China's market orientation. This strategy rescues the locale from being pinned down as the socialist memory of the nation—the "other" of the developed, coastal area. Furthermore, this construction of regional character proves useful in explaining the material success of Linyi and in staking out new subjectivities that are compatible with the market economic order, yet still embodying socialist legacies. Seen along these lines, the *laoqu* identity stands for trustworthiness, self-sacrifice, commitment, and competitiveness, which have collectively taken the place of class as the central organizing ideology for model citizenry.

## FORGING NEW SUBJECTIVE POSITIONS

To transmogrify the revolutionary past by invoking traditional ethics or an essential local identity is useful not only for smoothing out the disjuncture created by the outmoding of class discourse but also for integrating Linyi into the market economy. In other words, a political brand name such as "Hong Sao" has become a commercial brand. In the same manner that the image of Shajiabang is packaged for the market, as discussed in chapter 4, the revolutionary heritage in Linyi has become commodified and is now sold in the marketplace in the form of products, images, and experiences. This grand project to appropriate revolutionary history includes a master plan to promote Linyi as a destination for a "Red cultural tour," to package commercial products with revolutionary imagery and to churn out artistic works depicting local revolutionary events.

In each of these marketing schemes, the local cultural identity features prominently as the new "selling point." In September 2007, Linyi municipality undertook a packaged tour promotion that was built on the theme of "beautiful landscape, loving people" (*lingxiu shanshui, qinqing Yimeng*). What is significant is that not only did this image-making campaign hinge on the historical significance of Linyi as a revolutionary hub, but also, and more importantly, it tried to emphasize Linyi's "local traits"—the recuperated traditions and the people who embodied these traditions. Here, cultural memory was being selectively used as cultural capital. The target audience—tourists who might spend their weekend in Linyi—were not being enticed by the bitterness of the war or the poverty of the region, but by the simplicity of its people. Meanwhile, Linyi municipality has initiated twenty-four projects capitalizing on local Red culture, of which ten have been completed. These include Yimeng Old Base brand wine, Hong Sao wine, and the organic food product series named after revolutionary sites such as Jiujianpeng and Lijiazhai. These names, their publicity originally gained from Mao-era propaganda, but carried over to the present in public memory, bring positive connotations to the product; they are metonyms of the local people, who are known for their trustworthiness, their single-minded devotion and commitment, and their honesty—something of a rarity in a profit-driven market society. Jing Wang astutely describes the moment in early 1992 when the state started to embrace this culture of symbolic capital, and she argues that economic, political, and cultural capital are now mutually convertible.[32] Hong Sao wine serves as a textbook example of her argument.

Furthermore, this construction of regional character proves useful in explaining the material success of Linyi and in staking out new subjectivities which are compatible with the market economic order yet still embody socialist legacies. These characteristics are used to explain the locals' achievement in "catching up" with the economically advanced regions; they are thus qualities necessary for the new age. Meanwhile, the self-invented cultural traits, although they embrace the individual successes, still avow the authority of the Party and socialist ideals of self-sacrifice and collectivism, demonstrating a kind of market ethos with socialist characteristics.

This kind of *laoqu* moral leadership is showcased in the image of Wang Tingjiang,[33] a villager in Linyi Luozhuang District, who donated his six million yuan chinaware factory to the village, causing quite a stir in the local area. Jiang Zemin, the president at the time, met Wang during his visit to Linyi in 1992. Wang is hailed as personifying the Yimeng Spirit, exemplified in his endeavor to "return favor," yet another mythic trait of the Yimeng people. It serves as an example of how the remote cultural myth is garnered for the needs of the Party in subject making.

Another case in point is the Yimeng Spirit Exhibition. Leaders of the local Propaganda Department found the original conception of the exhibition unsatisfactory because it focused only on the revolutionary past. The Yimeng Spirit must extend to the present, manifesting itself in transforming Linyi in an entirely different type of context, that of the market. In the end, the curators had to include the last section, "The Great Practice of the Reform Era," to showcase a transformed Linyi and the new urbanized landscape resulting from economic progress. Similar advice was also given to scriptwriters of the *Yimeng* television drama series. They were told the story needed to reflect the "earth-shattering changes" that have taken place since the reform era.

## CONCLUSION

In this chapter, I have discussed some new developments in the production and consumption of revolutionary culture by using the city of Linyi as case study. Linyi is a locale wrought with conflicting identities, as a direct result of the government's contradictory attitudes toward its revolutionary past. On the one hand, as a revolutionary base for the CCP, it figures prominently as a symbol of the Party's solidarity with the oppressed in the discourse of class struggle. On the other hand, this legacy has been rendered obsolete in the hegemonic ideology of global capitalism. Linyi's revolutionary past still features prominently both in the Party's official governance and in everyday life. As long as the centralized political structure is still in place, the need to legitimize the homogenous narrative of official history and myth of the founding of the nation remains strong and perhaps more acute because market forces have threatened to encroach on the old fabric of everyday life and social relations that came into being in the socialist era. However, revolutionary culture needs to be reconfigured to appeal to the populace in a society that has already embraced the market, commodities, and consumerism. This reconfiguration takes place not only consciously at the official level but also as an everyday practice, when individuals attempt to make sense of the changes and negotiate their subjectivity in a drastically changing society.

Television dramas such as *The Red Sun* and *Yimeng* play an indispensable role in recreating Linyi's past for the present. The contemporary fascination with TV drama, its capacity to provide both edification and pleasure, is the most important motive behind the production of *The Red Sun* and *Yimeng*.

In reading the Red Classics TV drama adaptations, the interpretative community in Linyi has demonstrated a desire to transgress the revolutionary bound locality. To transcend the class discourse around which the Red Classics formerly revolved, the locals now resort to humanism and other traditional ethics to recast a socialist subject originally distinguished by its solidarity with the Party. Traditional ethics were both expelled and recalled into service in socialist realism when the discourse of class struggle reigned. In revolutionary discourse, the discourse of class is used to transform and displace familial ethics and kinship bonds. The idea of class in Marxist terms is based on relations of production, not on blood; love and hatred are based on class differences. On the other hand, the class struggle, being such a new concept, was expressed in terms of familial ethics to appeal to the masses. Locals have embraced the recuperated Confucian traditions and invented local traits as new ideologies and subject positions. This recourse to locality and cultural essence is useful in imposing cohesion on the memory of the past. The official historiography reflected in the major works of the Red Classics, which reduced history to the CCP's struggle, leaves gaps for individuals to fill when they seek to reconcile the conflicts between national narrative and local memory on a daily basis. This is especially true in Linyi, where revolutionary sites and cultural products are everywhere and readily accessible. A natural cultural essence and locality appears to be adopted by the locals as a strategic response to overcome this predicament. TV drama serials, such as *The Red Sun* and *Yimeng*, both constitute and are constitutive of this discursive strategy. This effort to suture the disjunctions between "socialist legacy and neoliberal strategies" seems to be prevalent at both the production and consumption level.

This new discourse is also enabling, in that it opens up new subject positions for the individuals living in the locality. The reframing of the revolutionary legacy through a cultural myth marks a shift from a class-based subject position to one of productive capitalist labor. It offers a subjectivity that locals readily take on in order to be seen as fitting in with this new ideology of economic development. TV dramas such as *Yimeng* thus construct a discursive space that satisfies the conflicting demands of local identity, global capitalism, and socialist citizenship.

*Chapter 6*

# The Question of Faith in
# TV Drama Series

By the early 2000s, nearly all the core texts of the canonical Red Classics had had their TV adaptations. For a long period, this genre was a fixed market niche with a specific audience group, though by now it was beginning to seem as though revolutionary drama was no longer capable of grabbing the public's attention to the extent that it had. Despite this, the development of a broad collection of revolutionary TV productions was still progressing, and through this development emerged a refreshed subgenre that once again placed revolutionary drama in the spotlight. This time it was spy drama.

From 2006 to 2018, spy genre TV dramas had become a truly popular phenomenon, particularly after the airing of *The Silent War* [*An suan*] in 2006. Based on the critically acclaimed novel of the same name by Mai Jia, this series had all the familiar tropes of Chinese spy fiction and film, namely an intriguing plot involving mind games between the usual suspects: the Communists, the Kuomintang, the Soviets, and the Japanese. This series in particular shone, with its superb cast and fascinating unpredictable plot. The success of *The Silent War* led to a deluge of spy series, including *Lurk* [*Qian Fu*, 2008], *The Cliff* [*Xuan ya*, 2012], *Red* [*Hong se*, 2014] and *The Kite* [*Feng Zheng*, 2017].

Spy films were a significant sector of the Chinese film industry. The genre had begun in the early PRC days stemming from a paranoia that, even though the enemy with weapons had been wiped out, there was still a hidden enemy actively engaged in a desperate struggle with the new regime. These fears produced the first spy genre film *The Invisible Battleline* [*Wuxing de zhanxian*, 1949], based around the story of the hunt for a group of spies deployed in the new Republic by the Kuomintang. The film ushered in the use of espionage as a plot device. The popularity of the genre was heightened by the events of the time, the ambience of rivalries and intrigues between major power camps during the Cold War and the fresh memory of brutal conflict between Kuomintang/Japanese and the Communists.

The espionage genre, in film as well in TV, received a new boost in the mid-1980s, when the pressure of economic reform pushed the "entertainment film" to the fore.[1] With the sentiment and memories of the consumer base now far removed from the warring period, these films adopted novel strategies to relate to audiences. Thematically, the spy films and TV drama series still narrated the national struggle against foreign aggression and the CCP's battle with the Kuomintang, however, the overriding imperative now was to provide a forward-driven narrative similar to that of thrillers or politico-thrillers. The spy genre had amassed a corpus of works and a nationwide audience. Such works include the film *Spitting Blood in the Black Valley* [*Diexue heigu*, 1985] and twenty-part TV drama series *Remorseless Pursuit* [*Wuhui zhuizong*, 1997]. Similar to previous spy works, the primary formula of these films carried a mandate to educate and inform. However, the protagonists of these series had become more atomized characters with specialized skills and dogged wills, rather than the exemplary hero archetype of the proletarian class.

The overriding imperative driving this resurgence of interest is to provide entertainment rather than education.[2] To achieve this goal, TV drama series need to speak to the structure of feelings that are shaping the lives of the public in the new millennium. The prevailing sentiment of the public is heavily shaped by China's turbulent past; China's modernization was gained through a radical revolutionary program. Furthermore, as a result of numerous periods of colonization, anti-imperialist sentiment dominates feelings about the previous century. The memory of this history is filled with narratives of humiliation, rebellion, agony, sacrifice, and progress. The international political and economic tensions, as well as social unrest in the new millennium could well trigger sentiments often encapsulated in the spy genre.

Since the onset of this third wave of popularity for espionage drama in the new millennium, TV has now overtaken film as the principle medium of choice. With the third wave of spy series, the clash of universal ideologies as a central theme has gradually receded to the background. After the 2004 SAPPRFT (State Administration of Press, Publication, Radio, Film and Television), 2013–2018, previously SARFT) ban on popular criminal investigation TV series for displaying excessive violence, spy series had become the outstanding successor by grafting the criminal investigation genre with the Red Classics genre.[3] Cai sees the genre as a new mode of propaganda, that "indicate an innovative bond between the CCP official rhetoric and the commercial media entity" to facilitate a "dominant reading."[4] The spy series certainly relies on the fusion between mainstream ideology and commercial strategies, however, the dominant reading remains complex and vague. I argue that the success of the espionage genre lies exactly in this indecision on a clear ideological agenda. For example, Ni[5] explores this ambiguity and looked at how the idea of "revolutionary belief"—the Communist ideal central to all the Red Classics narrative—is now hollowed out and infused with personal spiritual pursuit. Television's inability to articulate a clear position on the Communist belief system is a true reflection of the public confusion and anxiety on the issue of belief. The tangled relationship between the traditional ethics and political belief has troubled the public for some time in the post-Mao era. There is a general tendency to state political beliefs in terms of or displace it with personal spirituality. Ironically, TV drama fulfills its role as the storyteller of the contemporary society by catching the zeitgeist of the time. What characterizes the spy series since the new millennium, apart from the intricate schemes and ruses, are the moral complexities: the individual hero's moral choices with regard to belief, love and trust. To understand these drama series, one must look at the moral anxiety that has defined the zeitgeist in the last three decades.

## MORALITY, A MURKY SCENE

The thirty-five years of the post-Mao era were with filled with the angst of searching for a moral compass. An initial sense of moral panic pervaded the public discourse in the 1980s, when commercialization and marketization radically changed the Maoist moral order centered on collectivism and asceticism.[6] For the first time, economic development superseded politics as the force in command. However, as the economic reform deepened in the 1990s, the anxiety temporarily eased. The public gradually accepted economic development as the "absolute principle," as proclaimed by Deng Xiaoping.

By the early 2000s, the public perception of a complete breakdown of morality suddenly became acute. It was clear that by then, neither the transcendent Confucian values of moral duty nor Communist ethics of altruism and asceticism could provide the moral anchor for a society increasingly more competitive and individualistic. Moral malaise was perceived to be abundant. Social trust crises set off round after round of heated debates on the debasement of humanity and the loss of meaning and innocence. In April 2011, the ex-premier Wen Jiabao gave warnings on the serious moral decline and the lack of social trust in Chinese society.[7] Since then, the discussion of moral decline has become a common topic and accepted fact in the public domain. Mao's utopian project had been largely abandoned and materialism and pragmatism have only led to cynicism and hedonism.[8] People, especially the younger generation, were weary of ideals, as socialism lost its currency. Religious belief was largely in a void. The enormous energy spent on the Communist utopian project had been seemingly wasted and could now only be channeled into the seeking of material comfort. However, the logic of the market and the principle of self-interest could not serve as a belief to live or die for. Hedonism could only lead to a meaningless existence and exhaustive mental state.[9] It was a confluence of these factors that has led Chinese to desperately seek a meaningful spiritual life.

The atmosphere of constant moral dilemma was taken on by the spy television dramas. Arguably, the most important way of storytelling in contemporary China, television has always played a crucial role in various social formations in China.[10] TV drama is seen as the medium that deals with the fundamental social issues of China, its texts the manifestation of collective unconsciousness.[11] Hooking viewers with sensitive social issues or arousing their historical memories, TV drama epitomizes the aesthetic consciousness, cultural modality, social consensus, and ideology of our times. As a result, the protagonists of TV spy dramas are invariably torn by the moral struggles around ideas of "faith," "ideal," "responsibility," and "love," and it is in these struggles that the viewers find echoes in their own lives. These stories are thus not just a recounting of history, but are representations of what concerns the Chinese public in a high metaphorical sense.

The remainder of the chapter will demonstrate how the spy genre of TV drama poses ethical and moral questions related to contemporary daily life, through textual analysis and viewer responses. It will contend with scholars who see "something profoundly wrong with the Chinese spirit."[12] I argue that the concept of political belief remains a major point of concern in these revolutionary spy dramas. The connotation of belief is often hollowed out, and belief is certainly shown in tension with Confucian moral ethics, nonetheless, there is a desire to give credit to political belief as the ultimate source of a revolutionary's strength and will. There is also a genuine desire to understand the pressure of living a lie, and price paid for defying the ethical laws of ordinary life. However, the overall message seems to be that the lack of political aspirations contributes to the moral slide in China rather than political belief itself as the main cause of it as scholars have argued.[13] This group of spy dramas speaks to the public anxiety about the moral transformation of individuals in the consumerist society and has created a moral self that attends to Confucian ideals, socialist moral legacy, and neoliberal values at the same time.

## POLITICAL BELIEF AND ITS MORAL COST

It almost feels reductive to call *The Kite* a spy drama. Certainly, there are set pieces, but in terms of the intricacies of espionage, the plot is not short of holes, compared to other series. *The Kite* at heart is a story about the Communist faith and the moral torment the protagonists have to go through in leading the double lives that espionage mandates. The Communist under-cover agent Zheng Yaoxian, code name "Kite," infiltrates the Kuomintang army's Bureau of Investigation and Statistics of Military Affairs Commission or *Juntong*, and becomes invaluable to its chief Dai Li, the spymaster. Only his director contact, Doctor Lu, and Zheng' fiancée are aware of his mission and his identity. In the meantime, Kuomintang spy Han Bing is planted in the Yan'an headquarters with the code name "Shadow." Each mole works hard to gain an advantage in intelligence over the other side and to find the moles in their respective organization.

Known for his mercilessness and wit, Zheng wins the trust and admiration of his peers in *Juntong*. While under cover, he has taken many of these "coworkers" under his wing, and some of them are prepared to die for him in the name of fraternity. In particular, one minion Gong Shu has been assigned to be his left hand by the chief and develops a strong mentor-mentee relationship with Zheng. This protégé turns out to be a ruthless master spy just like Zheng, except he is on the opposite side. In the meantime, Zheng's name evokes deep frustration and resentment on the part of the Communist spies who do not know his true identity. Believed to be the mastermind behind much successful sabotage and arrests, Zheng is at the top of the "to-kill" list for the unknowing CCP task force.

The story unfolds with Zheng outwitting everyone around him until about one-third of the way into the series. With the death of the two people who know his true identity, Zheng hangs on for his mission and his life. He becomes effectively a "kite cut loose." Disaster can occur at any time, and eventually, he is forced to flee as a fugitive from *both* sides, shot in the knee by a CCP squad and crippled. After the communists take over, Zheng continues to stay under cover as an ex-Kuomintang librarian, his mission, to help the police to track down the remaining spies including the paramount Shadow, who almost certainly penetrated into the core espionage body, lurking around and waiting for opportunities to deal some fatal blows to the new regime.

*The Kite* is not especially rigorous in honoring the themes of espionage thrillers. Nor is this the main concern of this drama series. From episode 19 onward, it becomes more about the exploration of the cost of espionage, personal and otherwise, and political faith. Over the course of three decades, Zheng Yaoxian lives in an infernal world, losing two lovers and estranged from his only daughter, all for his Communist political convictions. Not that he does not complain. Once, when in touch with his CPC contact:

> I have endured for a decade now. I don't know how many decades I have to continue to endure this? How many decades does one have in a life? When can I live like a human being?

From this point onward, the narrative revolves around the aporia with which Zheng has to come to terms. In order to reach the Communist utopia that gives meaning to his life, he has to do things that threaten to smother moral scruples, including those that are considered most basic to human nature. It is thus a tale about the burden of tough choices. It pits the political belief and collective goal against nearly all the obligations defined as cardinal to traditional Confucian ethics: those between husband and wife, father and child, friends, and siblings. Director Liu made this focal point clear by putting a capper in the subtitles before the credits roll at the end of each episode:

> Political belief rules supreme. But to what level does it need to be elevated for one to have the conviction to sacrifice the fundamental relations that makes up the core of your humanity?

The tension between moral order and the political is an important issue that the CCP feels the need to resolve when it communicates its authority to the masses. Literature and art is a major means through which the elites articulate their principle of behaviors to persuade the people to adopt a Communist theodicy, "a cultural system that addresses the problem of meaning at the highest level—that is, at the level of existence."[14] Meng Yue[15] and Lee[16] provide insightful analysis on how the cultural agents of the state have revamped the "ethical order" in rural societies, for example, "repackaging" a local ghost story such as *The White-haired Girl* into a story about class struggle. On the other hand, both Li Yang[17] and Liu Fusheng[18] argue against a dichotomic relation between the rural ethical order and revolutionary ideology. Instead, revolutionary ideals revise, restore, and reconstitute the traditional moral order. *The Kite* zooms in on the dialectical relations between Communist utopian as a transcendent moral vision and the "self" that is called upon to make sacrifices for the good of the collective, but at the cost of abandoning his moral obligations. Over half a century, Zheng Yaoxian is tortured by the tough decisions he has to make as a matter of political imperative, and the distressing consequences those decisions incur.

The most harrowing moral challenge comes from the "betrayal" of brotherhood. For example, in episode 33, Song Xiao'an, one of Zheng's blood-sworn colleague and a mole planted in the mainland by Kuomintang after 1949, gets approval to go back to Taiwan to look after his aged mother. Zheng's intimate knowledge of Song helps him to crack a coded message Song relays to Taiwan regarding when and where he is to leave the mainland. On the day, Zheng goes with his team to the dock where Song plans to embark on his trip back to Taiwan, to help identify him. However, Zheng's daughter happens to appear on the scene and recognizes him while he is disguised as a beggar, which creates a commotion amidst all the travelers on the docks. Alerted,

Song also recognizes Zheng. Song mistakes Zheng's CCP team as being in waiting for Zheng. To cover a Zheng escape, Song fires to draw attention to himself and urges Zheng to leave with his daughter. Refusing to submit to the pursuers, Song is shot to death at the scene. But he dies without fear or regret. His last words are: "The Lord had mercy to give me the chance to see my Sixth Elder Brother before I die!" Once again, Zheng accomplishes his mission to perfection. But while Song Jianzhi is being shot to pieces, the supposed victor Zheng hides himself behind a rock and cries his heart out. As the mission wraps up, with death on both sides, the distressed Zheng bares his soul to a buddy on how political belief always stands above the bonds of brotherhood:

> The most outstanding spy . . . may have to endure the misunderstanding on the part of his family and friends for life and face whatever mishaps this profession might bring. But when the state needs you, do you have any other option? No. Not everyone qualifies to make this kind of sacrifice for the nation. If you have done it, it testifies to your value. There is no other reward more perfect than this feeling of self-worth.

The series are peppered with poignant moments like this one. Every now and then, Zheng has to contemplate the cost of serving the country and his commitment to an ultimate Communist utopia. For years and years, he has to live a deceitful double life as an ex-Nationalist librarian, leaving his only daughter in the care of a neighbor. During the Cultural Revolution, his daughter turns away from him because of his "shameful" past. Sacrificing one's own life for the Party's mission is not new in works of the Red Classics genre. In fact, the tension between political fealty and private attachments is a recurring theme. Works in the socialist canon, in particular the *Bildungsroman* genre such as *The Song of Youth*, tell the story of the growth of the main character from a flawed "individual" to a mature human fully equipped with class consciousness.[19] Transformation from unreconstructed spontaneity to socialist consciousness is an important theme of the Stalin-era socialist novel.[20]

As discussed in previous chapters, the post-Mao revision of the Red Classics represents a conscious reversal of political indoctrination, by attempting to restore, with varying degrees of success, the humanity, and agency of the revolutionary subject. The commercialized revolutionary discourse is often expressed at the narrative level in the sexualization of the heroines, the unleashing of primitive vitality in the heroes, and love that transcends nationality and class division. *The Kite* adds a new dimension to the revised revolutionary semantics by focusing on Zheng's struggle with cross-camp fraternity, which in essence, is the tension between an historical ideal and the lived experience. That the protagonist is troubled by the cross-camp fraternity is no small matter. It questions the value and validity of ideology as the meaning of a life and highlights the alienating nature of the realpolitik.

The world presented in *The Kite* is ambiguous, ironic, and open to multiple readings. Hardly any of the protagonists can be easily labeled as good or bad. Nearly all of Zheng's alliances in the Kuomintang camp are endowed with a heart-breaking humanity so that each death comes with weight and impact on Zheng's conscience. They often serve as the obverse of Zheng—loyal to friends, filial to parents, and committed to their spouses and lovers. For example, Zhao Jianzhi, Zheng's buddy, commits suicide when he was arrested by the CCP, to avoid betraying Zheng under Communist interrogation. Zheng's daughter is in the care of Gao Junbao, son of a former Kuomintang chief spy who plotted against Zheng but was ensnared by Zheng's schemes and gets shot by Zheng's disciple Gong Shu. Only a young boy at the time, Gao Junbao is traumatized, and this returns to haunt him often when he becomes an adult. Gao grows up burning to take revenge. But thirty years later, when he finally sets it up so as to shoot Zheng at the same spot where his father was shot, in the presence of Zheng's grandson, he could not bear the thought of inflicting the same pain on this little boy and shoots himself instead. Gao shows more compassion than Zheng, leaving the die-hard Communist again ravaged by his guilt.

Like many of the Red Classics works on the history of the Civil War (1946–1949), *The Kite* interrogates the same issue: How the Communists prevailed over the nationalists. Unlike the previous works though, *The Kite* takes "faith in Communism" as the ultimate reason for victory rather than Party unity, incorruptibility, or superb combat skills. However, the drama series lay bare the discrepancy between worldview and actual experience by stripping the safety nets of family and friends from the protagonist. The righteousness of the Communist meaning making system does not work as a panacea for ameliorating the moral dilemmas Zheng has to face. In fact, it often sounds hollow every time it is cited to remind Zheng of his duty or to fix his broken psyche. One such critical moment comes in episode 40: instructed by Taiwan, Zheng's disciple Gong Shu returns from Hong Kong to the mainland to look for Zheng, who has been entrusted to lead a restoration of the Nationalist spy network. Knowing that Zheng has the personal trust of Gong, the CCP instructs him to serve as a bait for Gong. Seeing through his inner struggle, his superior warns Zheng that he should put "national interest above all and reserve his deepest feeling 'for the people.'" As expected by Zheng, Gong Shu has been waiting for days at the tomb site where Zheng turns up to pay tribute to his dead wife on the traditional Tomb-sweeping Day. Here Zheng has one of the hardest conversations with his old-time buddy after fourteen years of separation.

"You have managed to escape from (mainland), why on earth did you come back?" Zheng's painful expression seems to suggest that he wishes Gong did not.

*Gong:* "I would rather die than come back if it were for somebody else. But you are different. You are my Sixth Elder Brother, the one who put me in a high position without taking a cent from me . . . "

*Zheng:* "What are your plans?"

*Gong:* "I'll continue to assist you as before."

    . . . .

Gong says, in tears: "I told Jianzhi, we two have been like morning and evening stars that never meet in the sky. I thought I'd never be able to see you in my life. But then lord had mercy! There's always the exception. I have come across you after all!" At this point, CCP soldiers lying in wait start to close in on Gong. Startled by them, Gong pulls out his rifle, telling Zheng to stay put and that he will protect him. While Gong is scanning the surroundings, Zheng points his gun at Gong's head. Gong turns back dumbfounded. With visible difficulty, Zheng tells him "This is my duty!" Bewildered at first and then coming to realization, Gong drops his gun without protest. The ambushers take Gong away, leaving Zheng holding his gun with a shaking hand, still pointing at the empty space where Gong had been standing.

The conundrum between moral obligation/personal attachment and political discipline/faith does not stop at cross-camp conflict or mateship. The script has the two ultimate opponents—Kite and Shadow, fall in love with each other. To hunt the mole "Shadow," Zheng remains under cover as ex-Kuomintang until the Cultural Revolution ended. His identity brings him endless punishment during the waves of political campaigns. At the same time, his ultimate opponent Shadow, now a highly valued mastermind in the Communist secret agency, known as Han Bing in her duplicate life, is suspected of betrayal and banished to the same political labor camp as Zheng. In the face of political madness, the two outcasts help each other to survive hard labor, corporal punishment, and social condemnation. The series end with each figuring out the other's identity. The fulfillment of their political mission thus ironically precludes their matrimony. But the love ritual is still completed and consummated—Zheng asks for a moment of solitude with Han before she is arrested. Han commits suicide after both have confessed and confirmed their feelings to each other. The human frailty in the form of empathy was allowed to surface.

*The Kite* was produced in 2013 but withheld by the censors until it was released by the Oriental Satellite Channel and Beijing Satellite Channel in 2017. The original fifty-one-part series submitted for inspection later made its way to the Internet. The controversy revolving around *The Kite* has drawn a lot of public interest. Viewers have posted online the vignettes that have been sanitized for comment. But the real knotty issue, the contentious relationship between morality and political belief, is too complex to fix with small tinkerings here and there by the production team based on the advice of the censor. Zheng's conundrum seems to suggest that political faith or the political project does not necessarily command the moral high ground, and in fact, it might be contradictory to traditional moral codes of conduct. This has stretched the convention of socialist realism since, thus far, Confucian social order has always been subordinate to the communist code of belief in the Red Classics works. It is a target to be transformed, overcome, or integrated into the communist code of conduct, but not something that can challenge its righteousness or ultimate legitimacy. For example, love across different classes almost never works out such as in *The Song of Youth*, and kinship bound by blood is not as close as the bond based on class. *The Kite*'s success comes from its attempt to show the difficulty in reconciling the two.

The relationship between traditional morality and Communist political faith was discussed extensively in Ci Jiwei's delineation of the moral order in Chinese society before and after revolution. Ci sees Confucian moral structure as a three-level construct, with Li (propriety) providing the code of conduct, Ren (benevolence) as code of virtue, giving meanings and justification to Li, and Tian (heaven) residing at the top as a code of belief and granting meaning to the virtues. Provided the code of conduct is sufficient for people to behave morally, there is no need for the other two to exist. The Confucian code of conduct is closest to embodiment in that it offers more elaborate rules for people to act accordingly in their everyday living. The Communist code of conduct, crude but fit for wartime, offered few rules to follow at the first two levels in the postrevolution period. This resulted in a kind of moral vacuum, with a disembodied, abstract, and distant code of belief attached to the political programs.[21] In Ci Jiwei's reflection on the trajectory of Chinese consciousness, Communist utopianism in the Maoist era and early reform era had already given way to nihilism which lasted until the years before 1989, and by now has been completely taken over by hedonism.[22]

Even though utopianism is giving way to nihilism and hedonism is a big way, political belief is still held up as the source of strength for the revolutionaries and for critiquing social ills as the country progresses to capitalism and consumerism. The question of political belief has been a common theme that anchors all the spy series. Utopia, or belief, is explicitly dealt with in TV drama series such as *Lurk*[*Qianfu*], *Before Dawn* [*Liming zhi qian*], and *The Kite*. In *The Kite*, political faith as the code of belief is still held as sacred. In spite of everything, Zheng Yaoxian's last wish before his death is to watch the national flag raising ceremony on Tian'anmen Square. In fact, in nearly all the successful spy series, the question of political belief is treated as the raison d'etre for the altruistic sacrifice the revolutionaries make. The protagonists are all portrayed as being in constant danger, teetering on the edge of death, yet a mention of *"xin yang"* (faith) usually suffices to explain their dedication. In other words, moral scruples are important qualities that accentuate human character, but political faith still reigns as a far higher purpose. Morality does not constitute a zero-sum relationship as Ci suggests. The protagonist endures a broken psychology, fighting, sometimes literally, his private attachments for the ultimate public good. This is a price he has paid, and it endows him with a "demigod" spirituality. Through his morality, people are led to an understanding of him. Because of his sacrifice, people admire him. What is interesting is this "political faith" is at the same time depoliticized. It does not matter if it is Communist belief, or Nationalist. What determines the outcome is not ideological differences, but which party could pursue it more doggedly.

The supremacy of the Communist political belief in the revolutionaries is the hardest to convey in the postrevolutionary and depoliticized era. In his close-reading of how spy series such as *"Lurk,"* appeal to viewers, Ni Wenjian[23] observes that in today's complex ideological landscape, TV drama series can only try to convince an audience by starting with an "ordinary viewer's" everyday logic. It initially tells its story by observing closely the common logic of everyday life, and then creates moments of epiphany by replacing this everyday logic with a revolutionary's.[24] This often comes as a shock to viewers.

The everyday logic in *The Kite* comes in the form of the sociality permitted and by traditional Chinese notions of morality. It allows an average viewer to relate to the dehumanizing experience of living a double life—The stress of being constantly under scrutiny; the desperate loneliness, the frustration of being despised by your own folk, the pain of being and the guilt in sending those who love you to their deaths. After satisfying the viewers' voyeuristic desire to "spy" into the life of a spy, it then invites the audience to consider the price an individual human has to pay as the cog at the center of the larger scheme, in this case, the collective struggle for a utopian future. The similar kind of exploitation of individual justified for collective need is depicgted in John Le Carre's *The Spy Who Came in from the Cold.*[25] As discussed in previous chapters, the adaptation of Red Classics often taps into commercial interest by "subverting the revolutionary sublime."[26] Strategies to humanize both hero and enemy in spy series, seem to be a genuine effort to historicize revolutionary subjectivity, imperfect, and agonized over moral choice, yet in many ways convincing.

The protagonists in spy series largely fall into two categories: those who already have a Communist conviction and those who come to acquire this political belief through a serials of significant life events. *The Kite* belongs to the first category. The protagonist Zheng Yaoxian is a dedicated Communist believer through and through from the very beginning. However, his subjectivity in forming has to withstand various challenges, including the struggle with the meaning of the bodily self. The second category has a different focus. It usually tells how an ordinary person is tempered into a socialist subject. In the canonical Red Classics, a typical protagonist is usually a peasant, oppressed and dispossessed, who can see that revolution could lift him out of misery and bring him/her freedom. In the current depoliticized social milieu, however, the notion of class struggle has been rendered ineffective and even criticized, and the vision of "fanshen"[27] or "being liberated and made free" has lost its appeal in the public imaginary. The story of the "transformed" subject thus needs another kind of nominal figure and another source for instigating political proselytization. Here I argue that the primordial peasant, the typical figure to be transformed, has now been replaced by an apolitical middle-class urbanite. The rallying point for individuals is the code of virtue. The code of belief is avowed by the moral, but is significantly downplayed.

## MORALITY VERSUS POLITICAL BELIEF: THE VIEWERS

*The Kite* enjoyed instant ratings success when it was first aired on a provincial satellite channel. No doubt Director Liu Yunlong's reputation as a spy series mastermind and the long scrutiny of the censors helped to whet the appetite of viewers. The series also experienced a spontaneous boost online, where *Douban*, one of the most influential web 2.0 websites, rated it 8.8/10. It was referred to as "quality domestic product" by netizens. Unlike the adaptations of the canonical Red Classics, which targeted a niche market comprised of middle-aged or older people, the viewers of spy series span a much wider range of urbanites who are savvy Internet users and more likely to make comments and exchange views on public forums. The comments show that some "unlikely" viewers of this genre turned on to watch the series because of the good reviews on online platforms such as *Douban*, a public domain populated by users who share a similar taste, viewing habit and level of cultural sophistication as theirs.

The question of belief and its paradoxical relationship with morality are hardly missed by the viewers. Zhihu.com, a Chinese Q & A social media platform, has garnered over 20,000 posts on the series, with most of these comments revolving around the issue of political belief and morality/humanity. Within the question stream "What do you think of TV drama 'The Kite'?," Viewers not only identified "belief" as the main theme, but also confirms that it has made the series a cut above other spy series, in that it deals with more serious issues that all need to be discussed and debated. Many have commented that Director Liu Yunlong should be congratulated on his courage in tackling a sensitive and difficult subject. Some viewers provided detailed analysis of illogical plot lines and flaws in characterization in the series, but still believe that overall it was worth watching because it got them to reflect on history and values. For example, one viewer wrote, "From a genre perspective, *The Kite* does not necessarily surpass the other excellent spy genre classics produced in the past. But if we put aside our pre-conceived ideas of the genre, we will find that *The Kite* has in a sense gone much further" (哈影小十君).

Some have written long, philosophical reflections, deliberating on the purpose of life, human nature, and ethics. This is an interesting point to note. Given that the prime role of TV drama is to provide entertainment, it seems the viewers still expect more than just exciting and suspenseful stories from historical, revolutionary-themed works.

While most of the posts commend the series for its exploration of the issue of political belief, there is a great deal of ambiguity over what really constitutes Zheng Yaoxian's political beliefs. Communism as an ideologically coherent body of political beliefs does not always come with a readily available answer. The ambivalence of the positions taken by *The Kite* seems to encourage the viewers to make their own interpretations and judgments. As a result, the comments focus much more on the underlying significance of the serial rather than on plot, acting, and other technical aspects. Quite a few viewers have attempted to define what political belief is; nevertheless, the concept seems to remain a variable from person to person. Even the mainstream official media failed to spell out clearly what political belief should be in the show. A review article in *The People's Daily* praised the TV series for its philosophical probing of whether belief is a necessity for human existence, but it did not provide a definition of "belief." Most viewers tended to define it as a generalized, abstract idea like this one: "For Zheng Yaoxian, political belief is a goal, and to achieve this goal he could sacrifice everything, for people not even related to him." Another viewer made the comment that "belief" is a neutral word. If it goes to the extreme, it will become a "superstition." Whether the "belief" is right or normal depends on the historical period." "Belief" is presented as an abstract structure that resembles "religion," which gives meaning and moral purpose to human existence. The hollowing out of the political construct of "belief" allows viewers to see both Zheng Yaoxian and his opponents as admirable figures as long as they are committed to their political convictions. The depoliticized understanding of "belief" in effect blurred the demarcation between the "positive characters" and "negative characters." Kuomintang agents and communists are essentially the same in nature, it was just a matter of "ge wei qi zhu" (*each serving his own master*).

There exists a common anxiety surrounding the lack of any belief in the Chinese society. Viewers expressed frustration over the hedonism prevalent in a commercialized society, such as this comment: "Belief is an ill-suited topic in a society such as ours, for most people have only desires, not beliefs, or simply take desire as belief" (开膛手贝塔). These viewers commend Zheng Yaoxian for his steadfast commitment to his political faith and claim that the prevalent social ill is materialism and hedonism (樊家齐). These viewers are not so much concerned with the definition, but use the drama series to reflect and critique greed, and the loss of spiritual pursuits.

Just as some viewers expressed a yearning for the times of faith, others showed strong distrust and even disgust over Zheng's fervent political faith at the cost of human feelings and social relations. These viewers were weary of the excessive politicization of everyday life in the high socialist era. "My belief is humanity. If a certain belief runs counter to the most basic human feeling, then that belief is wrong." (AJIX) "The series is about revolutionary scumbags against counter-revolutionary *junzi,* the ideal man that embodied the Confucian moral principles. The beliefs of the likes of Zheng Yaoxian's character may appear lofty, yet they still do not justify the extreme actions. This is victory by any means." (Anonymous) This viewer made the astute observation that contradictions lie in two value systems—traditional ethics which hold a person of noble character as a moral ideal against the Communist ideological system that takes political belief as being above any individual needs. These viewers identify with traditional Confucian ethics, regarding self-cultivation, moral integrity, and harmonious relationships as the utmost ideal. While seeking identification with traditional ethics, the cultural revivalism frames political ideology, including the revolutionary ideal, as an aberration of these cultural roots. They see political beliefs, regardless of their content, as inherently in tension with ethics. "Those who stick by their beliefs are often too stubborn and crazy. They would do anything to achieve their goal. We could all become victims of these die-hards!" (问行不问心)

## CONCLUSION

By the early 2000s, the consensual boundary of what can and cannot be done has been carefully drawn with Red Classics TV adaptations. These television series seldom make sensational headlines anymore, for either mishap or success. This chapter argues that it is the spy subgenre which has found a way to address the unique Chinese revolutionary experience by speaking to the postrevolutionary moral order and middle-class personhood.

The success of spy serials represents a larger trend and innovative thrust in Chinese TV on the revolution. Like the Red Classics adaptations, it aims to provide escapism from consumer society by providing an intricate plot and interesting characters. Yet what distinguishes these serials from the rest is its way of engaging political concepts. Like most adaptations of the Red Classics, these spy serials resort to a de-politicizing historical outlook that was prevalent in the 1980s and 1990s, which favored "universal" and "humanistic" values over ideological dogma and state rule. However, the stories have moved away from simply "spicing up" the ascetic life of the revolutionaries with romantic relations or presenting a more humane landlord.

Operating in multiple, complex discursive environments, the spy series succeed in winning an audience by taking contradictory and vague ideological stances. It appears to deal with the fundamental issue of "belief," yet it puts the pursuing of faith in direct conflict with human morality. The resolution of this tension is never resolved and is kept in perpetual suspension. However, by touching on the anxiety that is at the center of the zeitgeist in contemporary China, it hit a nerve, and in a way struck a chord with a postmillennium audience. The popularity and controversy surrounding the spy series *The Kite* has provided a fine example of how the revolutionary stories can be successful by staying ambiguous, a sharp contrast with its predecessors.

# Conclusion

A collection of Red Songs ushered in "Mao Fever" and the revival of Red Classics in the late 1990s. Despite some liberal-thinking critics' concerns that dangers lurked in this revival of the "totalitarian" Left, the Red Classics craze was largely swept along as part of market reform and became just another cultural commodity for consumption. In 2015, musicians created a Red Song called *Uncle Xi Loves Mummy Peng*, and it has been played more than 20 million times since it was posted on the Internet. Although lyricist Song Zhigang claimed the work is a "true expression of my innermost feelings,"[1] the phenomenon sparked multiple interpretations, including suspicions of outright flattery on the part of a creator who favored the emergence of a Xi cult, or, at the other end of the spectrum, that it was straight sarcasm.

One thing is certain: none of these cultural phenomena can be simply dismissed as a historic shift to the left. In fact, the world has been experiencing what Stuart Hall called "the swing to the right" since 1970s, which "no longer looks like a temporary swing in the political fortunes, a short-term shift in the balance of forces."[2] This statement is open to application in China. According to Wang Hui,[3] China's reform years have been marked with a continuing and totalizing de-revolutionary process. In this process, the CCP has largely given up its class-based representative character to become a party that derives its legitimacy from its performance in managing the economy. Under such circumstances, political divisions between left and right have become indistinct. The mainstream ideology has been searching for a set of dominant narratives compatible with the changes, ranging from Deng Xiaoping's "Development is the absolute principle," to Jiang Zemin's "Three representatives," to Hu Jintao's "A scientific outlook on development," and "Harmonious society," and Xi Jinping's "Chinese dream." Increasingly, the state ideology has intentionally steered toward a more "de-politicized" language that privileges modernization and the market.

The mainstream culture is transformed in these new circumstances. The control of the media and culture sphere is not primarily ideological, but rather is based on the need to maintain stability.[4] As a result, the role of the state apparatus is not so much about advancing a political agenda, but is more a pragmatic approach to exercise political power in the name of national interest and cultural values. The control of the state is often exercised in an ad hoc manner, lacking a coherent ideological conviction.

Cultural life since the 1990s has been heterogeneous and contradictory in nature. However, a simple binary approach that only foregrounds ideological opposition between the left and right still underlies academic understanding of cultural transformation. The available cultural critiques still suffer from the lack of an effective theoretical framework and language properly describing the emerging phenomena. The mainstay of mass culture in the Maoist era, the working-class culture, which was subjugated to Marxist and Maoist ideology, has given way to a new consumerist culture that favors a middle class. However, this transformation is "an uneven, partial and gradual process" where the cultural form, operation, and ideology of the present eras interweave with those of the past in often irregular patterns.[5] In the decades since the 1990s, state-directed mainstream cultural products have successfully appropriated and incorporated elements of popular and mass culture. The production of mainstream culture has to negotiate the dual forces of state directives and the market, but the state's vision of modernity has changed with the market reforms, resulting in the revision of various categories of subjectivity, including class, gender, place, and belief.

## GROUNDING MEDIA STUDIES IN SOCIAL TRANSFORMATION

The key to deciphering a cultural phenomenon like the TV adaptation of Red Classics is to go beyond simply associating it with certain political leanings, that is, to view it simply as "totalitarian nostalgia," but to embed it in China's social transition. The revision of the revolutionary cultural heritage such as the Red Classics is always tied up with concurrent developments and debates over broadcasting, media and cultural policies, global capital flow, cultural memory, and emerging consumption tastes. The Red Classics works are not simply outdated products of the Cold War, but rather, they are works that convey collective anxiety and aspirations and continue to have contemporary relevance. For this reason, it is equally problematic to view the TV adaptations as driven purely by commercial motives to tap into a cultural resource, as some of the existing analysis has suggested. To tease out the connections between the rewriting of the Red Classics and the general discourse of privatization and commercialization, I have opted to link TV drama's interpretation of the Red Classics to the particular contemporary values on which the adaptations are based. A society's major movements are usually closely tied with popular culture. This is especially true with a genre such as the Red Classics, which was produced and disseminated to perform important cultural work. From its inception, the genre has had a political and pedagogical function, and it always operates within and embodies the structure of power at large. In over half a century, these cultural texts have changed from ideological tools produced with rather rigid prescriptions to deliver political messages, to cater to various cultural tastes, as an element of commercial narrow-casting for a nostalgic audience, or a hybrid light entertainment form catering to populist nationalist sentiment, or even as the target of political parody or satire, all the while retaining their symbolic value as a revolutionary cultural heritage. The implication of connecting these various manifestations in this way is that it lays bare the power relations and vested interests that underlie the process of re-inscribing national icons such as the Red Classics.

Through examining the cultural process in which key markers of subjectivity, such as class and gender, were changed in the TV adaptations, this study links the critique of capitalist marketization with the general social transformation of Chinese society. The forces lying behind the changed subjectivities in the TV adaptations are seen as not only economically motivated (propelled by the pursuit for profit) but also deeply political and ideological. For example, the fact that TV adaptations have sought to restore the ambiguity in revolutionary heroes is a result of a general reaction against the class discourse with no shades of ambiguity, which is further linked with how class and class struggle are occluded, sidelined, and replaced in current Chinese politics and ideology. The rejection of class discourse derives from the urgent need to cover up the reality of a deeply fractured and stratified society that has emerged in China since the onslaught of neoliberalism. The transgressive refashioning of the past has in effect transcended the official/popular dichotomy. It no longer reiterates the old official discourse, because the discourse of class and class struggle has been discarded as ultra-leftist ideology and excluded from the consumerist discourse that has inundated cultural media, both official and commercial. The populist appeal of the Red Classics adaptations lies in its ability to maneuver the tension between the official and the unofficial, to transgress in certain areas and to a certain extent, so that the TV adaptation is taken in innovative directions on the surface, while at the same time maintaining a benign political message. Its logic is not that of a carnivalesque celebration of the inversion of the established order, but a product of many determinations, particularly the politics of consumption.

The adaptation does not constitute a means of resisting dominance through transgression, but contributes to the further displacement and fragmentation of revolutionary culture.

Similarly, my analysis has suggested that the boundaries of femininity and sexuality set out for revolutionary women in the Red Classics have been significantly redrawn due to the backlash against state feminism, the commodification of women's bodies, and the recovery of sexuality in the reform era. These changes favor a depoliticized neoliberal subjectivity within a traditional moral boundary. Likewise, people living in the heart of the revolutionary base areas seek a new identity because the neoliberal symbolic order valorizes attributes that are favorable to economic development and tourism. In addition, the old class-based subjectivity has grown outmoded and put residents of the old revolutionary base areas at a disadvantage. The "schizoid"attitude toward revolutionary legacy has also manifested itself in narrating "Communism" as a belief system in the newly produced Red Classics-type of drama series.

However, my analysis indicates clearly that these changes do not represent a radical, one-dimensional disjuncture—that the grand narratives, the perfect heroes, and the idealistic projects represented by the Red Classics were not all of a sudden transformed into commodities. Indeed, the process has been protracted and nonlinear, full of contradictions, tensions, ambiguities, and difficulties, just like the painful social changes it embodies. In addition, the driving forces of this process, the Party-state and the market, have complex relationships. At times, they contest and challenge each other, but at other times, they accommodate each other, co-opt each other, and form coalitions. A critical understanding of the interplay of power must delve into the cultural politics at the micro level, foregrounding the subtle strategies of desublimation and disintegration of the former dominant ideology and related institutions. By explicating the media's role in the decline and dissipation of socialist morals, this study has made a link between the media and social processes. The focus in this book on the analytical categories of class, gender, locality, and faith is quite deliberate.[6]

## COMPLICATING THE STATE-MARKET DICHOTOMY

Chinese society has experienced the most profound changes since the late 1980s. These changes are most acutely manifested in people's outlook, mentality, feelings, and the way they relate to the outside world. As scholar Chen Xiaoming observes, the "utopian faith and idealistic passion were replaced by practical interest and the fanatical social mobilisation was dissolved by individual opportunism."[7] Many cultural critics prophesized the end of history, society, collectivism, and all the grand narratives that had been part of ordinary Chinese life. Under such circumstances, it is easy to see this revolutionary nostalgia as a cultural fad, some kind of postmodern appropriation of popular cultural icons and images. However, I share Liu Kang's view that revolutionary culture is more than just "residual and irrelevant." Instead, it is "deeply ingrained in the Chinese cultural imaginary and constitutes a significant dimension in the contradiction-ridden cultural arenas,"[8] particularly in terms of the aesthetic forms, structures, and institutions responsible for its production and dissemination. Mass culture in the socialist era has also profoundly shaped the values, meanings, and lived experiences of the population growing up during the Maoist period. Throughout the political and social struggles, the Red Classics, the core component of the revolutionary legacy, have had their fair share of ups and downs. After being given an initial "cold shoulder" in the years immediately after the Cultural Revolution, a strong nostalgic sentiment for the revolutionary past emerged. The Maoist era was remembered as a kind of "Golden Age" for its allegedly clean government, strong leadership, and egalitarian pursuits. However, the resurgence of revolutionary icons, symbols, and texts occurred when commercialization and consumerism were rampant in Chinese society. As a result, these elements took on new faces. The variegated forms the Red Classics take nowadays defy any demarcation between commercial and propagandist. The boundaries between official, commercial, and popular culture have been transgressed in unprecedented ways. The crossover between revolutionary culture and commercial and unofficial culture has produced a cultural "anomaly"[9] that, paradoxically, is becoming the norm.

In her study of Chinese television drama, Zhong Xueping[10] has identified four major forces that future studies on mainstream/popular culture need to take into consideration: the officials, the media, the industry, and the academy. Each of the four analytical chapters in this book has engaged with these forces in different ways. The book describes the creative use of Red culture by the state media, intellectual elite, and ordinary consumers, and demonstrates the complexity of boundary negotiations and transgressions. The examples examined are in no way formulaic, however useful they are in mapping for us the complex power struggles inherent in appropriating the Red Classics. If anything, they should remind us how ideological struggle pervades every aspect of cultural production and consumption in the contemporary era. The criss-crossing of boundaries between official and nonofficial culture, between consumerism and socialist nostalgia, expresses precisely the chaos and ambiguities of the cultural landscape.

By exploring the transformation of the Red Classics genre, I argue that the interplay between the original texts and the more recent copies (the TV drama versions) of them resonates with the interplay of social forces between state power and market rationality in contemporary China. The relationship between the originals and the TV adaptations is that of transgression. The changes in this genre result from and are largely in step with China's transition from socialism to neoliberalism. This process is not linear, but full of negotiations at various stages of development. Neither can it be simplified as the market's successful takeover of political control. In this process, the boundary which was set in the socialist era between what is correct, acceptable, and legitimate has shifted and is gradually but dramatically being reworked, refined, renegotiated, and re-managed.

In choosing to study media transformation through a genre such as the Red Classics, this study answers the call by media and communication scholars to re-engage in researching China's revolutionary history and its lasting influence on contemporary Chinese society.[11] While focusing on the triumph of transnational capitalism and neoliberal governance, scholars are yet to fully recognize that China's march toward modernity is unique and influenced by China's recent past. For instance, the CCP has gained its legitimacy through revolution, and this historical legacy not only "continues to shape the political economic and discursive transformations of the Chinese communication system, but also continues to define the parameters of control and resistance in Chinese communication politics."[12] This historical legacy is fundamental in understanding the state's handling of the TV adaptations of the Red Classics, themselves part of this legacy. As I argued in the Introduction, the whole process of rewriting the Red Classics is premised on the CCP's contradictory approach to the socialist legacy: on the one hand, the national icons in the Red Classics are symbols of the Party's solidarity with the oppressed, and thus cannot be denied outright; on the other hand, some of the key aspects of this legacy have been rendered irrelevant by the Party's capitalist pursuits. The genre of the Red Classics provides a unique angle from which to examine the changing nature of the CCP's rule and allows us to challenge the binary distinction between the state and the market.

## NARRATING REVOLUTION, CONSTRUCTING EVERYDAY

Compared with literature and film, TV drama is the real core of mass culture in contemporary China. Its appeal lies in its ability to endow everyday life with a commonsense logic, despite its relatively new narrative style. The omnipresence of TV in everyday living spaces makes watching TV drama more than a "spectating" process, but a very basic act of everyday life.[13] Since its rise in the 1990s, TV drama has become one of the most effective mechanisms for the production and distribution of meaning and values. It is not an exaggeration to say that TV drama alone assumes the important function of reconstructing China's imagination of itself, of reality, and of history, as cultural critics agree.[14]

The TV drama series narrating revolution have occupied a fairly central position among the major genres, claiming a big share of the market. This recourse to revolutionary history has further diverged into different subgenres to serve different niches. At least three subgenres have matured and enjoyed high popularity in today's mainstream cultural scene. These subgenres include the Red Classics adaptations, which are melodramatic contemporary productions of a revolutionary theme, and remain important. All serving to suture the disjuncture between the historical revolutionary narratives and popular imaginations of this history, each of the subgenres has nevertheless been assigned different cultural remits in the media ecology.

Besides Red Classics adaptations, contemporary productions of revolutionary-themed TV drama serials constitute another main thrust in narrating a revolutionary past through the current value system. For example, spy thrillers such as *Lurk* and *Cliff*, are real crowd pleasers. Boasting intricate plotlines, in-depth explorations of characters' psychological inner workings and romantic entanglements, these tell tales of underground Communists working in the heart of enemy territory during the Civil War or Anti-Japanese War. Although revolutionary core values such as "belief in Communism" and "self-sacrifice" are still promoted as the main theme, they appear to be abstract concepts largely emptied of meaning and relevance. Instead, critics tend to believe that these thrillers do not construct a revolutionary subjectivity, but reference successful people who are calculating and good at scheming in today's workplace; and also speak to and mirror the precarious existence of the contemporary Chinese.[15]

More recently, another genre referred to as "over-the-top anti-Japanese plays" (*kangri shenju*) represents a more extreme form of commercial exploitation of revolutionary-themed topics. As its name suggests, this genre uses ridiculous plotlines such as a female Communist soldier tearing a Japanese soldier apart using her bare hands or throwing a grenade into the air to down a Japanese airplane. The subgenre has adopted the officially sanctioned anti-Japanese War theme to get past the regulators, while trying to up the viewing rate by packing in abundant sex, kungfu, and displays of supernatural power in a Hollywood type style. While this over-entertaining take on the revolutionary past seems to have found followers, it finally irritated the TV regulators enough and in 2013, State Administration of Press and Publication, Radio, Film and Television (SAPPRFT) criticized the "excessively entertaining" tendency and demanded that broadcasters "rectify" the content and even take it off their schedule.

Like the Red Classics adaptations, these subgenres have shown a depoliticizing tendency to various degrees. However, they do offer a chance to revisit revolutionary history, albeit in fragmented forms. Sometimes, as historian Wang Hui[16] pointed out, some of these televisual historical accounts may be more accurate in detail than those of the elites, as they wouldn't be skewed by overt official ideology. Rather than simply mapping these subgenres on the ideological spectrum of left, center, and right, it is more useful to ask questions such as what sort of values are these drama serials perpetuating? In what ways are these values implicated in social transformation and articulated to social identity? How are the cultural imaginaries created? How does TV as cultural technology mediate relations between politics, social identities, and citizenship? What cultural resources have been appropriated in the genre's reconstruction of history, and what is the underlying motivation and logic?

The previous chapters endeavored to address some of these questions. Even during the course of this project, the Red Classics adaptation phenomenon has been continually evolving: new situations are emerging and boundaries are forming and reforming all the time. For example, before 2004, during the initial stage of the adaptation craze, the TV adaptations were focused primarily on ratings. This purely commercial approach was widely criticized. After SARFT issued two notices to rein in the production of the genre, the production units were more tactful and restrained in their treatment of sensitive subjects, such as the hero's personal life or emotional entanglement. At the same time, the Hu Jintao-Wen Jiabao government had consolidated its rule since 2005. In an attempt to counter the negative consequences of reform caused by rampant commercialization, the Hu-Wen government promoted the concept of building a "harmonious society." Part of their corrective measures also included bringing the revolutionary legacy back into line and reinstating its symbolic value. Concurrent with the promotion of Red culture in the public sphere, the TV adaptations have come under more stringent control, not least because peasants, workers, and soldiers, once the masters of society in the Red Classics, are being marginalized in society, but still retain their relevance as the "power base of the socialist state."[17] In this context, how to reconstruct their subjectivity in the TV adaptations is a significant issue.

As pointed out above, the Red Classics adaptations rely on popular nostalgia for the socialist past. This nostalgia is often triggered by nothing else but the changed reality of society—the loss of socialist morals, the loss of collective purpose and aspirations, and the spiraling social conflicts and polarization in a society that once boasted about its egalitarianism. In the wake of the bursting neoliberal bubble in 2008, the search for a new model to replace the Washington Consensus[18] has gained new urgency. There is no denying that the revolutionary legacy is an important part of China's experience on the road to modernity. Under such circumstances, it is perhaps not enough to just conclude that the boundaries of the Red Classics have been rewritten and the genre has been turned into a hybrid. In the special issue on Red culture in China Perspectives, Barmé raised a series of questions on the relevance of the Red Classics and their remakes in contemporary Chinese society, pondering

whether these remakes will normalize the official historiography, or are commercialized fun for a market niche, or if they have the potential to revitalize
the concepts of social justice, fairness, and freedom.[19] There is no easy answer
to any of these questions. But precisely because the CCP has been strategi-
cally appropriating and interpreting the theoretical basis of Marxism,[20] the
corpse of the Red Classics could be taken in different directions.

Besides cultural critique that looks at the alternative meanings of images,
the next step then may be to ask whether the Red Classics could serve as the
potential site for protest and agency. A more nuanced, ethnographic study
of how this genre is consumed would shed light on whether the subjectivity
of the subaltern social classes articulated by the Red Classics still appeals to
workers and peasants and could potentially grant them power and legitimacy.
Another interesting phenomenon to examine is the newly created revolutionary genre on TV, which has not only captured a big proportion of the broadcasting schedule but also gained high ratings.

Looking into the future, a recent chance encounter proved to be a powerful
indication of the potent force that the revolutionary legacy maintains and the
new references it subsumes in the reform era. During a conference in China
in 2009, I took a day off to visit a small village, Youlong, on the border of
Jiangxi and Anhui Provinces. Situated in a serene, lush-green mountainous
part of central China, it has been an agrarian, tea-growing location for hundreds of years. The tracks of the "Ancient Tea-horse Road" that once linked
southwest China and Tibet and India are still visible. Like many of its coun-
terparts all over China, the village is now left to the elderly, the women, and
the children, as most young people have gone to the cities to work as migrant
workers. As I walked past one wooden house with its door open, I saw a big
poster of Mao Zedong on the wall. I stopped to speak with the old man sit-
ting in the dark front hall of the house watching me and other visitors walk
past: "Grandpa, you have Chairman Mao's picture up on the wall. Why?"
He answered in a serious tone: "Chairman Mao is good! He cares about
ordinary folks like us." I did not stop to have a chat with the old man. But I
could not help wondering what kinds of stories he would have to tell. At his
age, he would have lived his life seeing his identity come full circle: first as a
subaltern, then as master of society, and now again denigrated to a subaltern.
Perhaps he may not be able to articulate this process clearly, but he certainly
must feel it. I have no doubt that in the moment he hung the picture up on the
wall, he had some misgivings about what was going on in China. This example indicates to me that the Red Classics, as one of the main components of
the socialist legacy, will continue to be a site for protest and agency. Research
into the Red Classics is far from complete. How this genre is remembered and
interpreted, and for what purposes, remain crucial questions both for scholars
and for the future history of the Chinese state.

# Notes

## INTRODUCTION: REVOLUTION AND TV DRAMA

1. Raymond Williams, *The Long Revolution*. New edition with a foreward by Anthony Barnett ed. (Cardigan, UK: Parthian, 2013), 69–91.

2. Hui Wang, "Depoliticized Politics, from East to West," *New Left Review* 41, September-October (2006), 35.

3. Francis Fukuyama, *The End of History and the Last Man* (New York: The Free Press, 1992), xi.

4. Bonnie S. McDougall and Kam Louie, *The Literature of China in the Twentieth Century* (New York: Columbia University Press, 1997), 194–198.

5. Hong Hou and Bin Zhang, "Hongse Jingdian: Jieshuo, Gaibian Ji Chuanbo [Red Classics: Definition, Adaptation and Propagation]," *Contemporary Cinema* , no. 6 (2004): 79–82.

6. Shuo Liu, "Shiting Huayu Chanshi Yu Jingshen Chuancheng [Studies and Thoughts on Adaptation of *the Red Classics*]," *Dang Dai Dian Ying (Contemporary Cinema)* 136, no. January (2007): 71.

7. Yanfeng He, "Jiexi Hongse Jingdian [Analysing the Red Classics] " *Chinese Television* no. 3 (2005): 27–29.

8. Liu, "Shiting Huayu Chanshi Yu Jingshen," 71.

9. Film and Television State Administration of Radio, "Guanyu "Hongse Jingdian" Gaibian Dianshiju Shencha Guanli De Tongzhi [Notice on the Censorship and Management of Television Drama Adaptation of the "Red Classics"]," ed. Film and Television State Administration of Radio (2004).

10. Sihe Chen, "Wo Bu Zancheng "Hongse Jingdian" Zhege Tifa [I Do Not Agree with the Naming of "Red Classics"]," *Nanfang Zhoumo*, May 6 2004, C14.

11. Geremie R. Barmé, *In the Red: On Contemporary Chinese Culture* (New York: Columbia University Press, 1999), 235–254.

12. See Andrew Jones, *Like a Knife: Ideology and Genre in Contemporary Chinese Popular Music* (Ithaca: Cornell University East Asia Program, 1992).

13. Ibid, 247.

14. Ching Kwan Lee and Guobin Yang, *Re-Envisioning the Chinese Revolution: The Politics and Poetics of Collective Memories in Reform China* (Stanford: Stanford University Press, 2007).

15. Guimei He, *Renwenxue De Xiangxiangli: Dandai Zhongguo Sixiang Yu Wenxue Wenti (the Imagination of Humanities: Issues on Contemporary Chinese Thoughts, Culture, and Literature)* (Kaifeng: Henan University Press, 2005), 207–209.

16. Kang Liu, *Globalization and Cultural Trends in China* (Honolulu: University of Hawai'i Press, 2004), 93.

17. Ruoyun Bai, and Geng Song, eds. *Chinese Television in the Twenty-First Century: Entertaining the Nation* (London and New York: Routledge, 2015).

18. James Lull, *China Turned On: Television, Reform and Resistance* (London: Routledge, 2013), 155. Ying Zhu, Michael Keane, and Ruoyun Bai, eds., *TV Drama in China* (Hong Kong: Hong Kong University Press, 2008), 1.

19. Michael Keane, "Television Drama in China: Remaking the Market," *Media International Australia* Culture and Policy, no. 115 (2005): 82.

20. Raymond Williams coined the term "structure of feeling" the 1970s. Raymond Williams, *Marxism and Literature* (Oxford: Oxford University Press, 1977), 132. It refers to the meanings and values as lived and felt, as well as the affective elements of consciousness and relations, shared by a generation within a culture. "It was a structure in the sense that you could perceive it operating in one work after another which weren't otherwise connected—people weren't learning it from each other; yet it was one of feelings more than of thought—a pattern of impulses, restraints, tones, for which the best evidence as of the actual conventions of literary or dramatic writing." *Politics and Letters: Interview with New Left Review, with an Introduction by Geoff Dyer* (London: Verso, 2015), 159.

21. Weiliang Gong, "Suipian, Paohui, Wenhua Zhengzhi Yu "Shehuizhuyi": Dui "Dibajie Zhongguo Wenhua Luntan: Dianshiju Yu Dandai Wenhua" De Shuping (Fragments, Cannon Fodder, Cultural Politics and "Socialism": A Review on "the Eighth Chinese Culture Forum: TV Drama and Contemporary Culture")," Renwen yu Shehui (Humanity and Society), last modified November 1, 2012, http://wen.org. cn/modules/article/view.article.php/3581/c20.

22. Liu, *Globalization*, 48.

23. Moral economy in this context refers to the ways in which customs and cultural mores compel the cultural producers to conform to traditional norms at the expense of profit.

24. Linda Hutcheon, *A Theory of Adaptation*, 2nd ed. (London and New York: Routledge, 2013), 4.

25. Liu, *Globalization*, 8–9.

26. Binchun Meng, "Regulating Egao: Futile Efforts of Recentralization," in *China's Information and Communications Technology Revolution: Social Changes and State Responses*, ed. Xiaoling Zhang and Yongnian Zheng (New York, NY: Routledge, 2009), 52–67.

27. Gail Hershatter, "The Subaltern Talks Back: Reflections on Subaltern Theory and Chinese History," *Positions* 1 no. 1 (1993): 103–130.

28. Xiaobing Tang, *Chinese Modern: The Heroic and the Quotidian* (Durham, NC: Duke University Press, 2000), 3.

29. Williams, *The Long Revolution*, 70.

30. Ibid., 72.

31. Ibid. 72–75.

32. See Yang Li, *50 Niandai—70 Niandai Zhongguo Wenxue Jingdian Zai Jiedu [Rereading: Chinese Literary Classics from 50s to 70s]* (Shandong: Shandong Education Publishing House, 2003). Xiaobing Tang, ed. *Zai Jiedu: Dazhong Wenyi Yu Yishixingtai (Rereading: The People's Literature and Art Movement and Its Ideology)* (Beijing: Peking University Press, 2007). Richard King, *Milestones on a Golden Road: Writing for Chinese Socialism 1945–80* (Vancouver: University of British Columbia Press). Xiang Cai, *Revolution and Its Narratives: China's Socialist Literary and Cultural Imaginations* trans. Rebecca Karl and Xueping Zhong (Durham, NC and London: Duke University Press, 2016).

33. Barmé, *In the Red*, 316–344.

34. Ban Wang and Xueping Zhong, "Why Does Socialist Culture Matter Today," in *Debating the Socialist Legacy and Capitalist Globalization in China*, ed. Xueping Zhong and Ban Wang (New York: Palgrave Macmillan, 2014), 1–18.

35. Rosemary Roberts and Li Li, eds., *The Making and Remaking of China's "Red Classics": Politics, Aesthetics, and Mass Culture* (Hong Kong: Hong Kong University Press, 2017).

36. Xueping Zhong, *Mainstream Culture Refocused: Television Drama, Society, and the Production of Meaning in Reform-Era China* (Honolulu: University of Hawai'i Press, 2010), 27.

37. Richard Johnson, "What Is Cultural Studies Anyway?," *Social Text* Winter (1986–1987), no. 16 (1987): 55.

38. Doreen Massey, *Space, Place and Gender* (Cambridge, UK: Polity Press, 1994).

39. Chun Lin, *The Transformation of Chinese Socialism* (Durham, NC and London: Duke University Press, 2006).

40. Shaun Breslin, "Serving the Market or Serving the Party: Neo-Liberalism in China," in *The Neo-Liberal Revolution*, ed. Richard Robison (London: Palgrave Macmillan, 2006), 114–131; David Harvey, *A Brief History of Neoliberalism* (Oxford: Oxford University Press, 2007); Aihwa Ong, *Neoliberalism as Exception: Mutations in Citizenship and Sovereignty* (Durham, NC: Duke University Press, 2006); Yuezhi Zhao, "Neoliberal Strategies, Socialist Legacies: Communication and State Transformation in China," in *Global Communications: Towards a Transcultural Political Economy*, ed. Paula Chakravarty and Yuezhi Zhao (Lanham, MD: Rowman & Littlefield, 2008), 23–50.

41. Massey, *Space, Place and Gender*, 22.

42. Jinhua Dai, "Dai Jinhua, Kang Honglei, Gan Yang, Wang Xiaoming Tan Zhongguo Dianshiju [Dai Jinhua, Kang Honglei, Gan Yang, Wang Xiaoming on Chinese Television Drama]," *Chinese Readers Gazette*, Sept 12, 2012, 13.

# CHAPTER 1

1.  Jing Wang, *Brand New China: Advertising, Media and Commercial Culture* (Cambridge, MA: Harvard University Press, 2008); Yuezhi Zhao, *Communication in China: Political Economy, Power, and Conflict* (Lanham: Rowman & Littlefield Publishers, 2008); Xueping Zhong, *Mainstream Culture Refocused*; Ying Zhu and Chris Berry, eds., *TV China* (Bloomington and Indianapolis: Indiana University Press, 2009); Ying Zhu, Michael Keane, and Ruoyun Bai, eds., *TV Drama in China* (Hong Kong: Hong Kong University Press, 2008).

2.  Paul du Gay, Stuart Hall, Linda Janes, Hugh Mackay, and Keith Negus, eds., *Doing Cultural Studies: the Story of the Sony Walkman* (London: Sage Publications, 1997).

3.  Ann-Marie Brady, *Marketing Dictatorship* (Lanham: Rowman & Littlefield Publishers, Inc., 2008), 1.

4.  Yuezhi Zhao, *Media, Market and Democracy in China: Between the Party Line and the Bottom Line* (Urbana: University of Illinois Press, 1998), 1.

5.  Yu Huang, "Peaceful Evolution: The Case of Television Reform in Post-Mao China," *Media, Culture & Society* 16, no. 2 (1994): 217–241.

6.  Hong Yin, "Yiyi, Shengchan Yu Xiaofei—Dangdai Zhongguo Dianshiju De Zhengzhi Jingji Xue Fenxi (Ideology, Production and Consumption: A Political Economic Analysis of Contemporary Chinese Television Drama)," [Meaning, Production and Consumption: A political economic analysis of contemporary Chinese television drama.] *Xiandai Chuanbo [Modern Communication]* 2001, no. 4 (2001): 1–7.

7.  Lull, *China Turned On*, 20.

8.  Hong Zhu, "Huihuang De Chengjiu, Canlan De Weilai: Zhongguo Dianshi Shiye Fazhan Chengjiu [Brilliant Achievement, Bright Future: Development Trajectory of China's Television Industry]," *Dianshi Yanjiu [Television Studies]*, no. 5 (2006): 10–12.

9.  Film and Television State Administration of Radio, "Quanguo Guangbo Dianshi Fugai Qingkuang [Data on Broadcasting and Television Population Coverage 2008]," (Beijing: State Administration of Radio, Film and Television, 2008).

10. Ying Zhu, "Yongzheng Dynasty and Chinese Primetime Television Drama," *Cinema Journal* 44, no. 4 (2005): 4–5.

11. Yuezhi Zhao, "From Commercialization to Conglomeration: The Transformation of the Chinese Press within the Orbit of the Party State," *Journal of Communication* 20, no. 2 (Spring 2000) (2003): 3–26.

12. Di Lu, *Zhongguo Dianshi Chanye De Weiji Yu Jiyu [the Crises and Opportunities for Chinese Television Industry]*. (Beijing: China People's University Press, 2002), 90.

13. Unable to fund the increasing television coverage, the four-tier policy aims to involve various social groups to invest in the broadcasting industry by allowing provinces, cities, and counties to run full-scale TV stations.

14. Michael Keane and Christina Spurgeon, "Advertising Industry and Culture in Post-WTO China," *Media International Australia* 111, no. May (2004): 104–117.

15. Ian Weber, "Reconfiguring Chinese Propaganda and Control Modalities: A Case Study of Shanghai's Television System. Journal of Contemporary China," *Journal of Contemporary China,* 11, no. 30 (2002): 53–75.

16. Yin, "Yiyi, Shengchan Yu Xiaofei," 1–7.

17. Zhu, "Huihuang De Chengjiu," 10–12.

18. Lu, *Zhongguo Dianshi Chanye*, 120–121.

19. Wang, *Brand New China*, 279–280.

20. Haibo Liu, "Zhengzhi Yu Ziben De Boyi [Two Forces and Their Mutual Action: Influencing on Chinese TV Drama]," in *Zhongmei Dianshiju Bijiao Yanjiu [Comparative Research on Television Drama between China and America]*, ed. Chunjing Qu and Ying Zhu (Shanghai: Shanghai Sanlian Bookstore, 2005), 454–470.

21. Ibid.

22. Brady, *Marketing Dictatorship*, 71.

23. Yuezhi Zhao, "Caught in the Web: The Public Interest and the Battle for Control of China's Information Superhighway," *Info* 2, no. 1 (2000): 41–65.

24. Ruoyun Bai, "Media Commercialization, Entertainment, and the Party-State: The Political Economy of Contemporary Chinese Television Entertianment Culture," *Global Media Journal* 4, no. 6 (2005): 8.

25. Zhao, *Communication in China*, 97.

26. Michael Keane, *The Chinese Television Industry* (London: Palgrave Macmillan, 2015), 37.

27. Zhao, *Communication in China*, 99–108.

28. Bai, "Media Commercialization, Entertainment, and the Party-State," 19–38.

29. Junhao Hong, *The Internationalization of Television in China: The Evolution of Ideology, Society, and Media since the Reform* (Westport: Praeger, 1998).

30. Junhao Hong, Yanmei Lü, and William Zou, "CCTV in the Reform Years: A New Model for China's Television? ," in *TV China*, ed. Ying. Zhu and Chris. Berry (Bloomington and Indianapolis: Indiana University Press, 2009), 40–50.

31. Chin-Chuan Lee, Zhou He, and Yu Huang, ""The Chinese Party Publicity Inc." Conglomerated: The Case of the Shenzhen Press Group," in *Political Regimes and Media in Asia*, ed. Krishna Sen and Terence Lee (New York: Routledge, 2008), 12.

32. Keane, "Television Drama in China," 82–93.

33. The sixty-five–second advertising spots after the prime-time news and leading up to the weather forecast are the most expensive in the country. Adopting a voluntary auction method to set the advertising-spot prices, CCTV was able to earn 6.8 billion yuan ($860 million) in 2006. See Wang, *Brand New China*, 263.

34. Wanning Sun, "Significant Moment on CCTV," *International Journal of Cultural Studies* 10, no. 2 (2007): 187–204.

35. Bai, "Media Commercialization, Entertainment, and the Party-State," 21–22.

36. Zhu, Keane, and Bai, *TV Drama in China*, 1.

37. Zhao, *Communication in China*, 6–7.

38. Wanning Sun and Yuezhi Zhao, "Television with Chinese Characteristics: The Politics of Compassion and Education," in *Television in the Post-Broadcasting Era*, ed. Graeme Turner and Jinna Tay (London: Routledge, 2009), 96–104.

39. Jing Wang, "The State Question in Chinese Popular Cultural Studies," *Inter-Asia Cultural Studies* 2, no. 1 (2001): 37.

40. Zhao, *Communication in China*, 212–216. Liu, "Zhengzhi Yu Ziben De Boyi," 458–464.

41. Ruoyun Bai, *Staging Corruption: Television Drama and Politics* (Hong Kong: Hong Kong University Press, 2015), 58–60.

42. Brady, *Marketing Dictatorship*, 214.

43. State Administration of Radio, Film and Television. "Guanyu Renzhen Duidai "Hongse Jingdian" Gaibian Dianshiju Youguan Wenti Tongzhi [Notice on Management and Approval Procedures of Adaptation of the Red Clasics]." May 26, 2004 http://www.people.com.cn/GB/14677/22114/33943/33945/2523858.html.

44. Lull, *China Turned On*, 132.

45. Zhu, Keane, and Bai, *TV Drama in China*, 4.

46. Keane, "Television Drama in China," 3.

47. Jianying Zha, *China Pop: How Soap Operas, Tabloids, and Bestsellers Are Transforming a Culture* (New York: New Press, 1995), 33–38.

48. Jing Wang, *High Culture Fever: Politics, Aesthetics, and Ideology in Deng's China* (Berkeley: University of California Press, 1996), 266–268.

49. Xuetong Zhou, "Guanzhong Bu Fan "Jiqing Ranshao De Suiyue" Lianbo Wubian [Viewers Not yet Had Enough: Five Reruns of "Passion" Series in a Row]," last modified May 23, 2002, www.people.com.cn/GB/wenyu/64/128/20020827/80 8984.html.

50. Geremie Barmé, *In the Red: On Contemporary Chinese Culture* (New York: Columbia University Press, 1999), 179–200, 235–254.

51. Hong Yin and Daihui Yang, "Zhongguo Dianshiju Yishu Chuantong," in *Zhongmei Dianshiju Bijiao Yanjiu*, ed. Chunjing Qu and Ying Zhu (Shanghai: Shanghai Sanlian Bookstore, 2005), 315–344.

52. Sheldon Hsiao-peng Lu, "Global Postmodernization: The Intellextual, the Artist, and China's Condition," in *Postmodernism & China*, ed. Arif Dirlik and Xudong Zhang (Durham and London: Duke University Press, 2000), 145–174.

53. Barmé, *In the Red*, 307–308.

54. Wang, *Brand New China*, 251.

55. Zhu, Keane, and Bai, *TV Drama in China*, 9.

56. Michael Keane, "Send in the Clones: Television Formats and Content Creation in the People's Republic of China," in *Media in China: Consumption, Content, and Crisis*, ed. Stephie Donald, Michael Keane, and Hong Yin (London: RoutledgeCurzon, 2002), 80–90.

57. Lull, *China Turned On*, 92–94.

58. Yin and Yang, "Zhongguo Dianshiju Yishu Chuantong," 315–344.

59. Yin and Yang, "Zhongguo Dianshiju Yishu Chuantong," 317.

60. In a survey on rural viewing habits conducted in seven provinces and municipalities in 2006, 67.36 percent of the respondents ranked TV drama and film reruns as the preferred programs, making them the most watched genres for rural families, see Weiqing Zhao, Xinxun Wu, and NiYu, "Qi Sheng Shi Qu Nongcui Dianshi Shoushi Xiguan Diaocha Baogao [Survey Report on Rural Television Viewing Habits in

Seven Provinces, Municipalities and Autonomous Regions]," *TV Research* 201, no. 8 (2006): 38–41.

61. Wang, *Brand New China*, 27.

62. Yin and Yang, "Zhongguo Dianshiju Yishu Chuantong," 315–344.

63. Lisa Rofel, *Desiring China: Experiments in Neoliberalism, Sexuality, and Public Culture* (Durham, NC: Duke University Press, 2007), 62–63.

64. Perry Link, *The Uses of Literature* (Princeton: Princeton University Press, 2000), 30.

65. Paul Clark, *The Chinese Cultural Revolution: A History* (Cambridge: Cambridge University Press, 2008), 56–62.

66. Cun Chen, "Kan Dianying (Watching Films)," in *Everyday China: Dailylife of the Common People in the 1970s*, eds. Liang Wu, Yun Gao, and Huaming Gu (Jiangsu: Jiangsu Fine Arts Press, 1999), 84.

67. Yingjin Zhang, *Chinese National Cinema* (London: Routlege, 2004), 203.

68. Tang, *Chinese Modern*, 110.

69. Rofel, *Desiring China*, 48.

70. Ibid., 48.

71. Yuezhi Zhao, "Rethinking Chinese Media Studies: History, Political Economy and Culture," in *Internationalizing Media Studies*, ed. Daya Kishan Thussu (London and New York: Routledge, 2009), 94.

72. Wanning Sun, "The Curse of the Everyday: Politics of Representation and New Social Semiotics in Post-Socialist China," in *Political Regimes and the Media in Asia*, ed. Krishna Sen and Terence Lee (New York: Routledge, 2008), 31–48.

73. Yuezhi Zhao, "Neoliberal Strategies, Socialist Legacies", 30.

74. Harriet Evans and Stephie Donald, *Picturing Power in the People's Republic of China: Posters of the Cultural Revolution* (Lanham: Rowman and Littlefield, 1999), 20.

75. Ien Ang, "Living Room Wars: New Technologies, Audience Measurement and the Tactics of Television Consumption," in *Consuming Technologies: Media and Information in Domestic Spaces*, ed. Roger Silverstone and Eric Hirsch (London: Routledge, 1992), 343–351.

76. Rofel, *Desiring China*, 45.

77. Janice Hua Xu, "Building a Chinese "Middle Class": Consumer Education and Identity Construction in Television Land," in *TV China*, ed. Ying Zhu and Chris Berry (Bloomington and Indianapolis: Indiana University Press, 2009), 150–176.

## CHAPTER 2

1. McDougall and Louie, *Literature of China*, 196.

2. Li, *50 Niandai*, 177.

3. Wang, "Depoliticized Politics," 29–45.

4. Lin, *The Transformation of Chinese Socialism*; Lee, He, and Huang, "The Chinese Party Publicity Inc," 17–26. Mark Selden and Elizabeth Perry, eds., *Chinese Society: Change, Conflict and Resistance (Asia's Transformations)* 3rd Edn (London:

Routledge, 2010); Dorothy Solinger, "Labour Market Reform and the Plight of the Laid-Off Proletariat," *The China Quarterly* 170 (2002): 304–326.

5.     Liu Kang suggests that various forms of street dance popular among the elderly in the post-Mao era have their roots in the dancing balls of the revolutionary period. He also argues that the origin of karaoke can be traced to the collective forms of entertainment popular in the revolutionary period. Liu, *Globalization and Cultural Trends in China*, 87.

6.     See Yu Liu, "Maoist Discourse and the Mobilisation of Emotions in Revolutionary China," *Modern China* 36, no. 3 (2010): 329–362. See also Tang, *Chinese Modern* and Ban Wang, *The Sublime Figure of History: Aesthetics and Politics in Twentieth-Century China* (Stanford: Stanford University Press, 1997).

7.     "Structure of feeling" is a term created by Williams, *Marxism and Literature*, 132. It refers to meanings and values as lived and felt, as well as the affective elements of consciousness and relations.

8.     Liu, *Globalization and Cultural Trends in China*, 94.

9.     Kang Liu, "Reinventing 'Red Classics' in the Age of Globalization," *Comparative Literature in China* 26, no. 1 (2003): 13–30.

10.     Jinhua Dai, "Jiushu Yu Xiaofei [Redemption and Consumption]," in *Meijie Zhexue [Media Philosophy]*, ed. Yuechuan Wang (Kaifeng: Henan University Press, 2004), 68–80.

11.     Dai, "Jiushu Yu Xiaofei," 68.

12.     Ban Wang, *Illustrations from the Past: Trauma, Memory, and History in Modern China* (Stanford: Stanford University Press, 2004), 120.

13.     Jin Ba, *Sui Xiang Lu [Random Thoughts]* (Beijing: Writers Publishing House, 2005). 563.

14.     Claire Huot, *China's New Cultural Scene: A Handbook of Changes* (Durham, NC: Duke University Press, 2000), 160–161.

15.     Wang, *Illustrations from the Past*, 103.

16.     The New Left scholar Wang Hui has argued that the intellectual movement of the 1980s has a complicit relationship with the state's modernisation project and reform agenda, despite its self-claimed autonomous stance. See Hui Wang, *China's New Order: Society, Politics, and Economy in Transition* (Cambridge, MA: Harvard University Press, 2003).

17.     Wang, *Illustrations from the Past*, 105.

18.     See Rofel, *Desiring China*.

19.     Perry Link points out that "pure art" was defined negatively as "non-Maoist, non-political, non-didactic and non-instrumental," a counter reaction to the extreme oppressive political culture in the high Maoist era. Link, *The Uses of Literature*, 139.

20.     Sheldon Lu, "Soap Opera in China: The Transnational Politics of Visuality, Sexuality, and the Masculinity," *Cinema Journal* Fall 2000, no 1 (2000): 25–47.

21.     Barmé, *In the Red*, 224.

22.     Zongwei Zhang, "Yiqi Shixian Zhangyang De Wenhua Shijian: Toushi 'Hongse Jingdian' Gaibian [A Drummed-up Cultural Event: On the Adaptation of the Red Classics]," *Contemporary Cinema* 2007, no. 1 (2007): 74–79.

23.     Barmé, *In the Red*, 251.

24. Ibid., 252–253.
25. Dongfeng Tao, "Hou Geming Shidai De Geming Wenhua [Revolutionary Culture in a Post-Revolutionary Age]," in *Dangdai Zhongguo Wenyi Sichao Yu Wenhua Redian [Contemporary Trends in Literature and the Arts and Key Cultural Issues]* ed. Dongfeng Tao (Beijing: Beijing University Press, 2008), 196–211.
26. Barmé, *In the Red,* 319.
27. Fei Yang, "Jinhou Wunian Hongse Lüyou Jiang 'Hong' Bian Huaxia Dadi [Red Tour Popular across the Country in the Next Five Years]," www.people.com.cn, February 25, 2005, http://travel.people.com.cn/GB/41636/41637/44670/44672/3202881.html.
28. According to statistics provided by China Central Television (CCTV), the ratings for *The Making of a Hero* were 9–12 percent across the country. *Shajiabang* captured around 10 percent of TV audiences in the Beijing area on its first airing, and *Tracks in the Snowy Mountain* achieved about the same rate.
29. Lu, "Soap Opera in China." See also Ning Wang, "The Mapping of Chinese Postmodernity," in *Postmodernism and China,* eds. Arif Dirlik and Xudong Zhang (Durham, NC and London: Duke University Press, 2000), 21–40.
30. Liu, *Globalization and Cultural Trends in China,* 93.
31. Wang and Zhong, "Why Does Socialist Culture Matter Today," 1–18.
32. "Political pop" is a term coined by critic Li Xianting in his 1992 article, "Apathy and deconstructive consciousness in post-1989 art." It describes a social trend in the 1990s, when artists began to make connections between the ideological and iconic status attributed to Mao Zedong and the fetishization of consumer commodities. An artistic movement emerged thereafter, characterized by a satirical treatment of Maoist subjects and style by using Pop Art techniques. See Xianting Li, "Apathy and Deconstruction in Post-'89 Art: Analyzing the Trends of 'Cynical Realism'and 'Political Pop' " in *Contemporary Chinese Art: Primary Documents,* ed. Hong Wu and Peggy Wang (New York: Museum of Modern Art, 1992/2010), 157–166.
33. Liu, *Globalization and Cultural Trends in China,* 94.
34. Barmé used the "gray" to describe the prevailing sentiments of the early 1990s. These sentiments included the "doubtful, ironic, lackadaisical and the cynical elements of society." Barmé, *In the Red,* 100. The gray sentiments resulted from the complex negotiation between orthodox Party culture and the rising commercial culture, represented by popular culture originating from Hong Kong and Taiwan, avant-garde culture and youth culture.
35. Jianli Hu, ""Gangtie" Chengwei Zhuxuanlü Jingpin ["The Making of a Hero" Becomes "Main Melody" Top Pick] " *Life Times,* March 16, 2000, http://ent.sina.com.cn/film/old/5436.html.
36. Hongmei Yu, "Dujie Women Shidaide Jingshen Zhenghou: Dui Dianshi Lianxuju 'Gangtie Shi Zenyang Lianchengde'Jieshoufankui De Sikao[Reading and Understanding the Spiritual Syndrome of Our Times: Reflections on the Reception of the Television Drama 'the Making of a Hero.']," in *Shuxie Wenhua Yingxiong [Writing About Cultural Hero: Cultural Studies at the Turn of the Century],* ed. Jinhua Dai, Contemporary Popular Media Criticism (Nanjing: Jiangsu People's Press, 2000), 192–227; Zhao, *Communication in China,* 217–219.

37.   Vanke Film and Television Co Ltd was formerly Vanke Cultural Communication Co Ltd. Established in 1992, the company specialises in film and television planning and production. It has branches in Beijing and Hong Kong. See http://mt.vanke.com/.

38.   Yu, "Dujie Women Shidaide Jingshen Zhenghou," 194.

39.   Ibid., 196.

40.   Weidong Ren, "Shenzhen, Bao'er, Wukelan: You Yige Chuntian De Gushi [Shenzhen, Pavel, Ukraine: Another Story of Spring]," *People's Daily*, May 29 2000, 5.

41.   Lan Guan, "Zheng Kainan: Fanxing Cai Shi Chenggong Zhimu [Zheng Kainan: Reflection Is the Mother of Sucess]," *Finance* (2005), November 18, 2005, http://finance.sina.com.cn/money/lcexpr/20051118/17272131068.shtml.

42.   Yu, "Dujie Women Shidaide Jingshen Zhenghou," 195–197.

43.   Ibid., 195.

44.   Ibid., 196–197.

45.   Frederik H. Green, "The Cultural Indigenization of a Soviet "Red Classic" Hero: Pavel Korchagin's Journey through Time and Space," in *The Making and Remaking of China's "Red Classics"*, ed. Rosemary Roberts and Li Li (Hong Kong: Hong Kong University Press, 2017), 136–155. Also Zhao, *Communication in China*, 218.

46.   Main melody or leitmotif TV dramas were drama series on revolutionary history or contemporary changes based on official policies and guidelines.

47.   Zhao, *Communication in China*, 215.

48.   Ying Chang, "'Wode Changzheng' Daxing Dianshi Huodong Chuangzuo Beijing ['My Long March' Publicity Behind the Scenes]," CCTV, April 18, 2006, http://www.cctv.com/news/other/20060418/101844.shtml.

49.   Keane, "Send in the Clones," 80–90.

50.   Chang, "Wode Changzheng".

51.   Ibid.

52.   Meng, "Regulating Egao," 52–67. See also Paola Voci, "Quasi-Documentary, Cellflix and Web Spoofs: Chinese Movies' Other Visual Pleasures," *Senses of Cinema* October-December, no. 41 (2006), http://sensesofcinema.com/2006/film-history-conference-papers/other-chinese-movies-pleasures/ and Xuelin Zhou, "'From Behind the Wall': The Representation of Gender and Sexuality in Modern Chinese Film," *Asian Journal of Communiction* 11, no. 2 (2001): 1–16.

53.   Meng, "Regulating Egao," 63.

54.   Voci, "Quasi-Documentary."

55.   xxxx

56.   *Super 6+1* is a popular weekend entertainment program on CCTV 3. Its format is a mixture of game show and talent competition. The host of the show, Li Yong, is one of the most popular TV personalities in China.

57.   Zhi Jiang, "Lei Feng Ye Ceng Shi Shimao Qingnian, Chulian Nüyou Zhaopian Shouci Gongkai [Lei Feng Was Once a Trendy Youth, Photo of First Love Made Public]," *Southern Metropolis Daily* March 1, 2006, http://www.southcn.com/news/community/shgc/200603010360.htm.

58.   Wei Su, "The School and the Hospital: On the Logics of Socialist Realism," in *Chinese Literature in the Second Half of a Modern Century: A Critical Survey*, ed. Pang-yuan Chi and David Der-wei Wang (Bloomington: Indiana Unviersity Press, 2000), 65–95.

59.   Zhao, *Communication in China*, 32.

60.   Ibid., 45.

61.   Meng, "Regulating Egao," 56.

62.   Ibid., 56.

63.   Xuejun Zhang, "E'gao 'Shanshande Hongxing,' Zuozhe Hu Daoge Xiang Baiyichang Daoqian [Author Hu Daoge Apologises to Baiyi Studio for Spoofing 'the Shining Red Star']," April 24, 2006, http://news.163.com/06/0424/10/2FFHLNQ90 0011229.html.

64.   Yanqin Zhang, "Lei Feng Zaoyu Le 'Hou Liuxing,' Dang Lei Feng Yushang Wangluo E'gao [Caught in the Post-Pop, When Lei Feng Meets the Online Spoofing Fad]," March 24, 2006, http://finance.sina.com.cn/media/cmpl/20060324/12042445 468.shtml.

65.   There is often a discrepancy between Chinese TV drama's ideal audience and the actual viewers. While there is no consensus on the size and definition of the middle class in China, the fascination over this social category's potential as the ideal consumer and its presumed stabilizing function within society has remained unabated. Media such as TV dramas have played an indispensable role in projecting the imaginary of such a social stratum.

## CHAPTER 3

1.   Yuezhi Zhao, "Chinese Modernity, Media and Democracy: An Interview with Lu Xinyu," *Global Media and Communication* 6, no. 1 (2010): 5–32.

2.   Lorenz Bichler, "Coming to Terms with a Term: Notes on the History of the Use of Socialist Realism in China," in *In the Party Spirit: Socialist Realism and Literary Practice in the Soviet Union, East Germany and China* ed. Hilary Chung, et al. (Amsterdam: Rodopi, 1996), 23–29.

3.   Williams, *The Long Revolution*, 319.

4.   Ibid., 320.

5.   Ibid., 319.

6.   Link, *The Uses of Literature*, 10.

7.   McDougall and Louie, *Literature of China*, 194–195.

8.   Weibao Fang, *Hongse Yiyi De Shengcheng: Ershi Shiji Zhongguo Zuoyi Wenxue Yanjiu [the Formation of the Meaning Red: A Study of the Twentieth Century Leftist Literature]* (Hefei: Anhui Education Press, 2004), 53–55.

9.   See Link, *The Uses of Literature*; Wang, *The Sublime Figure of History*.

10.   Literary critic Wang Ban argues that although the sublime is treated as a concept which originated from the West, Chinese aestheticians have nativized it to a large extent. In the context of the Red Classics, I adopt Wang's definition of the sublime as "an aesthetic that furnishes a gigantic image of the people, the figure of

the collective subject engaged in a world-transforming practice in order to carry out the telos of history" (1997, 8).

11. Tang, *Chinese Modern*; Wang, *The Sublime Figure of History*.

12. Wang, *The Sublime Figure of History*, 258.

13. Ying Du, "Yizhong Xin Wenyi Dianfan De Jiangou: Dui 1949 Nian Qianhou Wenyi Zuopin De Kaocha [the Construction of a New Model for Literature and the Arts: A Study of Literary and Art Works around the Year 1949]," *Wenyi Pinping [Literary Criticism]* 2010, no. 2 (2010): 83–89.

14. Fang, *Hongse Yiyi De Shengcheng*, 156.

15. Guangwei Cheng, *Wenxue Xiangxiang Yu Wenxue Guojia: Zhongguo Dangdai Wenxue Yanjiu [Literary Imaginary and Literary State: A Study of Chinese Contemporary Literature (1949–1976)]* (Kaifeng: Henan University Press, 2005), 63–68.

16. Yuchun Li, *Quanli, Zhuti, Huayu: 20 Shiji 40–70 Niandai Zhongguo Wenxue Yanjiu [Power, Subjectivity, Discourse: A Study of Chinese Literature from the 1940s to the 1970s]* (Wuhan: Central China Normal University Press, 2007), 95.

17. Ibid.

18. Wei Su, "The School and the Hospital: On the Logics of Socialist Realism," in *Chinese Literature in the Second Half of a Modern Century: A Critical Survey*, ed. Pang-yuan Chi and David Der-wei Wang (Bloomington: Indiana Unviersity Press, 2000), 69.

19. Li, *Quanli, Zhuti, Huayu*, 3.

20. Zhicheng Hong, *A History of Contemporary Chinese Literature* (Leiden and Boston: Brill, 2007), 106.

21. See Perry Link, Richard P. Madsen, and Paul G. Pickowicz, eds., *Popular China: Unofficial Culture in a Globalising Society* (Lanham: Rowman & Littlefield, 2002), 116. Lan Yang, "'Socialist Realism' Versus 'Revolutionary Realism Plus Revolutionary Romanticism,'" in *In the Party Spirit: Socialist Realism and Literary Practice in the Soviet Union, East Germany and China*, ed. Hilary Chung, et al. (Amsterdam, Netherland: Rodopi, 1996).

22. Clark, *The Chinese Cultural Revolution*, 34–35.

23. Lan Yang, "The Depiction of the Hero in the Cultural Revolution Novel," *China Information* 12, no. 68 (1998): 74.

24. Barmé, *In the Red*, 247.

25. Ibid.

26. Li, *50 Niandai*.

27. In an interview with *Beijing Daily* in 1957, Qu Bo told reporters that he could easily recite large chunks of these works, and it was his belief that workers, peasants, and soldiers were also fond of this vernacular style (Qu, as cited in Li, 2003, 5)

28. Ibid.

29. Ibid., 53.

30. Rofel, *Desiring China*.

31. *Tracks* is a joint production by Vanke Film and Television Co. Ltd., the Shenzhen Municipal Publicity Department (SMPD), and the Theatrical Company of the General Political Department (TCGPD). Like *The Making of a Hero*, this is a

project cofunded by an independent production unit (Vanke) and state organisations (SMPD and TCGPD). The producer, Zheng Kainan, is the director of *The Making of a Hero*.

32.    According to Bakhtin, the material bodily lower stratum is a fundamental component of the "uncrowning" of the official, the sublime, the sober, the sacred, and the exalted in *Rabelais and His World*. Bakhtin describes the material bodily lower stratum as a major thrust downward, a movement that manifests itself in fights, beatings, and blows, in curses and abuses, in carnival travesty, and in banquets and material bodily needs such as swallowing, farting, and birth-giving. Is "birth-giving" the term used in the original text? It seems a little odd in English—"giving birth" is more common. But if this is how it was put in the original text, no need to change it. Bakhtin believes that this strategy "liberates objects from the snares of false seriousness, from illusions and sublimations inspired by fear" (Bakhtin, 1984, 376). One could draw a parallel between Bakhtin's strategies with some major changes made to Yang Zirong's image in the TV adaptation: his dialect (not standard), his habit of swearing, his impure social background, his mastery of underworld language, his propensity to get drunk, his job as a chef, his love of indecent folk tunes and practical jokes, his ruffian style, and his emotional entanglement with his former lover. It can be argued that these characterizations were adopted to transform the perfect, godly hero embodying the proletarian class into an earthly human individual.

33.    It is interesting to note that Mao Zedong once said, "Revolution is not hosting a banquet or dining." In justifying the violence in the peasants' movement, Mao contrasted it with eating, which is relaxed and easy. Zedong Mao, "Hunan Nongmin Yundong Kaocha Baogao [Report on an Investigation of the Peasant Movement in Hunan]," in *Mao Zedong Xuanji Diyi Juan [Selected Works of Mao Tse-Tung, Vol. I]* (Beijing: Foreign Languages Press, 1975).

34.    Yang Li, "Gongye Ticai, Gongye Zhuyi Yu 'Shehuizhuyi Xiandaixing' [Industrial Subject, Industrialism, and 'Socialist Modernity': Rereading 'Braving the Winds and Waves']," *Wenxue Pinglun [Literary Critics]* 2010, no. 6 (2010): 46–53.

35.    Clark, *The Chinese Cultural Revolution*, 57–59.

36.    Li, *50 Niandai*.

37.    Fusheng Liu, "Tuibian Zhong De Lishi Fuxian: Cong 'Geming Lishi Xiaoshuo' Dao 'Xin Geming Lishi Xiaoshuo,'" *Wenxue Pinglun [Literary Critics]* 2006, no. 6 (2006): 65–72.

38.    Yiming Chen, "Cui Yongyuan: Zai Hongse Jingdian Qian [Cui Yongyuan: Facing Hongse Jingdian]," (2004), http://www.people.com.cn/GB/wenhua/22219 /2481780.html.

39.    Hongjingsuhongbudong'ai, "Hen Pi 'Linhai Xueyuan': Wu Qing Bu Cheng Xi, Bu Su Bu Suan Wan [Lashing Tracks in the Snowy Mountain: Without Love There Would Be No Drama; Unsatisfied Till It Is Vulgar]," March 10, 2004, http:// www.peopledaily.com.cn/BIG5/yule/1083/2382935.html.

40.    Bo Liu, "Qubo Airen: Yang Zirong Youqianghuadiao, Linhaixueyuan Gaibian Qiantuo [Yang Zirong with a Glib Tougue, the Reinvention of Tracks in the Snowy Mountain Is Improper]," March 26, 2004, http://ent.sina.com.cn/v/2004-03-26 /0902343957.html.

41.   Liwei Jin, "Linhai Xueyuan Ge Nianling Ceng Shoushi Diaocha, Hongse Jingdian Xinbian Nan [a Survey on Viewing of Tracks in the Snowy Mountain Based on Age Groups: Adapting Red Classics Is a Hard Job]," March 11, 2004, http://news.sina.com.cn/o/2004-03-11/17172025115s.shtml.

42.   Yong Zhao, "Shui Zai Shouhu 'Hongse Jingdian': Cong 'Hongse Jingdian' Ju Gaibian Kan Guanzhongde 'Zhengzhi Wuyishi' [Who is guarding the 'Red Classics': TV Adaptation Viewers' Political Unconsciousness]," *Southern Cultural Forum*, 2005, no. 6 (2005): 36–39.

43.   Chantal Mouffe, "Hegemony and New Political Subjects: Toward a New Concept of Democracy," in *Marxism and the Interpretation of Culture*, ed. Cary Nelson and Lawrence Grossberg (Urbana: University of Illinois Press, 1988), 98.

44.   Guangwei Cheng, "Ershi Shiji Liushi Niandai De Dianying Yu Wenhua Shishang [Film and Cultural Fad in 1960s]," *Journal of Xinyang Teachers' Colleage* 2002, no. 1 (2002): 96–101. Cheng discusses various readings of the Red Classics films in the 1960s that diverged from the dominant ideological operations. For example, Anti-Japanese War films such as *The Tunnel War* and *The Mine War* did not attract children with their grand narrative of revolution, but, rather, through their depiction of the magic military tactics of the guerrilla war and farcical scenes where Japanese soldiers flee helter-skelter. These scenes connected with the children's enjoyment of playful games. Cheng's observations should indicate that film or television texts are open and offer a variety of interpretations to the audience.

45.   Yingjie Guo, "Class, Stratum and Group," in *The New Rich in China: Future Rulers, Present Lives* ed. David Goodman, S. (London: Routledge, 2008), 38–52.

46.   Clark, *The Chinese Cultural Revolution*, 142–144.

47.   See Tang, *Chinese Modern*; Wang, *The Sublime Figure of History*.

48.   Wang, *China's New Order*, 57–58.

# CHAPTER 4

1.   Hershatter, "The Subaltern Talks Back," 103–130.

2.   Harriet Evans, *Women and Sexuality in China: Dominant Discourses of Female Sexuality and Gender since 1949* (Cambridge and Oxford: Polity Press, 1997), 5–6.

3.   Jinghua Dai, "Invisible Women: Contemporary Chinese Cinema and Women's Film," *Positions* 3, no. 1 (1995); Lydia H. Liu, "Writing and Feminism Invention and Intervention: The Female Tradition in Modern Chinese Literature," in *Gender Politicis in Modern China: Writing and Feminism*, ed. Tani E. Barlow (Durham, NC and London: Duke University Press, 1993); Yue Meng, "Female Images and National Myth," in *Gender Politics in Modern China*, ed. Tani E. Barlow (Durham, NC and London: Duke University Press, 1993).

4.   Xiaodong Zhu, "Tongguo Hunyin De Zhili," in *Shenti De Wenhua Zhengzhixue*, ed. Ming'an Wang (Kaifeng: Henan University Press, 2004); Xianglin Li, "Yangbanxi: Quanli Huayu He Xingbie Yishi De Jiaozhi [Model Revolutionary Works: Interaction between Power and Gender Discourses]," Aesthetic Studies Webpage, http://www.aesthetics.com.cn/s45c1143.aspx.

5. Zhu, "Tongguo Hunyin De Zhili."
6. Evans, *Women and Sexuality in China*, 18–19.
7. Some recent readings of *Yangbanxi* suggest that gender erasure was not total in these works. To various degrees, traditional ideas of gender difference still operate within these works. See Rosemary Roberts, "Positive Women Characters in the Revolutionary Model Works," *Asian Studies Review* 28, no. 4 (2004): 407–423. In revolutionary cinema, the gendered gaze is common and this socialist-realist erotic gaze is often expressed in the revolutionary romance between a young girl and a male Communist hero, as in *The Red Detachment of Women*. See Stephanie Hemelryk Donald, *Public Secrets: Public Spaces: Cinema and Civility in China* (Lanham: Rowman and Littlefield, 2000). Others have also argued that feminine beauty is always present in the revolutionary culture. See Hung-Yok. Ip, "Fashioning Appearances: Feminine Beauty in Chinese Communist Revolutionary Culture," *Modern China* 29, no. 3 (2003): 329–361.
8. Li, "Yangbanxi."
9. Evans, *Women and Sexuality in China*, 140–142.
10. See Yifei Shen, *Bei Jiangou De Nuxing: Dangdai Shehui Xingbie Lilun [The Woman That Is Constructed: Contemporary Gender Theory]* (Shanghai: Shanghai People's Press, 2005) and also Zheng Wang, "Gender, Employment and Women's Resistance," in *Chinese Society, 2nd Edition: Change, Conflict and Resistance*, eds. Elizabeth Perry, J. and Mark. Selden, Asia's Transformation (London and New York: Routledge, 2000), 159–182.
11. Rosemary Roberts, "Women's Studies in Literature and Feminist Literary Criticism in Contemporary China," in *Dress, Sex and Text in China Culture*, ed. Antonia Finnane and Anne McLaren (Clayton, Melbourne: Monash Asia Institute, 1999), 225–240.
12. Jinping Dong, "Huayu Yu Nuxingqizhi De Jiangou: Ershi Shiji Yilai Zhongguo Nuxingqizhi Bianqian De Fenxi [Discourse and the Construction of Femininity: An Analysis of the Transformation of Femininity in the 20th Century]," *Jianghua Luntan* 7, no. 2 (2007): 151.
13. Cara Wallis, "Chinese Women in the Official Chinese Press: Discursive Construction of Gender in Service to the State," *Westminster Papers in Communication and Culture* 3, no. 1 (2006): 94–108.
14. Liu Huifang, the heroine in the TV soap hit, Yearnings, who is gentle, virtuous, self-sacrificing, and forbearing became an overnight "saintly women icon" (Barmé, *In the Red*, 104) and was identified as the "ideal wife" by male audiences in a survey. This illustrates how the traditional view of women still held sway.
15. Zhou, "From Behind the Wall," 1–16.
16. Antonia Finnane and Anne McLaren, "Introduction," in *Dress, Sex and Text in Chinese Culture*, ed. Antonia Finnane and Anne. McLaren (Clayton: Monash Asia Institute, 1999), 18.
17. Zhizhong Zhang, "Dingwei Yu Cuowei: Yingshi Gaibian Yu Wenxue Yanjiu Zhong De "Hongse Jingdian" [Positioning and Mis-Positioning: TV Adaptations and Literary Research on the Red Classics]," *Wenyi Yanjiu [Literary and Art Research]* 2005, no. 4 (2005): 13–20.

18.   Jason Mcgrath, *Postsocialist Modernity; Chinese Cinima, Literature, and Criticism in the Market Age* (Stanford, California: Stanford University Press, 2008), 92.

19.   Clark, *The Chinese Cultural Revolution*, 31.

20.   Ibid.

21.   It premiered on Qilu Satellite TV channel on April 27, 2006.

22.   Xichao Ma, "Cong "Shajiabang" Dao 'Shajiabang': Banben Yange Zhong Geming Huayu Tixi De Bianzou [from "Shajiabang" to 'Shajiabang': The Transformation of Revolutionary Discursive System in the Edition Evolutions]," *Journal of Xi'an University of Electronic Technology (Social Sciences)* 2006, no. 5 (2006): 98–102.

23.   Hongzhen Ji, "Wang Zengqi Yu Yangbanxi [Wang Zengqi and Yangbanxi]," *Shu Wu [Book House]*2007, 76–82.

24.   Jiafang Dai, *Yangbanxi De Fengfeng Yuyu [The Vicissitudes of Yangbanxi]* (Beijing: Knowledge Publishing House, 1995).

25.   Sihe Chen, *Zhongguo Dangdai Wenxue Guanjianci Shijiang [Ten Lectures on Key Words in Contemporary Chinese Literature]* (Shanghai: Fudan University Press, 2002), 152–154.

26.   In a dialogue on ideologies behind films, Yao Xiaomeng and Hu Ke once remarked that to watch the scene "Battle of Wits" is to watch one woman flirt with three men, only in a very secretive way.

27.   Chen, *Zhongguo Dangdai Wenxue Guanjianci Shijiang*, 152–154.

28.   Xue Rong, as cited in Hanci Chen, "Xiaoshuo "Shajiabang" Zuozhe Xue Rong Shouci Dapo Chenmo Jie Xinbao Tan Chuanzuo [Novelette "Shajiabang" Author Xue Rong Breaks Silence for the First Time, Talk About His Writing through News Bulletin]," http://www.booktide.com/news/20030224/200302240001.html .para.4

29.   He Xiao, "Xiaoshuo "Shajiabang" Zai Xueyang Shenme? [What Does Novelette 'Shajiabang' Propagate]," *Zhejiang Daily* 2003, 8.

30.   Tiechuan Hao, "Xiaoshuo "Shajiabang" Bu Heli, Bu Hefa [Novelette Shajiabang Unreasonable and Illegitimate]," *Wenhui Gazette*, April 25 2003, 5.

31.   Stephanie Hemelryk Donald and John.G. Gammack, *Tourism and the Branded City* (Hampshire: Ashgate, 2007), 8.

32.   Yin Wang and Feiran Du, "Shajiabang "Xin" Gushi [the "New" Story of Shajiabang]," *Nanfang Weekend*, July 17 2003, D21.

33.   Yin Wang, "Shajiabang Xianchang," *Nanfang Weekend*, July 17 2003, D21.

34.   Yin Wang and Feiran Du, "Shajiabang "Xin" Gushi, ibid.

35.   Pan Jinlian is a character in two Chinese classic novels, *Stories from the Water Margin* and *The Plum in the Golden Vase,* and the quintessential adulterous wife in Chinese culture.

36.   Mcgrath, *Postsocialist Modernity,* 95.

37.   Ibid., 96.

38.   Ibid., 126.

39.   Yan Li, "Xinban "Hongse Jiangzijun" Gen Hongse Bu Tiebian [The New Version of "the Red Detachment of Woman" Has Nothing to Do with "Red"]," *Beijing Youth Daily*, July 3 2006, B6.

40. Nan Cai, "You Jian Qionghua: Dianying "Hongse Niangzijun" Beihou De Gushi [Qionghua Met Again: Stories Behind the Scene of Film "the Red Detachment of Women"]," *China Television News*, June 12 2006, 42.

41. Xin Pan, "Xinban Shajiabang Chengwei Zhushuiju [Shajiabang Watered Down in Its New Version]," *Dahe Bao*, September 12 2006, A24.

42. Ibid., A24.

43. ent.sina.com.cn, "Shajiabang Shoubo Yishi: Duihua Daoyan Shen Xinghao [Shajiabang Debut Ceremony: A Dialogue with Shen Xinghao]," (www.ent.sina.com, 2006).

44. Zhiqiang Peng, "Shajiabang Zuowan Zai Chuantai Kaibo [Series Shajiabang Started Running on Sichuan Television Yesterday Evening]," *Chengdu Commercial News*, July 8 2006, 15.

45. Xue as cited in Wang and Du, "Shajiabang "Xin" Gushi," D21.

46. Peng, "Shajiabang Zuowan Zai Chuantai," P15.

47. Pan, "Xinban Shajiabang," A24.

48. ent.sina.com.cn, "Xu Qing, Liu Jinshan, Cheng Qian Xinlang Liao "Shajiabang" Zhan Caiyi [Xu Qing, Liu Jinshan and Cheng Qian Talk About Shajiabang with Sina]," (Sina.com.cn, 2006).

49. Ibid.

50. Xue, as cited in Peng, "Shajiabang Zuowan Zai Chuantai," 15.

51. Wang, "Shajiabang Xianchang [on the Scene of Shajiabang]," A24.

52. Norbert Elias, *Power and Civility: The Civilising Process*, 2nd edn (New York: Pantheon Books, 1982).

53. Zhang, "Dingwei Yu Cuowei."

54. Fa Zhang, "Hongse Jingdian: 2004 De Yizhong Wenhua Xianxiangde Jiedu," *Literature and Art Research* 2005, no. 4 (2005): 21–25.

55. Tak-hung Leo Chan, *The Discourse on Foxes and Ghosts: Ji Yun and Eighteenth Century Literati Story-Telling* (Honolulu: University of Hawai'i Press, 1998), 11.

56. Roger. Silverstone, *Television and Everyday Life* (London: Routledge, 1994).

57. Sue Thornham and Tony Purvis, *Television Drama: Theories and Identities* (New York: Palgrave MacMillan, 2005), 66.

58. Raymond Williams, "Drama in a Dramatised Society," in *Raymond Williams on Television: Selected Writings*, ed. Alan. O'Connor (New York and London: Routledge, 1989), 3–13.

59. Christine Gledhill, *Home Is Where the Heart Is: Studies in Melodrama and the Woman's Film* (London: British Film Institute, 1987), 349.

60. Zhang, "Hongse Jingdian," 21–25.

61. Zhang, "Dingwei Yu Cuowei," 13–20.

62. Evans, *Women and Sexuality in China*, 130.

63. Ya.-Chien Huang, "Pink Dramas: Reconciling Consumer Modernity and Confucian Womanhood," in *TV Drama in China*, ed. Ying Zhu, Michael Keane, and Ruoyun Bai (Hong Kong: Hong Kong University Press, 2008), 103–114.

64. Harriet Evans, *The Subject of Gender: Daughter and Mothers in Urban China* (Lanham, MD: Rowman & Littlefield, 2008), 13.

65. Ying Hu, "Writing Erratic Desire: Sexual Poltics in Contemporary Chinese Fiction," in *In Pursuit of Contemporary East Asian Culture*, eds. Xiaobing Tang and Stephen Synder (Boulder, Colorado: Westview Press, 1996), 49–68.

66. Huang, "Pink Dramas," 103–114.

## CHAPTER 5

1. Sun and Zhao, "Television with Chinese Characteristics," 96–104.

2. He, *Renwenxue De Xiangxiangli*, 27–29.

3. Shufang Wu, "'Modernising' Confucianism in China: A Repackaging of Institutionalization to Consolidate Party Leadership," *Asian Perspective*, no. 39 (2015): 301–324; Qin Pampkin Pang, "The 'Two Lines Control Model' in China's State and Society Relations: Central States' Management of Confucian Revival in the New Century," *International Journal of China Studies* 5, no. 3 (2014): 627–55.

4. Rong Cai, "Make the Present Serve the Past: Restaging on Guard beneath the Neon Lights in Contemporary China," in *Chinese Television in the Twenty-First Century: Entertaining the Nation*, ed. Yuoyun Bai and Geng Song (London: Routledge, 2015), 149–157.

5. Lisa Hoffman, "Urban Transformation and Professionalization: Translocality and Rationalities of Enterprise in Post-Mao China," in *Translocal China: Linkages, Identities, and the Reimagining of Space*, ed. Tim Oakes and Louisa Schein (London: Routledge, 2006), 109–137.

6. My discussion of what the Red Classics mean for ordinary people, particular those in Linyi, is based mainly on my fieldwork in Linyi and Beijing from November 2008 to February 2009. The original plan was to carry out two focus group discussions and some in-depth interviews on the consumption of the Red Classics. After discussing my research with my local contacts, mostly my childhood friends and classmates, I realized that these friends, having lived in Linyi for decades, have developed a much larger local network, a valuable resource for my research. I thus asked them to distribute and collect a questionnaire, aimed at finding some general information on the locals' viewing habits and memories of the Red Classics and some initial response to the TV adaptations. Overall, seventy-one questionnaires were collected. The respondents mainly came from middle-class backgrounds, and worked in state-owned work units, including the Food and Drug Administration Bureau, the Bureau of Finance, a Polytechnic College, the Environmental Protection Bureau, and the Customs Administration. Most of the respondents were between twenty-five and forty-five years old. The majority had some form of tertiary education.

7. Wang, *China's New Order*, 78–84.

8. Considered one of the core works of the Red Classics, *The Red Sun* was originally a novel published in 1959. Combining history with fiction, the story focuses on the three major campaigns—Lianshui, Laiwu, and Menglianggu—fought between the CCP and the Nationalist armies in 1947 in Shandong Province. The novel gave a breathtaking account of the last campaign in Menglianggu, an isolated, rugged mountain area in Linyi. The Communist army fought against the Nationalist's

Seventy-Fourth division, led by military talent Zhang Lingfu. It was a cliff-hanging win for the CCP and the outcome of the campaign suggested the eventual downfall of the Nationalists. The novel, while largely maintaining the "class characteristics" of the characters, gave a more rounded persona to its major characters. The Nationalist army commander, Zhang Lingfu, was depicted as relatively capable, astute and resourceful, despite his evil class nature. The novel was adapted into a popular film in 1963.

9. The forty-two–episode TV drama serial, *Yimeng*, was commissioned by the Linyi Propaganda Department to narrate the locals' contribution to the founding of the nation in the Anti-Japanese War (1937–1945) and the Civil War (1946–1949) in a popular dramatic form. The story revolves around the vicissitudes of one family in a small village called Mamuchi during a chaotic period. Many of the wartime legends in the local area were dramatized and personified by the members of the fictitious family. The serial was shown during prime time on CCTV's Channel 8 in November 2009. Within weeks, it was CCTV's second highest-rating prime time drama (Wei Zhu and Jizhen Zhang, "Yimeng Shoushilu Yuju Yangshi Di'er: You Wang Rongying 2009 Nian Yangshi Huangjindang Dianshiju Shoushi Guanjun ['Yimeng' Jumped to Second Place in CCTV's Rating: Possible Number One in Cctv's 2009 Overall Primetime Drama Rating]," *Qilu Evening News*, Dec 8 2009, C02).

10. *Little Soldier Zhang Ga* was made in 1963. It is a story about a teenage boy who was caught in the middle of the Anti-Japanese War. For contemporary Chinese, it is one of the most memorable revolutionary themed children's movies. Yingchi Chu, Stephanie Hemelryk Donald, and Andrea Witcomb, "Children, Media and the Public Sphere in Chinese Australia," in *Political Communications in Greater China*, ed. Gary D. Rawnsley, and Ming-Yeh T. Rawnsley (London: Routledge-Curzon, 2003), 260–274.

11. In 2006, in Perth, West Australia, I conducted a focus group discussion and follow-up interviews based on the viewing of *Struggles in the Old City*, one of the seminal works in the genre. The results show that TV consumption is complex and unpredictable. TV dramas are charged with ambiguities and open to interpretation. And it is precisely these ambiguous moments and diverse ways of interpreting the Red Classics that have provided an important discursive space, where a range of new social identities can be constructed and contested.

12. Chu, Donald, and Witcomb, "Children, Media and the Public Sphere," 271.

13. Erik Mueggler, "Spectral Chains: Remembering the Great Leap Forward Famine," in *Re-Envisioning the Chinese Revolution: The Politics and Poetics of Collective Memories in Reform China*, ed. Ching Kwan Lee and Guobin Yang (Stanford: Stanford University Press, 2007), 50–68.

14. Wang, *China's New Order*, 57.

15. Arif Dirlik, "Looking Backward in the Age of Global Capital: Thoughts on History in Third World Cultural Criticism," in *In Pursuit of Contemporary East Asian Culture*, ed. Xiaobing Tang and Stephen Snyder (Boulder: WestviewPress, 1996); Arif Dirlik, "Mao Zedong in Contemporary Chinese Official Discourse and History," *China Perspectives* 2012, no. 2 (2012): 17–27.

16. Zhao, "Neoliberal Strategies, Socialist Legacies," 23–50.

17. Xueping Zhong and Ban Wang, eds., *Debating the Socialist Legacy and Capitalist Globalization in China* (London: Palgrave Macmillan, 2014), 1.

18. Chongyi Feng, "Jiangxi in Reform: The Fear of Exclusion and the Search for a New Identity," in *The Political Economy of China's Provinces: Comparative and Competitive Advantage*, ed. Hans Hendrischke and Chongyi Feng (London: Routledge, 1999), 249–276.

19. Hoffman, "Urban Transformation and Professionalization,"109–137.

20. David S.G. Goodman, "Shanxi as Translocal Imaginary: Reforming the Local," in *Translocal China: Linkages, Identities, and the Reimagining of Space*, ed. Tim S. Oakes and Louisa Schein (London: Routledge, 2006), 56–73.

21. For a detailed analysis of *Yimeng*, please see Qian Gong, "The Red Sister-in-Law Remakes: Redefining the 'Fish-and-Water' Relationships for the Era of Reform and Opening," in *The Making and Remaking of China's "Red Classics,"* ed. Rosemary Roberts and Li Li (Hong Kong: Hong Kong University Press, 2017), 156–176.

22. Wang, *The Sublime Figure of History*, 1–14.

23. These projects include a study of the pedagogical value of Yimeng Red Culture in contemporary society; an overview of Yimeng Red Culture resources; and a study of representative performances and theatrical works that have a revolutionary, historical theme.

24. I interviewed Professor Ji in a meeting room in the Social Development Institute on January 8, 2009. The quote below also comes from that interview.

25. This is the story of a child martyr, Wang Erxiao, who encountered a Japanese army troupe during the Anti-Japanese War. When a Japanese officer tried to trick him into giving them information about the hideout of the Eighth Route Army branch, Erxiao pretended he was taken in. He cleverly led the Japanese into an area that had been encircled by the Communist army. The Japanese were ambushed and suffered heavy losses. Erxiao died a heroic death. The story was later turned into a folk song, which has been popular with children for generations.

26. In countless films and television drama series, burnt village houses, locals screaming and scrambling, and soldiers chasing after the villagers' chickens for their food signify the presence of the Kuomintang army.

27. Huang is the surname of my interviewee, who preferred to be called Lao Huang. I interviewed Lao Huang at Linyi Normal College on January 8, 2008.

28. The exhibition was curated by the Linyi Municipal Party Committee as part of the nation's commemoration event series celebrating the Sixtieth Anniversary of Victory in the Anti-Fascist War in 2005.

29. Gayatri Chakravorty Spivak, "Can the Subaltern Speak?," in *Marxism and the Interpretation of Culture*, ed. Cary Nelson and Lawrence Grossberg (Basingstoke: Macmillan Education, 1988), 271–313.

30. Ibid.

31. Lao Li is an official working in the East China Revolutionary Martyr Cemetery, which houses the Yimeng Spirit show permanently in its exhibition hall. I interviewed Lao Li in his office on January 4, 2009.

32. See Wang, Jing, "Culture as Leisure and Culture as Capital." Positions: East Asia cultures critique 9, no. 1 (Spring 2001): 99–104.

33. Wang Tingjiang is a farmer-turned-entrepreneur in Shenquan Village, Luozhuang District of Linyi. He started his business in the late 1970s, transporting porcelain ware for sale with a hand-drawn cart. With the first profits he received from retailing and transportation, Wang set up a porcelain ware factory in 1986. By 1989, his assets were worth six million yuan. Wang, however, donated all his wealth to the village. The same year he was elected unanimously as the Director of the Village Committee and Party Secretary. He then led the villagers out of abject poverty through a series of entrepreneurial endeavors. Wang was the ideal moral model for the CCP in the current social environment; his success legitimizes Deng's neoliberal motto that "development is a hard truth," while his willingness to share his wealth overcomes the side-effects of disparity brought by the market and confirms the socialist egalitarian ideal of "get wealthy together" (*gongtong zhifu*). He thus embodies the compatibility of neoliberal strategy and socialist legacy.

# CHAPTER 6

1. Zhang, *Chinese National Cinema*, 239–240.
2. Ruoyun Bai and Geng Song, *Chinese Television in the Twenty-First Century: Entertaining the Nation* (London and New York: Routledge, 2015), 1–14.
3. Wei Ni, "Dangdai Diezhanju Zhong De Xinyan Yu Wenhua Zhenghou [The Idea of Belief and Cultural Symptoms in Spy TV Series]," in *Dianshiju Yu Dangdai Wenhua [TV Drama and Contemporary Culture]*, ed. Xiaoming Wang (Beijing: SDX Joint Publishing Company, 2014), 8.
4. Shenshen Cai, *State Propaganda in China's Entertainment Industry.* (New York: Routledge, 2016), 4.
5. Ni, "Dangdai Diezhanju", 7–18.
6. Yunxiang Yan, "The Chinese Path to Individualization," *The British Journal of Sociology* 61, no. 3 (2010): 489–512; ed. Yunxiang Yan, et al. (Berkeley: Los Angeles. London: University of California Press, 2011), 36–77.
7. Jiabao Wen, "Jiang Zhenhua, Cha Shiqing: Tong Guowuyun Canshi He Zhongyang Wenshi Yanjiuguan Guanyuan Zuotan Shi De Jianhua [Speak the Truth and Look for the True Situation; Speech Given During the Discussion Forum with Counselors of the State Council and Staff of the Central Research Institute of Culture and History]," (2011), http://www.gov.cn/ldhd/2011-04/17/content_184 6206.htm.
8. Jiwei Ci, *Dialectic of the Chinese Revolution: From Utopianism to Hedonism* (Stanford: Stanford University Press, 1994), 14–15.
9. Ibid.
10. Wanning Sun, "Significant Moment on CCTV," 187–204.
11. Wenjian Ni, et al., "'Zhongguo Dianshiju' De 'Zhongguo Qixi' [The 'Chinese Flavour' of 'Chinese Television Drama']," last modified 9 March, 2010, http://finance.ifeng.com/opinion/xzsuibi/20100309/1902074.shtml.
12. Ci, *Dialectic of the Chinese Revolution*, 2.

13. See Ci, *Dialectic of the Chinese Revolution*, 165–167. Haiyan Lee, *The Stranger and the Chinese Moral Imagination* (Stanford: Stanford University Press, 2014).

14. Lee, ibid, 49.

15. Meng, "Female Images and National Myth," 118–136.

16. Lee, *The Stranger*, 44–51.

17. Li, *50 Niandai*, 243–272.

18. Fusheng Liu, "Bixu Baowei Shehui: Huabei Xiaonong De Mingyun Yu Xiangcun Gongtongti De Chongjian [Guarding the Society: The Fate of Northern Chinese Peasants and the Reconstruction of Rural Community]," *iaoshuo Pinglun [Fiction Review]* 201, no. 3 (2018): 65–72.

19. Mingwei Song, *Young China: National Rejuvenation and the Bildungsroman, 1900–1959* (Cambridge: Harvard East Asia Center, 2016), 59.

20. Katerina Clark, *The Soviet Novel: History as Ritual* (Bloomington: Indiana University Press, 2000), 9–10.

21. Ci, *Dialectic of the Chinese Revolution*, 130–133.

22. Ibid, 166–167.

23. Wenjian Ni, "Xinyang Ruhe Chuanda? Xidu 'Qianfu' De Qishi [How to Convey the Idea of Belief? Some Inspirations from the Close Reading of 'Lurk']," in *Dianshiju Yu Dangdai Wenhua [Television Drama and Contemporary Culture]*, ed. Xiaoming Wang (Beijing: SDX Joint Publishing Company, 2014), 135.

24. Yifan Pan, "'Diezhan Beihou: Dianshiju Yu Dangdai Wenhua Luntan Diwuchang [Behind the Espionage War: Television Drama and Contemprary Culture Forum No 5],'" (2012), http://old.cul-studies.com/index.php?m=content&c=index&a=show&catid=39&id=213.

25. John Le Carre, *The Spy Who Came in from the Cold* (London: Penguin Random House, 2010).

26. Qian Gong, "A Trip Down Memory Lane: Remaking and Rereading the Red Classics," in *TV Drama in China*, ed. Ying Zhu, Michael Keane, and Yuoyun Bai (Hong Kong: Hong Kong University Press, 2008), 157–172.

27. See William Hinton, *Fanshen: A Documentary of Revolution in a Chinese Village* (New York: Vintage, 1966).

# CONCLUSION

1. Miao Liu, "'Xi Dada Aizhe Peng Mama' Yuanchuang: Xiwang Yangshi Kuailai Zhao Women [Author of 'Xi Dada Aizhe Peng Mama': Hope Cctv Will Visit Us Soon]," Nov 26, 2014, http://gd.people.com.cn/n/2014/1126/c123932-23016995.html.

2. Stuart Hall, "The Great Moving Right Show," *Marxism Today* 1979, no. 1 January (1979),14.

3. Wang, "Depoliticized Politics," 29–45.

4. Ibid.

5.     Tanya Lewis, Fran Martin, and Wanning Sun, eds. *Telemodernities: Television and Transforming Lives in Asia* (Durham, NC: Duke University Press, 2016), 261.

6.     However, these categories do not represent the only means to organise the study of change in contemporary China, nor are these categories mutually exclusive. Nationalism and ethnicity, for example, could well be used to examine these social transformations.

7.     Xiaoming Chen, "The Carefree 90s: The Void Brought by the End of History (Zizaide 90 Niandai: Lishi Zhongjie Zhihou De Xukong)," in *Trends in Criticism (Piping De Qushi)*, ed. Rui He (Beijing: Beijing Library Press, 2001), 44.

8.     Liu, *Globalization and Cultural Trends in China*, 19.

9.     Barmé, *In the Red*, 99.

10.     Zhong, *Mainstream Culture Refocused*, 162.

11.     Zhao, "Rethinking Chinese Media Studies," 175–195.

12.     Ibid., 176.

13.     Dai, "Dai Jinhua, Kang Honglei, Gan Yang".

14.     Jinhua Dai, "Shuoshuren De Juese: Dianshiju, Anxiang Yu Pingmu [The Role of Bard: Televsion Drama, Camera Obscura and Screen]," in *Dianshiju Yu Dangdai Wenhua [Tv Drama and Contemporary Culture]*, ed. Xiaoming Wang (Beijing: SDX Joint Publishing Company, 2014), 5.

15.     Wei Ni, "Dangdai Diezhanju Zhong De Xinyan Yu Wenhua Zhenghou," 15.

16.     Hui Wang, "Ping Lun [Discussion]," in *Dianshiju Yu Dangdai Wenhua [Tv Drama and Contemporary Culture]*, ed. Xiaoming Wang (Beijing: Beijing: SDX Joint Publishing Company, 2014), 23–24.

17.     Zhao, "Rethinking Chinese Media Studies," 185.

18.     The Washington Consensus generally refers to the orientation towards neo-liberalism from around 1980 to 2008. The policies associated with the Washington Consensus include market liberalisation, deregulation, privatisation, and fiscal austerity. See *Communication in China*, 5.

19.     Geremie R. Barmé, "Red Allure and the Crimson Blindfold," *China Perspectives* 2012, no. 2 (2012): 34–45.

20.     Dirlik, "Mao Zedong in Contemporary Chinese," 17–27.

# Filmography

## ORIGINAL TEXTS OF THE RED CLASSICS

### *Little Soldier Zhang Ga* (*Xiaobing Zhang Ga*) 小兵张嘎

**Synopsis**: The film is set against the background of the Anti-Japanese War (1937–1945). Zhang Ga, an orphaned boy who lives with his grandmother in northern China, witnesses her murder by the Japanese army after she covers for a Communist platoon leader's evacuation. To seek revenge for his grand-mother, Zhang Ga joins the Communist guerrillas. He becomes a brave and resourceful scout.

**Main characters**: Zhang Ga

**Production information**: A novel by Xu Guangyao published in 1958. Adapted into film in 1963 by Beijing Film Studio. Director: Cui Wei, Ouyang Hongying.

### *The Making of a Hero* (*Gangtie shi zenyang liangchengde*) 钢铁是怎样炼成的

Synopsis: Published as an autobiographical novel penned by Nicholas Ostravski, *The Making of a Hero* was an autobiographical account of a legendary young Communist, Pavel Korchagin, from his childhood in a working-class family to his role in the Russian Civil War (1918–1920), and in the subsequent reconstruction of the Soviet Union after the World War I. Despite suffering from rheumatism, typhoid fever, and becoming blind and bedridden later in life, he manages to dictate his life story.

**Main characters**: Pavel Korchagin, Tonya Tumanova

**Production information**: Novel by Nicholas Ostravski published in 1936. *The Making of a Hero*, Film released in 1942 in USSR; *Pavel Korchagin*, film released in 1956 in USSR; *The Making of a Hero*, TV series of six episodes broadcast in 1975 in USSR.

## The Red Crag (Hong yan) 红岩

Synopsis: Sister Jiang is the Communist heroine in *The Red Crag*. Her husband Peng Yongwu is assigned by the CCP to Chongqing to lead the underground struggle against the Nationalists. Peng is captured and killed by the Nationalists after his true identity is revealed. After his death, Sister Jiang takes over as the head of the underground agency. In the course of spying wars, Jiang and a few other Communist agents are arrested by the Nationalist secret police after betrayal by a fellow agent. Tortured in jail, she and the other inmates refuse to give in to the enemy and die as martyrs.

**Main characters**: Jiang Zhujun, Xu Yunfeng, Pu Zhigao

**Production information**: First published as a novel in 1961. A film adaptation with the title *Eternity in Flames* (Liehuo zhong yongsheng) by Beijing Film Studio was released in 1965.

## The Red Lantern (Hongdeng ji) 红灯记

**Synopsis**: The story is set in the 1930s, as the Japanese occupy Northeast China. Communist underground agent Li Yuhe is a railway signaler who uses the red lantern of the title to communicate with fellow Communists. He is given a mission to deliver a set of cipher codes to the Communist guerrilla detachment in the region. However, Li is betrayed by a traitor and is captured by the Japanese. Despite extreme pressure from the Japanese, Li refuses to surrender and dies. Li's adopted daughter Tiemei carries on with his father's mission and safely passes the code to the guerrillas.

Main characters: Li Yuhe, Li Tiemei, Hatoyama

Production information: Originally a film *The Revolution Has Successors* (Geming ziyou houlairen) by the Northeast' Changchun Film Studio. Adapted into an opera by Harbin Peking Opera Troupe. Made into Shanghai Opera (*Huju*) in 1962 by the Aihua Shanghai Opera Company. Transplanted into Yangbanxi around 1966. Filmed in 1968.

## The Red Sun (Hong ri) 红日

Synopsis: Considered one of the core works of the Red Classics, the Red Sun was originally a novel published in 1959, which combines history with fiction. The story focuses on the three major campaigns, Lianshui, Laiwu, and Menglianggu, fought between CCP and the Nationalist armies the 1947 in Shandong Province. The novel gives a breathtaking account of the last campaign in Menglianggu, an isolated, rugged mountain area in Linyi. The Communist army is pitted against the Nationalist's elite army, the 74th division, led by military talent Zhang Lingfu. It became a cliff-hanging win for the CCP and the outcome of campaign predated the eventual downfall of the Nationalist. The novel, while largely maintaining the "class characteristics" of the characters, gives more rounded personas to its major characters. The Nationalist army commander Zhang Lingfu is depicted as relatively capable, astute, and resourceful despite his "evil" class nature.

**Main characters**: Shen Zhenxin, Zhang Lingfu

**Production information**: Novel by Wu Qiang, published by China Youth Publishing House in 1957. Adapted into a popular film in 1963 by Tianma Film Studio, directed by Tang Xiaodan.

## *The Red Detachment of Women (Hongse Niangzijun)* 红色娘子军

Synopsis: The story is about Wu Qionghua, the daughter of a poor peasant who suffers as a slave girl at the hands of Nan Batian, a landlord despot in a village on south China's Hainan Island. She is rescued from a water-filled dungeon where Nan Batian has her incarcerated by Hong Changqing, the Communist Party representative. Wu then joins the revolutionary corps to seek personal revenge and under the influence and education of Hong Changqing, she gradually becomes a conscientious revolutionary fighter.

**Main characters**: Wu Qionghua, Hong Changqing, Nan Batian

**Production information**: Film version released in 1961, director Xie Jin, Tianma Film Studio. Adapted into ballet by Central Opera and Ballet Company in 1964. Adapted into Peking Opera and filmed in 1972, by Chinese People's Liberation Army August First Film studio.

## *Shajiabang (Shajiabang)* 沙家浜

Synopsis: The story unfolds during the Anti-Japanese War (1937–1945) in a prosperous country town of Shajiabang in Jiangsu Province along Yangtze River. Shajiabang is a battleground for competing guerrilla forces, including local bandits, the New Fourth Army led by the Communists, the Nationalists, and the Japanese. New Fourth Army commander Guo Jianguang and seventeen other sick and wounded soldiers are recuperating in the town from their wounds. When the Japanese become aware of the Communist presence, they move to mop up all the New Fourth Army soldiers in the area. Guo and his men are forced to take refuge in the nearby reed marshes. In the meantime,

the Nationalist Party, the supposed ally of Communists, send their spy Diao
Deyi to recruit local armed forces and keep watch on the movements of the
wounded Communist soldiers. Sister A Qing (the leading female role) is the
leader of the underground communist cell, who runs the teahouse as a cover
for a liaison station. With incredible intelligence and steadfastness, Sister A
Qing artfully disintegrates the different factions within the enemy camp. With
the information and help provided by Sister A Qing, Guo and his troupe rout
the enemy in a single battle.

**Main characters**: Communist undercover agent Sister A Qing, New
Fourth Army commander Guo Jianguang, Nationalist spy Diao Deyi, local
bandit leader Hu Chuankui.

**Production information**: First appeared as Shanghai opera (*Huju*) with
the title *Emerald Water and Red Flags* (Bishui hongqi) in 1960. It was
revised and staged as *Sparks amid the Reeds* (Ludang huozhong) in 1963. The
Peking opera version *Shajiabang* was on show in 1965.

## *Struggles in the Old-line City* (*Yehuo chunfeng dou gucheng*) 野火春风斗古城

Synopsis: In 1943, Communist army officer Yang Xiaodong is assigned
by the CCP to lead the anti-Japanese struggle in an ancient city in Hebei
Province in northern China. Central to his mission is to persuade Guan
Jingtao, the commander of the puppet army troops stationed in the city, of
uprising. With the help of Jinhuan and Yinhuan, twin sisters who are CCP's
underground agents, the Communist guerrillas capture Guan in an ambush
but releases him, hoping he will convince his army to defect. Due to the
betrayal of an insider, both Jinhuan and Yang are captured by the Japanese.
Trying to protect Guan, Jinhuan dies. This makes a great impact on Guan's
view of the CCP. After Yang is rescued by the Communist guerrillas, he and
Yihuan successfully win Guan over, and together they work out the plan for
his army to revolt and cross over to their side.

**Main characters**: Yang Xiaodong, Jinhuan, Yinhuan, Guan Jingtao

**Production information**: Novel by Li Yinru, published in 1958. Adapted
to film in 1963, directed by Yan Jizhou, by Chinese People's Liberation
Army August First Film Studio.

## *Tracks in the Snowy Mountains* (*Lin hai xue yuan*) 林海雪原

Synopsis: This is a story about the eradication of defeated Nationalist bandits who had joined professional brigands and landlord tyrants in Northeast
China's Manchuria during 1946. The bandits are trying to locate a large
amount of crude opium left by the Japanese army to finance their offensives

against the Communists. Meanwhile, the Communists and the bandits and the gangs are searching for a map marked with liaison stations of Kuomintang spies. The hero, Yang Zirong, is modeled on the life experiences of a real person who slips into the bandits' stronghold and wins the trust of the enemy leader. Based on the intelligence Yang provides, the Communist army is able to eliminate the bandit den.

Main characters: Yang Zirong, Shao Jianbo, Zuo Shandiao

Production information: First published as a novel by Qu Bo in 1957. Adapted into film in 1960 by Chinese People's Liberation Army August First Film Studio, directed by Liu Peiran. Peking opera version with entitled *Taking the Tiger Mountain by Strategy* was created by Shanghai Peking Opera Troupe in 1958.

# TV DRAMA ADAPTATIONS

## *Little Soldier Zhang Ga (Xiaobing Zhang Ga)* 小兵张嘎

**Production information**: Produced by Nanjing Film Studio. Director: Xu Geng. Premiered on CCTV Channel 8, July 27, 2004. Twenty episodes.

## *The Making of a Hero (Gangtie shi zenyang liangchengde)* 钢铁是怎样炼成的

**Production information**: Coproduced by Shenzhen Municipal Publicity Department, Film and Television Department of CCTV, China International Television Corporation. Director: Han Gang. Premiered on CCTV's Channel 1. Twenty episodes.

## *The Red Detachment of Women (Hongse Niangzijun)* 红色娘子军

**Production information**: Produced by Asian Union Film & Entertainment. Director: Yuan Jun. Premiered on South Film and Television Channel on June 15, 2005. Twenty-one episodes.

## *The Red Sun (Hong ri)* 红日

**Production information**: Produced by Zhejiang Great Wall Film and Television Company. Director: Su Zhou. Premiered on Zhejiang Satellite TV on February 2, 2009. Thirty-five episodes.

## *Shajiabang (Shajiabang)* 沙家浜

**Production information**: Coproduced by Beijing Zhushi United Media Co. Ltd. and Beijing Huancong Film and Television Co. Ltd. Director: Shen Xinghao. Premiered on Qilu Satellite TV, on April 27, 2006. Thirty episodes.

## *Tracks in the Snowy Mountain (Lin hai xue yuan)* 林海雪原

**Production information**: Coproduced by Vanke Film and Television Co. Ltd., Shenzhen Municipal Publicity Department (SMPD) and the Theatrical Company of General Political Department (TCGPD). Director: Li Wenqi. Premiered on Beijing Television's Channel 2 on March 4, 2004. Thirty episodes.

## MAIN TELEVISION DRAMA PRODUCTIONS ANALYZED IN THE THESIS

## *Days of Burning Passion (Jiqing ranshao de suiyue)* 激情燃烧的岁月

Synopsis: The twenty-two-episode TV series is a sustained dramatic representation of the troubled marital life and relationship between a military commander and his wife. Division commander Shi Guangrong falls in love at the first sight with Chu Qin, a dancer from an art troupe, much younger in age. Pressed by various parties including her parents, Chu marries Shi reluctantly. This causes great resentment to Xie Feng, Chu's ex-lover. Xie is subsequently killed in a military action in the Korean War. Chu blames Xie's death on Shi and herself. Chu's guilt torments her. Besides, huge differences exist between Chu and Shi in age, education, family background, upbringing, temperament, and experience. All these plus Shi's patriarchal behavior toward children means the decades of marriage life together is never peaceful. But over the years, the two gradually reconcile on the realization of their love toward each other.

   **Main characters**: Shi Guangrong, Chu Qin

   **Production information**: Based on a novelette by Shi Zhongshan published in 1998. Produced by Xi'an Chang'an Film and Television Production Co Ltd. Director: Kang Honglei. Premiered on Beijing Television's Channel 4 on October 8, 2001. Twenty-two episodes.

## *The Sky of History (Lishi de tiankong)* 历史的天空

**Synopsis**: The story focuses on two military commanders, Big-tooth Jiang and Chen Mohan and spans 1937 to the contemporary period. The epic begins with the two young men killing a few Japanese soldiers to save a young girl from being raped. Having no other choice, the two flee the scene to join the army. Chen, having exposure to revolutionary theory in his schooling, wants to join the Communist New Fourth Route Army, while the lackadaisical-style Jiang wants to join the Nationalist Army so he can enjoy a soldier's pay and provisions. However, by a series of odd coincidences, Jiang runs into the Communists while Chen meets the Nationalist. Attracted by a female Communist soldier Dongfang Wenying and impressed by the charisma of the Communist leader Yang Tinghui, Jiang stays on in the Communist troupe. Chen, on the other hand, is drawn into the whirlpool of power struggles within the Nationalist army branches. The two troops have a brief period of cooperation but remain chief enemies the rest of the time. During the Civil War, Chen gets disgusted at the corruption within the Nationalist armies and decides to revolt and cross over to the Communists. Jiang's love Dongfang dies in a battle in aid of Chen's troop. Jiang believes Chen is responsible for her death and harbors a personal grudge against him. During the Korean War, Jiang is again forced to fight side by side with Chen. The two are persecuted during the Cultural Revolution and are banished to the same farm to work. Their misunderstandings are gradually resolved. After the Cultural Revolution, the two commit themselves to building the modern army.

**Main characters**: Big-tooth Jiang, Chen Mohan

**Production information**: Based on a novel with the same title by Xu Guixiang, published in 2000. Produced by Shanghai Tianshi Cultural & Media Co. Ltd. Director: Gao Xixi. Premiered on Kunming Television August 1, 2004. Thirty-two episodes.

## *Sword Show (Liang jian)* 亮剑

**Synopsis**: The story starts in the Anti-Japanese War in the 1930s when Li Yunlong loses his command because of his misconduct and is working in a quilt-making factory for the Communist army. He is summoned back to take charge of the demoralized Communist regiment after a humiliating defeat by a Japanese force in north China's Shanxi Province. With superb military strategy, Li leads the regiment to victory in a major battle against Japanese. Later, he and the Nationalist commander Chu Yufei capture an important town heavily defended by the Japanese. The two become friends.

In the winter of 1941, Li's guard is killed by bandits incorporated into the Communist-led Eighth Route Army. Li defies orders and kills the bandits responsible in revenge. As a result, he is again relieved of his command of the regiment.

In the subsequent Civil War, Li meets his Nationalist counterpart Chu in the major battle Huaihai Campaign. He is nearly killed in a battle and is taken to hospital to recuperate. He meets a nurse Tian Yu and marries her. After the end of the war, Li becomes bored with the humdrum of everyday life. His request to fight in the Korean War is rejected, and instead, he is ordered to further his study in a military college. Li is bitterly disappointed at first, but soon finds the challenge rewarding.

**Main characters**: Li Yunlong, Chu Yunfei,

**Production information**: First published as a novel by Dou Liang in 2005. Produced by Hairun Film and Television Production Co Ltd. Director: Zhang Qian, Chen Jian. Premiered on CCTV Channel 1 on September 12, 2005. Thirty-six episodes.

## *Yearnings (Kewang)* 渴望

Synopsis: Yearnings is a fifty-episode TV series produced after the June 4 Incident in 1989 when tensions over public culture were high. Set in Beijing from 1960s to 1980s, the melodramatic story revolves around the lives of two families who are brought together by serendipity. Huifang, a kind-hearted girl from a worker's family marries Husheng, a college student whose family is under political persecution. She adopts an abandoned child, Xiaofang, who is later paralyzed by an accident. After the Cultural Revolution, Husheng's intellectual family resumes their privileged status, and Husheng leaves Huifang for his college sweetheart. Huifang is determined to raise the disabled Xiaofang by herself when it is found that Xiaofang was the lost child of Husheng's sister. Medical treatment cures Xiaofang, but Huifang is crippled by a staged traffic accident. Acclaimed by some critics as China's first soap opera, it is often recognized as TV drama's turning of attention from the public to private lives, personal feelings, and experiences.

**Main characters:** Liu Huifang, Wang Husheng, Wang Yaru, Song Dacheng

**Production information:** Produced by Beijing Television Art Centre. Director: Lu Xiaowei. Premiered on CCTV's channel 1 on December 6, 1990. Fifty episodes.

## *Yimeng (Yimeng)* 沂蒙

Synopsis: The forty-two–episode TV drama series *Yimeng* was commissioned by the Linyi Propaganda Department to narrate the locals' contribution to founding of the nation in the Anti-Japanese War (1937–1945) and the Civil War (1946–1949) in a popular dramatic form. The story revolves around vicissitude of one family in a small village called Mamuchi during a period full of chaos. The protagonist is an old woman Yu Baozhen, the head of the family in everything but name. Strong and able, she manages the big house of three sons and daughters, two daughter-in-laws, and a rather weak and a good-for-nothing husband. In 1938, the Japanese army makes incursions into the Yimeng Mountainous Area. In one of the looting expeditions to the village, several Japanese soldiers murder Yu's youngest daughter after raping her. The enraged villagers kill one Japanese soldier in retaliation. In the subsequent series of battles with the Japanese, Yu's eldest son Li Jichang, second son Li Jishan, and daughter Li Yue have all joined the Communist Eighth Route Army. Yu's husband dies in a mission to deliver supplies to the Communist army. Yu's eldest son and his wife are captured by Li Jizhou, the village chief's son, who is now a Nationalist army commander, and handed over to the Japanese. Refusing to surrender, the couple die martyrs. However, despite the personal feud, Yu saves Li Jizhou from death when his army is ambushed by the Japanese. The villagers are united as never before.

Meanwhile, Yu and her two daughter-in-laws, Xintian and Xin'ai, organize a Women's Resistance Association in the village to supply provisions and assist the Communist army. In one of the battles, Xintian finds a Communist soldier in a hideout unconscious and dying of dehydration, she feeds the soldier her own milk to save his life. When the Communist army are retreating from the revolutionary base area, Yu and her two daughter-in-laws provide foster care to a dozen children of Communist army officers. When the Japanese soldiers take villagers at gunpoint, threatening to shoot them if they do not reveal the whereabouts of the Communist children, Xin'ai offers her own adopted son as the Communist cadre's son and sees him taken away by the Japanese.

In the Civil War (1946–1949), Yu and villagers continue to give all they have to the Communist troops, offering their last handful of grain and last piece of cloth to the army and sending their last male to the battlefield. Decades pass. A general comes back to the village to find his savior. Somebody suggests Yu. But after a close look, he finds she is not the one. He looks for several days, but cannot locate the woman who saved him. However, he meets so many locals who supported and sacrificed for the Communist army. Many of the wartime legends in the local area were dramatized and personified by the members of the fictitious family.

**Main characters**: Yu Baozhen, Li Zhonghou, Li Jishan, Li Jichang, Li Yue, Xintian, Xin'ai.

**Production information**: Main producers: Shandong Film and Television Group, Linyi Municipal Department of Publicity. Director: Guan Hu. First exhibited during prime time on CCTV's Channel 8 on November 27, 2009. Forty-two episodes.

# Bibliography

Anagnost, Ann. *National Past-Times: Narrative, Representation, and Power in Modern China*. Durham, NC and London: Duke University Press, 1997.

Ang, Ien. "Living Room Wars: New Technologies, Audience Measurement and the Tactics of Television Consumption." In *Consuming Technologies: Media and Information in Domestic Spaces*, edited by Roger Silverstone and Eric Hirsch, 343–351. London: Routledge, 1992.

Ba, Jin. *Sui Xiang Lu [Random Thoughts]*. Beijing: Writers Publishing House, 2005.

Bai, Ruoyun, and Geng Song. *Chinese Television in the Twenty-First Century: Entertaining the Nation*. London and New York: Routledge, 2015.

Bai, Ruoyun. "Media Commercialization, Entertainment, and the Party-State: The Political Economy of Contemporary Chinese Television Entertianment Culture." *Global Media Journal* 4, no. 6 (April, 2005): 1–54.

Bai, Ruoyun. *Staging Corruption: Television Drama and Politics*. Hong Kong: Hong Kong University Press, 2015.

Barmé, Geremie R. *In the Red: On Contemporary Chinese Culture*. New York: Columbia University Press, 1999.

———. "Red Allure and the Crimson Blindfold." *China Perspectives* 2 (2012): 29–40.

Bichler, Lorenz. "Coming to Terms with a Term: Notes on the History of the Use of Socialist Realism in China." In *In the Party Spirit: Socialist Realism and Literary Practice in the Soviet Union, East Germany and China*, edited by Hilary Chung, Karin Mcpherson, Michael Falchikov and Bonnie S. McDougall, 23–29. Amsterdam: Rodopi, 1996.

Brady, Ann-Marie. *Marketing Dictatorship*. Lanham: Rowman & Littlefield Publishers, Inc., 2008.

Breslin, Shaun. "Serving the Market or Serving the Party: Neo-Liberalism in China." In *The Neo-Liberal Revolution*, edited by Richard Robison, 114–131. London: Palgrave Macmillan, 2006.

Cai, Nan. "You Jian Qionghua: Dianying 'Hongse Niangzijun' Beihou De Gushi [Qionghua Met Again: Stories Behind the Scene of Film 'the Red Detachment of Women']." *China Television News*, June 12 2006, 42.

Cai, Rong. "Make the Present Serve the Past: Restaging on Guard beneath the Neon Lights in Contemporary China." In *Chinese Television in the Twenty-First Century: Entertaining the Nation*, edited by Yuoyun Bai and Geng Song, 149–157. London: Routledge, 2015.

Cai, Shenshen. *State Propaganda in China's Entertainment Industry*. New York: Routledge, 2016.

Cai, Xiang. *Revolution and Its Narratives: China's Socialist Literary and Cultural Imaginations*, Trans. Rebecca Karl and Xueping Zhong. Durham, NC and London: Duke University Press, 2016.

Chang, Ying. "'Wode Changzheng' Daxing Dianshi Huodong Chuangzuo Beijing ['My Long March' Publicity Behind the Scenes]." *CCTV*, http://www.cctv.com/news/other/20060418/101844.shtml.

Chen, Cun. "Kan Dianying (Watching Films)." In *Everyday China: Dailylife of the Common People in the 1970s*, edited by Liang Wu, Yun Gao and Huaming Gu Jiangsu, 83–86. Jiangsu: Jiangsu Fine Arts Press, 1999.

Chen, Hanci. "Xiaoshuo 'Shajiabang' Zuozhe Xue Rong Shouci Dapo Chenmo Jie Xinbao Tan Chuanzuo [Novelette 'Shajiabang' Author Xue Rong Breaks Silence for the First Time, Talk About His Writing through News Bulletin]." Last modified February 24, 2003. http://www.booktide.com/news/20030224/200302240001.html.

Chen, Sihe. "Wo Bu Zancheng 'Hongse Jingdian' Zhege Tifa [I Do Not Agree with the Naming of 'Red Classics']." *Nanfang Zhoumo*, May 6, 2004.

———. *Zhongguo Dangdai Wenxue Guanjianci Shijiang [Ten Lectures on Key Words in Contemporary Chinese Literature]*. Shanghai: Fudan University Press, 2002.

Chen, Xiaoming. "The Carefree 90s: The Void Brought by the End of History [Zizaide 90 Niandai: Lishi Zhongjie Zhihou De Xukong]." In *Trends in Criticism [Piping De Qushi]*, edited by Rui He. Beijing: Beijing Library Press, 2001.

Chen, Yiming. "Cui Yongyuan: Zai Hongse Jingdian Qian [Cui Yongyuan: Facing Hongse Jingdian]." (2004). http://www.people.com.cn/GB/wenhua/22219/2481780.html.

Cheng, Guangwei. "Ershi Shiji Liushi Niandai De Dianying Yu Wenhua Shishang [Film and Cultural Fad in 1960s]." *Journal of Xinyang Teachers' College*, 22, no. 1 (2002): 96–101.

———. *Wenxue Xiangxiang Yu Wenxue Guojia: Zhongguo Dangdai Wenxue Yanjiu [Literary Imaginary and Literary State: A Study of Chinese Contemporary Literature (1949-1976)]*. Kaifeng: Henan University Press, 2005.

Chu, Yingchi, Stephanie Hemelryk Donald, and Andrea Witcomb. "Children, Media and the Public Sphere in Chinese Australia." In *Political Communications in Greater China*, edited by Gary D. Rawnsley and Ming-Yeh T. Rawnsley, 260–274. London: Routledge-Curzon, 2003.

Ci, Jiwei. *Dialectic of the Chinese Revolution: From Utopianism to Hedonism*. Stanford: Stanford University Press, 1994.

Clark, Katerina. *The Soviet Novel: History as Ritual*. Bloomington: Indiana University Press, 2000.

Clark, Paul. *The Chinese Cultural Revolution: A History*. Cambridge: Cambridge University Press, 2008.

Corner, John. "Television and Culture: Duties and Pleasures". In *British Cultural Studies: Geography, Nationality and Identity*, edited by David Morley and Kevin Robins, 261–272. Oxford: Oxford University Press, 2001.

Dai, Jiafang. *Yangbanxi De Fengfeng Yuyu [the Vicissitudes of Yangbanxi]*. Beijing: Knowledge Publishing House, 1995.

Dai, Jinghua. "Invisible Women: Contemporary Chinese Cinema and Women's Film." *Position*s 3, no. 1 (1995): 255–280.

———. "Dai Jinhua, Kang Honglei, Gan Yang, Wang Xiaoming Tan Zhongguo Dianshiju [Dai Jinhua, Kang Honglei, Gan Yang, Wang Xiaoming on Chinese Television Drama]." *Chinese Readers Gazette*, Sept 12 2012.

———. "Dai Jinhua, Kang Honglei, Gan Yang, Wang Xiaoming Tan Zhongguo Dianshiju." *Chinese Readers Gazette*, Sept 12 (2012): 13.

———. "Jiushu Yu Xiaofei [Redemption and Consumption]." In *Meijie Zhexue [Media Philosophy]*, edited by Yuechuan Wang, 68–80, Henan: Henan University Press, 2004.

———. "Shuoshuren De Juese: Dianshiju, Anxiang Yu Pingmu [the Role of Bard: Televsion Drama, Camera Obscura and Screen]." In *Dianshiju Yu Dangdai Wenhua [TV Drama and Contemporary Culture]*, edited by Xiaoming Wang, 3–6. Beijing: SDX Joint Publishing Company, 2014.

Ding, Fengyun, Hong Huang, Jingzhi Zhang, Xixi Zheng, and Guanghong Cui, eds. *Yimeng Spirit [Yimeng Jingshen]*. Beijing: People's Press, 2008.

Dirlik, Arif, and Xudong Zhang. "Introduction: Postmodernism and China." In *Postmodernism & China*, edited by Arif Dirlik and Xudong Zhang, 1–21. Durham, NC and London: Duke University Press, 2000.

Dirlik, Arif. "Mao Zedong in Contemporary Chinese Official Discourse and History." *China Perspectives* 2012, no. 2 (2012): 17–27.

———. "Looking Backward in the Age of Global Capital: Thoughts on History in Third World Cultural Criticism." In *In Pursuit of Contemporary East Asian Culture*, edited by Xiaobing Tang and Stephen Snyder, 183–215. Boulder: WestviewPress, 1996.

———. *Marxism in the Chinese Revolution*. Lanham: Rowman and Littlefield, 2005.

Donald, Stephanie Hemelryk. *Public Secrets: Public Spaces: Cinema and Civility in China*. Lanham: Rowman and Littlefield, 2000.

Donald, Stephanie Hemelryk, and John.G. Gammack. *Tourism and the Branded City*. Hampshire, UK: Ashgate, 2007.

Dong, Jinping. "Huayu Yu Nuxingqizhi De Jiangou: Ershi Shiji Yilai Zhongguo Nuxingqizhi Bianqian De Fenxi [Discourse and the Construction of Femininity: An Analysis of the Transformation of Femininity in the 20th Century]." *Jianghua Luntan* 7, no. 2 (2007): 146–151.

du Gay, Paul., Stuart Hall, Linda Janes, Hugh Mackay, and Keith Negus, eds. *Doing Cultural Studies: the Story of the Sony Walkman*. London: Sage Publications, 1997.

Du, Ying. "Yizhong Xin Wenyi Dianfan De Jiangou: Dui 1949 Nian Qianhou Wenyi Zuopin De Kaocha [the Construction of a New Model for Literature and the Arts: A Study of Literary and Art Works around the Year 1949]." *Wenyi Pinping [Literary Criticism]* 2010, no. 2 (2010): 83–89.

ent.sina.com.cn. "Shajiabang Shoubo Yishi: Duihua Daoyan Shen Xinghao [Shajiabang Debut Ceremony: A Dialogue with Shen Xinghao]." www.ent.sina .com, 2006.

———. "Xu Qing, Liu Jinshan, Cheng Qian Xinlang Liao 'Shajiabang' Zhan Caiyi [Xu Qing, Liu Jinshan and Cheng Qian Talk About Shajiabang with Sina]." Sina .com.cn, 2006.

Evans, Harriet, and Stephanie Donald. *Picturing Power in the People's Republic of China: Posters of the Cultural Revolution*. Lanham: Rowman and Littlefield, 1999.

———. *The Subject of Gender: Daughter and Mothers in Urban China*. Lanham: Rowman & Littlefield, 2008.

———. *Women and Sexuality in China: Dominant Discourses of Female Sexuality and Gender since 1949*. Cambridge and Oxford: Polity Press, 1997.

Fang, Weibao. *Hongse Yiyi De Shengcheng: Ershi Shiji Zhongguo Zuoyi Wenxue Yanjiu [The Formation of the Meaning Red: A Study of the Twentieth Century Leftist Literature]*. Hefei: Anhui Education Press, 2004.

Feng, Chongyi. "Jiangxi in Reform: The Fear of Exclusion and the Search for a New Identity." In *The Political Economy of China's Provinces: Comparative and Competitive Advantage*, edited by Hans Hendrischke and Chongyi Feng, 249–276. London: Routledge, 1999.

Finnane, Antonia., and Anne McLaren. "Introduction." In *Dress, Sex and Text in Chinese Culture*, edited by Antonia Finnane and Anne McLaren, 1–21. Clayton: Monash Asia Institute, 1999.

Fukuyama, Francis. *The End of History and the Last Man*. New York: The Free Press, 1992.

Gledhill, Christine. *Home Is Where the Heart Is: Studies in Melodrama and the Woman's Film*. London: British Film Institute, 1987.

Gong, Qian. "A Trip Down Memory Lane: Remaking and Rereading the Red Classics." In *TV Drama in China*, edited by Ying Zhu, Michael Keane and Yuoyun Bai, 157–172. Hong Kong: Hong Kong University Press, 2008.

Gong, Qian. "The Red Sister-in-Law Remakes: Redefining the 'Fish-and-Water' Relationships for the Era of Reform and Opening." In *The Making and Remaking of China's "Red Classics"*, edited by Rosemary Roberts and Li Li, 156–176. Hong Kong: Hong Kong University Press, 2017.

Gong, Weiliang. "Suipian, Paohui, Wenhua Zhengzhi Yu 'Shehuizhuyi': Dui 'Dibajie Zhongguo Wenhua Luntan: Dianshiju Yu Dandai Wenhua' De Shuping [Fragments, Cannon Fodder, Cultural Politics and 'Socialism': A Review on 'the Eighth Chinese Culture Forum: TV Drama and Contemporary Culture']." *Renwen yu Shehui [Humanity and Society]*. Last modified December 2006, http://wen.org. cn/modules/article/view.article.php/3581/c20.

Goodman, David S. G. "Shanxi as Translocal Imaginary: Reforming the Local." In *Translocal China: Linkages, Identities, and the Reimagining of Space*, edited by Tim Oakes and Louisa Schein, 56–73. London: Routledge, 2006.

Green, Frederik. H. "The Cultural Indigenization of a Soviet 'Red Classic' Hero: Pavel Korchagin's Journey through Time and Space." In *The Making and*

*Remaking of China's "Red Classics"*, edited by Rosemary Roberts and Li Li, 136–155. Hong Kong: Hong Kong University Press, 2017.

Guan, Lan. "Zheng Kainan: Fanxing Cai Shi Chenggong Zhimu [Zheng Kainan: Reflection Is the Mother of Sucess]." *Finance* (2005). Last modified November 18, 2005. http://finance.sina.com.cn/money/lcexpr/20051118/17272131068.shtml.

Guo, Yingjie. "Class, Stratum and Group." In *The New Rich in China: Future Rulers, Present Lives*, edited by S. David Goodman, 38–52. London: Routledge, 2008.

Hall, Stuart. "The Great Moving Right Show." *Marxism Today* 1979, no. Jan (1979): 14–20.

Hao, Tiechuan. "Xiaoshuo 'Shajiabang' Bu Heli, Bu Hefa [Novelette Shajiabang Unreasonable and Illegitimate]." *Wenhui Gazette*, Apirl 25 2003, 5.

Harvey, David. *A Brief History of Neoliberalism*. Oxford: Oxford University Press, 2007.

He, Guimei. *Renwenxue De Xiangxiangli: Dandai Zhongguo Sixiang Yu Wenxue Wenti [The Imagination of Humanities: Issues on Contemporary Chinese Thoughts, Culture, and Literature]*. Kaifeng: Henan University Press, 2005.

He, Yanfeng. "Jiexi Hongse Jingdian [Analysing the Red Classics]." *Chinese Television*, no. 3 (2005): 27–29.

Hershatter, Gail. "The Subaltern Talks Back: Reflections on Subaltern Theory and Chinese History." *Positions* 1 no. 1 (1993): 103–130.

Hinton, William. *Fanshen: A Documentary of Revolution in a Chinese Village*. New York: Vintage, 1966.

Hoffman, Lisa. "Urban Transformation and Professionalization: Translocality and Rationalities of Enterprise in Post-Mao China." In *Translocal China: Linkages, Identities, and the Reimagining of Space*, edited by Tim Oakes and Louisa Schein, 109–137. London: Routledge, 2006.

Hong, Junhao, Yanmei Lü, and William Zou. "CCTV in the Reform Years: A New Model for China's Television?" In *TV China*, edited by Ying Zhu and Chris Berry, 40–50. Bloomington and Indianapolis: Indiana University Press, 2009.

Hong, Junhao. *The Internationalization of Television in China: The Evolution of Ideology, Society, and Media since the Reform*. Westport: Praeger, 1998.

Hongjingsuhongbudong'ai. "Hen Pi 'Linhai Xueyuan': Wu Qing Bu Cheng Xi, Bu Su Bu Suan Wan [Lashing Tracks in the Snowy Mountain: Without Love There Would Be No Drama; Unsatisfied Till It Is Vulgar]." Last modified March 10, 2004, http://ent.sina.com.cn/v/2004-03-10/0716326362.html.

Hou, Hong, and Bin Zhang. "Hongse Jingdian: Jieshuo, Gaibian Ji Chuanbo [Red Classics: Definition, Adaptation and Propagation]." *Contemporary Cinema* 2004, no. 6 (2004): 79–82.

Hu, Jianli. "'Gangtie' Chengwei Zhuxuanlü Jingpin ['the Making of a Hero' Becomes 'Main Melody' Top Pick]," March 6, 2000. http://ent.sina.com.cn/film/old/5436.html.

Hu, Ying. "Writing Erratic Desire: Sexual Poltics in Contemporary Chinese Fiction." In *In Pursuit of Contemporary East Asian Culture*, edited by Xiaobing Tang and Stephen Synder Boulder, 49–68. Boulder: Westview Press, 1996.

Huang, Ya.-Chien. "Pink Dramas: Reconciling Consumer Modernity and Confucian Womanhood." In *TV Drama in China*, edited by Ying Zhu, Michael Keane and Ruoyun Bai, 103–114. Hong Kong: Hong Kong University Press, 2008.

Huang, Yu. "Peaceful Evolution: The Case of Television Reform in Post-Mao China." *Media, Culture & Society* 16, no. 2 (1994): 217–241.

Huot, Claire. *China's New Cultural Scene: A Handbook of Changes*. Durham, NC: Duke University Press, 2000.

Hutcheon, Linda. *A Theory of Adaptation*. 2nd ed. London and New York: Routledge, 2013.

Ip, Hung-Yok. "Fashioning Appearances: Feminine Beauty in Chinese Communist Revolutionary Culture." *Modern China* 29, no. 3 (2003): 329–361.

Ji, Hongzhen. "Wang Zengqi Yu Yangbanxi [Wang Zengqi and Yangbanxi]." *Shu Wu [Book House]*, 2007, 76–82.

Jiang, Zhi. "Lei Feng Ye Ceng Shi Shimao Qingnian, Chulian Nüyou Zhaopian Shouci Gongkai [Lei Feng Was Once a Trendy Youth, Photo of First Love Made Public]." *Southern Metropolis Daily* (2006). Published electronically March 1, 2006. http://www.southcn.com/news/community/shgc/200603010360.htm.

Jin, Liwei. "Linhai Xueyuan Ge Nianling Ceng Shoushi Diaocha, Hongse Jingdian Xinbian Nan [A Survey on Viewing of Tracks in the Snowy Mountain Based on Age Groups: Adapting Red Classics Is a Hard Job]." Last modified March 11, 2004. http://news.sina.com.cn/o/2004-03-11/17172025115s.shtml.

Johnson, Richard. "What Is Cultural Studies Anyway?" *Social Text* no. 16 (Winter 1986–1987): 38–80.

Jones, Andrew. *Like a Knife: Ideology and Genre in Contemporary Chinese Popular Music* Ithaca: Cornell University East Asia Program, 1992.

Keane, Michael, and Spurgeon Christina. "Advertising Industry and Culture in Post-WTO China." *Media International Australia* 111, no. May (2004): 104–117.

———. "Send in the Clones: Television Formats and Content Creation in the People's Republic of China." In *Media in China: Consumption, Content, and Crisis*, edited by Stephie Donald, Michael Keane and Hong Yin, 80–90. London: RoutledgeCurzon, 2002.

———. "Television Drama in China: Remaking the Market." *Media International Australia Culture and Policy*, 115, no. 1 (2005): 82–93.

———.*The Chinese Television Industry*. UK: Palgrave Macmillan, 2015.

King, Richard. *Milestones on a Golden Road: Writing for Chinese Socialism 1945-80*. Vancouver: University of British Columbia Press, 2013.

Kwok, Vivian Wai-in. "Hot Bidding for China TV Ads." *Forbes.com*. Last modified November 20, 2006, https://www.forbes.com/2006/11/20/cctv-advertising-television-markets-emerge-cx_vk_1120markets20.html#1b83c7464877.

Le Carre, John. *The Spy Who Came in from the Cold*. London: Penguin Random House, 2010.

Lee, Chin-Chuan., Zhou He, and Yu Huang. "'The Chinese Party Publicity Inc.' Conglomerated: The Case of the Shenzhen Press Group." In *Political Regimes and Media in Asia*, edited. by Krishna Sen and Terence Lee, 11–30. New York: Routledge, 2008.

Lee, Ching Kwan, and Guobin Yang. *Re-Envisioning the Chinese Revolution: The Politics and Poetics of Collective Memories in Reform China.* Washington, DC and Stanford: Woodrow Wilson Center Press, Stanford University Press, 2007.

Lee, Haiyan. *The Stranger and the Chinese Moral Imagination.* Stanford: Stanford University Press, 2014.

Lewis, Tanya, Fran Martin, and Wanning Sun. *Telemodernities: Television and Transforming Lives in Asia.* Durham, NC: Duke University Press, 2016.

Li, Xianglin. "Yangbanxi: Quanli Huayu He Xingbie Yishi De Jiaozhi [Model Revolutionary Works: Interaction between Power and Gender Discourses]." *Aesthetic Studies* Webpage. Last modified http://www.aesthetics.com.cn/s45c11 43.aspx.

Li, Xianting. "Apathy and Deconstruction in Post-'89 Art: Analyzing the Trends of 'Cynical Realism' and 'Political Pop'". In *Contemporary Chinese Art: Primary Documents*, edited by Hong Wu and Peggy Wang, 157–165. New York: Museum of Modern Art, 1992/2010.

Li, Xuemeng. "TV Series 'Yimeng' Features Vivid Portrayal of Locals (Daxing Dianshi Ju 'Yimeng' Huzhiyuchu)." *Jinan Daily*, May 6, 2008, 1.

Li, Yan. "Xinban 'Hongse Jiangzijun' Gen Hongse Bu Tiebian [the New Version of 'the Red Detachment of Woman' Has Nothing to Do with 'Red']." *Beijing Youth Daily*, July 3 2006, B6.

Li, Yang. *50 Niandai - 70 Niandai Zhongguo Wenxue Jingdian Zai Jiedu [Rereading: Chinese Literary Classics from 50s to 70s].* Shandong: Shandong Education Publishing House, 2003.

———. "Gongye Ticai, Gongye Zhuyi Yu 'Shehuizhuyi Xiandaixing' [Industrial Subject, Industrialism, and 'Socialist Modernity': Rereading 'Braving the Winds and Waves']." *Wenxue Pinglun [Literary Critics]* 2010, no. 6 (2010): 46–53.

Li, Yuchun. *Quanli, Zhuti, Huayu: 20 Shiji 40-70 Niandai Zhongguo Wenxue Yanjiu [Power, Subjectivity, Discourse: A Study of Chinese Literature from the 1940s to the 1970s].* Wuhan: Central China Normal University Press, 2007.

Lin, Chun. *The Transformation of Chinese Socialism.* Durham, NC and London: Duke University Press, 2006.

Link, Perry. *The Uses of Literature.* Princeton: Princeton University Press, 2000.

Link, Perry., Richard.P. Madsen, and Paul.G. Pickowicz, eds. *Popular China: Unofficial Culture in a Globalising Socieity.* Lanham: Rowman & Littlefield, 2002.

Liu, Bo. "Qubo Airen: Yang Zirong Youqianghuadiao, Linhaixueyuan Gaibian Qiantuo [Yang Zirong with a Glib Tougue, the Reinvention of Tracks in the Snowy Mountain Is Improper]". Last modifed March 26, 2004. http://ent.sina.com.cn/v/ 2004-03-26/0902343957.html.

Liu, Fusheng. "Bixu Baowei Shehui: Huabei Xiaonong De Mingyun Yu Xiangcun Gongtongti De Chongjian [Guarding the Society: The Fate of Northern Chinese Peasants and the Reconstruction of Rural Community]." *Xiaoshuo Pinglun* [Fiction Review] 201, no. 3 (2018): 55–64.

Liu, Haibo. "Zhengzhi Yu Ziben De Boyi [the Battling between Politics and Capital]." In *Zhongmei Dianshiju Bijiao Yanjiu [Comparative Research on Television Drama between China and America]*, edited by Chunjing Qu and Ying Zhu, 454–470. Shanghai: Shanghai SDX Joint Publishing Co., 2005.

Liu, Kang. *Globalization and Cultural Trends in China*. Honolulu: University of Hawai'i Press, 2004.

———. "Reinventing 'Red Classics' in the Age of Globalization." *Comparative Literature in China* 26, no. 1 (2003): 13–30.

Liu, Lydia H. "Writing and Feminism Invention and Intervention: The Female Tradition in Modern Chinese Literature." In *Gender Politicis in Modern China: Writing and Feminism*, edited by Tani E. Barlow, 33–57. Durham, NC and London: Duke University Press, 1993.

Liu, Miao. "'Xi Dada Aizhe Peng Mama' Yuanchuang: Xiwang Yangshi Kuailai Zhao Women [Author of 'Xi Dada Aizhe Peng Mama': Hope CCTV Will Visit Us Soon]." Last modified November 26, 2014. http://gd.people.com.cn/n/2014/1126/c123932-23016995.html.

Liu, Shuo. "Shiting Huayu Chanshi Yu Jingshen Chuancheng [Studies and Thoughts on Adaptation of the Red Classics]." *Dangdai Dianying [Contemporary Cinema]* 136, no. January (2007): 69–74.

Liu, Yu. "Maoist Discourse and the Mobilisation of Emotions in Revolutionary China." *Modern China* 36, no. 3 (2010): 329–362.

Lu, Di. *Zhongguo Dianshi Chanye De Weiji Yu Jiyu [The Crisis and Opportunities for Chinese Television Industry]*. Beijing: China People's University Press, 2002.

Lu, Sheldon Hsiao-peng. "Global Postmodernization: The Intellextual, the Artist, and China's Condition." In *Postmodernism & China*, edited by Arif Dirlik and Xudong Zhang, 145–174. Durham, NC and London: Duke University Press, 2000.

Lu, Sheldon. "Soap Opera in China: The Transnational Politics of Visuality, Sexuality, and the Masculinity." *Cinema Journal* Fall 2000, no. 1 (2000): 25–47.

Lull, James. *China Turned On: Television, Reform and Resistance*. London and New York: Routledge, 2013.

Ma, Xichao. "Cong 'Shajiabang' Dao 'Shajiabang': Banben Yange Zhong Geming Huayu Tixi De Bianzou [from 'Shajiabang' to 'Shajiabang': The Transformation of Revolutionary Discursive System in the Edition Evolutions]." *Journal of Xi'an University of Electronic Technology (Social Sciences)* 2006, no. 5 (2006): 98–102.

Mao, Zedong. "Hunan Nongmin Yundong Kaocha Baogao [Report on an Investigation of the Peasant Movement in Hunan]." In *Mao Zedong Xuanji Diyi Juan [Selected Works of Mao Tse-Tung, Vol. I]*, 23–29. Beijing: Foreign Languages Press, 1975.

Massey, Doreen. *Space, Place and Gender*. Cambridge, UK: Polity Press, 1994.

McDougall, Bonnie S., and Kam Louie. *The Literature of China in the Twentieth Century*. New York: Columbia University Press, 1997.

Mcgrath, Jason. *Postsocialist Modernity: Chinese Cinema, Literature, and Criticism in the Market Age*. Stanford: Stanford University Press, 2008.

Meng, Binchun. "Regulating Egao: Futile Efforts of Recentralization." In *China's Information and Communications Technology Revolution: Social Changes and State Responses*, edited by Xiaoling Zhang and Yongnian Zheng, 52–67. New York: Routledge, 2009.

Meng, Yue. "Bai Mao Nu Yanbian De Qishi." In *Zai Jiedu: Dazhong Wenyi Yu Yishi Xingtai [Rereading: The People's Literature and Art Movement and Its Ideology]*, edited by Xiaobing Tang, 68–89. Hong Kong: Oxford University Press, 1993.

———. "Female Images and National Myth." In *Gender Politics in Modern China*, edited by Tani E. Barlow, 118–136. Durham, NC and London: Duke University Press, 1993.

Mouffe, Chantal. "Hegemony and New Political Subjects: Toward a New Concept of Democracy." In *Marxism and the Interpretation of Culture*, edited by Cary Nelson and Lawrence Grossberg, 89–101. Urbana: University of Illinois Press, 1988.

Mueggler, Erik. "Spectral Chains: Remembering the Great Leap Forward Famine." In *Re-Envisioning the Chinese Revolution: The Politics and Poetics of Collective Memories in Reform China*, edited by Ching Kwan Lee and Guobin Yang, 50–68. Stanford: Stanford University Press, 2007.

Ni, Wei. "Dangdai Diezhanju Zhong De Xinyan Yu Wenhua Zhenghou [the Idea of Belief and Cultural Symptoms in Spy TV Series]." In *Dianshiju Yu Dangdai Wenhua [TV Drama and Contemporary Culture]*, edited by Xiaoming Wang. Beijing: SDX Joint Publishing Company, 2014.

Ni, Wenjian, Gang Luo, Jian Mao, Lianhong Zhang, and Xiaoming Wang. "'Zhongguo Dianshiju' De 'Zhongguo Qixi' [The 'Chinese Flavour' of 'Chinese Television Drama']." Last modified March 9, 2010. http://finance.ifeng.com/opini on/xzsuibi/20100309/1902074.shtml.

Ni, Wenjian. "Xinyang Ruhe Chuanda? Xidu 'Qianfu' De Qishi [How to Convey the Idea of Belief? Some Inspirations from the Close Reading of 'Lurk']." In *Dianshiju Yu Dangdai Wenhua [Television Drama and Contemporary Culture]*, edited by Xiaoming Wang, 133–135. Beijing: SDX Joint Publishing Company, 2014.

Ong, Aihwa. *Neoliberalism as Exception: Mutations in Citizenship and Sovereignty*. Durham, NC: Duke University Press, 2006.

Pan, Xin. "Xinban Shajiabang Chengwei Zhushuiju [Shajiabang Watered Down in Its New Version]." *Dahe Bao*, September 12 2006, A24.

Pan, Yifan. "Diezhan Beihou: Dianshiju Yu Dangdai Wenhua Luntan Diwuchang [Behind the Espionage War: Television Drama and Contemporary Culture Forum No 5]." (2012). Published electronically July 17, 2012. http://old.cul-studies.com/index.php?m=content&c=index&a=show&catid=39&id=213.

Pang, Qin Pampkin. "The 'Two Lines Control Model' in China's State and Society Relations: Central States' Management of Confucian Revival in the New Century." *International Journal of China Studies* 5, no. 3 (2014): 627–655.

Peng, Zhiqiang. "Shajiabang Zuowan Zai Chuantai Kaibo [Series Shajiabang Started Running on Sichuan Television Yesterday Evening]." *Chengdu Commercial News*, July 8 2006, P15.

Ren, Weidong. "Shenzhen, Bao'er, Wukelan: You Yige Chuntian De Gushi [Shenzhen, Pavel, Ukraine: Another Story of Spring]." *People's Daily*, May 29 2000.

Roberts, Rosemary, and Li Li, eds. *The Making and Remaking of China's "Red Classics": Politics, Aesthetics, and Mass Culture.* Hong Kong: Hong Kong University Press, 2017.

Roberts, Rosemary. "Positive Women Characters in the Revolutionary Model Works." *Asian Studies Review* 28, no. 4 (2004): 407–423.

———. "Women's Studies in Literature and Feminist Literary Criticism in Contemporary China." In *Dress, Sex and Text in China Culture*, edited by Antonia Finnane and Anne McLaren, 225–240. Melbourne: Monash Asia Institute, 1999.

Rofel, Lisa, B. *Desiring China: Experiments in Neoliberalism, Sexuality, and Public Culture.* Durham, NC: Duke University Press, 2007.

Selden, Mark., and Elizabeth Perry, J., eds. *Chinese Society: Change, Conflict and Resistance (Asia's Transformations)* 3rd ed. London: Routledge, 2010.

Shen, Yifei. *Bei Jiangou De Nuxing: Dangdai Shehui Xingbie Lilun [the Woman That Is Constructed: Contemporary Gender Theory].* Shanghai: Shanghai People's Press, 2005.

Silverstone, Roger. *Television and Everyday Life.* London: Routledge, 1994.

Solinger, Dorothy. "Labour Market Reform and the Plight of the Laid-Off Proletariat." The *China Quarterly* 170 (2002): 304–326.

Song, Mingwei. *Young China: National Rejuvenation and the Bildungsroman, 1900–1959.* Cambridge, MA: Harvard East Asia Center, 2016.

Song, Xiaopeng. "'Linhai Xueyuan': Yingxiong Tufei Dou Bianxing, Guanzhong Kan Le Bu Daying [Tracks in the Snowy Mountain: Deformed Hero and Villian, a No-No for Audience"], *Daily New Mail*, March 31, 2004.

Spivak, Gayatri Chakravorty. "Can the Subaltern Speak?" In *Marxism and the Interpretation of Culture*, edited by Cary Nelson and Lawrence Grossberg, 271–313. Basingstoke: Macmillan Education, 1988.

State Administration of Radio, Film and Television. "Guanyu 'Hongse Jingdian' Gaibian Dianshiju Shencha Guanli De Tongzhi [Notice on the Censorship and Management of Television Drama Adaptation of the 'Red Classics']." Edited by Film and Television State Administration of Radio, 2004.

State Administration of Radio, Film and Television. "Quanguo Guangbo Dianshi Fugai Qingkuang [Data on Broadcasting and Television Population Coverage 2008]." Beijing: State Administration of Radio, Film and Television, 2008.

Su, Wei. "The School and the Hospital: On the Logics of Socialist Realism." In *Chinese Literature in the Second Half of a Modern Century: A Critical Survey*, edited by Pang-yuan Chi and David Der-wei Wang, 65–95. Bloomington: Indiana Unviersity Press, 2000.

Sun, Wanning, and Yuezhi Zhao. "Television with Chinese Characteristics: The Politics of Compassion and Education." In *Television in the Post-Broadcasting Era*, edited by Graeme Turner and Jinna Tay. London: Routledge, 2009.

Sun, Wanning. "Significant Moment on CCTV." *International Journal of Cultural Studies* 10, no. 2 (2007): 187–204.

———. "The Curse of the Everyday: Politics of Representation and New Social Semiotics in Post-Socialist China." In *Political Regimes and the Media in Asia*, edited by Krishna Sen and Terence Lee, 31–48. New York: Routledge, 2008.

Tang, Xiaobing. *Chinese Modern: The Heroic and the Quotidian*. Durham, NC: Duke University Press, 2000.

———, ed. *Zai Jiedu: Dazhong Wenyi Yu Yishixingtai [Rereading: The People's Literature and Art Movement and Its Ideology]*. Beijing: Peking University Press, 2007.

Tao, Dongfeng. "Hou Geming Shidai De Geming Wenhua [Revolutionary Culture in a Post-Revolutionary Age]." In *Dangdai Zhongguo Wenyi Sichao Yu Wenhua Redian [Contemporary Trends in Literature and the Arts and Key Cultural Issues]*, edited by Dongfeng Tao, 196–211. Beijing: Beijing University Press, 2008.

Thornham, Sue, and Tony Purvis. *Television Drama: Theories and Identities*. New York: Palgrave MacMillan, 2005.

Voci, Paola. "Quasi-Documentary, Cellflix and Web Spoofs: Chinese Movies' Other Visual Pleasures." *Senses of Cinema* October-December, no. 41 (2006), http://sensesofcinema.com/2006/film-history-conference-papers/other-chinese-movies-pleasures/.

Wallis, Cara. "Chinese Women in the Official Chinese Press: Discursive Construction of Gender in Service to the State." *Westminster Papers in Communication and Culture* 3, no. 1 (2006): 94–108.

Wang, Ban. *The Sublime Figure of History: Aesthetics and Politics in Twentieth-Century China*. Stanford: Stanford University Press, 1997.

———. *Illustrations from the Past: Trauma, Memory, and History in Modern China*. Stanford: Stanford University Press, 2004.

Wang, Ban, and Xueping Zhong. "Why Does Socialist Culture Matter Today," In *Debating the Socialist Legacy and Capitalist Globalization in China*, edited by Xueping Zhong and Ban Wang, 1–18. New York: Palgrave Macmillan, 2014.

Wang, Hui. "Depoliticized Politics, from East to West." *New Left Review* 41, September-October (2006): 49–45.

———. "Ping Lun [Discussion]." In *Dianshiju Yu Dangdai Wenhua [TV Drama and Contemporary Culture]*, edited by Xiaoming Wang, 22–25. Beijing: Beijing: SDX Joint Publishing Company, 2014.

———. *China's New Order: Society, Politics, and Economy in Transition*. Cambridge, MA: Harvard University Press, 2003.

Wang, Jing. "The State Question in Chinese Popular Cultural Studies." *Inter-Asia Cultural Studies* 2, no. 1 (2001): 35–52.

———. *High Culture Fever: Politics, Aesthetics, and Ideology in Deng's China*. Berkeley: University of California Press, 1996.

———. *Brand New China: Advertising, Media and Commercial Cu*lture. Cambridge, MA: Harvard University Press, 2008.

———., ed. *Chinese Popular Culture and the State (Special Issue of Positions)* vol. 1. Durham, NC: Duke University Press, 2001.

Wang, Ning. "The Mapping of Chinese Postmodernity." In *Postmodernism and China*, edited by Arif Dirlik and Xudong Zhang, 21–40. Durham, NC and London: Duke University Press, 2000.

Wang, Yin, and Feiran Du. "Shajiabang 'Xin' Gushi [the 'New' Story of Shajiabang]."
  *Nanfang Weekend*, July 17 2003, D21.
Wang, Yin. "Shajiabang Xianchang [on the Scene of Shajiabang]." *Nanfang
  Weekend*, July 17 2003, D21.
Wang, Zheng. "Gender, Employment and Women's Resistance." In *Chinese Society,
  2nd Edition: Change, Conflict and Resistance*, edited by Elizabeth Perry, J. and
  Mark Selden. 159–182. London and New York: Routledge, 2000.
Weber, Ian. "Reconfiguring Chinese Propaganda and Control Modalities: A Case
  Study of Shanghai's Television System. *Journal of Contemporary China*, 11, no.
  30 (2002): 53–75.
Wen, Jiabao. "Jiang Zhenhua, Cha Shiqing: Tong Guowuyun Canshi He Zhongyang
  Wenshi Yanjiuguan Guanyuan Zuotan Shi De Jianhua [Speak the Truth and
  Look for the True Situation; Speech Given During the Discussion Forum with
  Counselors of the State Council and Staff of the Central Research Institute of
  Culture and History]." (2011). Published electronically April 17, 2011. http://www
  .gov.cn/ldhd/2011-04/17/content_1846206.htm.
Williams, Raymond. "Drama in a Dramatised Society." In *Raymond Williams on
  Television: Selected Writings,* edited by Alan O'Connor, 3–13. New York and
  London: Routledge, 1989.
———. *Marxism and Literature*. Oxford: Oxford University Press, 1977.
———. *The Long Revolution New edition with a foreward by Anthony Barnett* ed.
  Cardigan, UK: Parthian, 2013.
———. Politics and Letters: Interview with New Left Review, with an Introduction
  by Geoff Dyer London: Verso, 2015.
Wu, Shufang. "'Modernising' Confucianism in China: A Repackaging of
  Institutionalization to Consolidate Party Leadership." *Asian Perspective*, 39, no.
  2 (2015): 301–324.
Xiao, He. "Xiaoshuo 'Shajiabang' Zai Xuanyang Shenme? [What Does Novelette
  'Shajiabang' Propagate]." *Zhejiang Daily*, February 18, 2003, P8.
Xu, Janice Hua. "Building a Chinese 'Middle Class': Consumer Education and
  Identity Construction in Television Land." In *TV China*, eds. Ying Zhu and Chris
  Berry, 150–167. Bloomington and Indianapolis: Indiana University Press, 2009.
Yan, Yunxiang. "The Changing Moral Landscape." In *Deep China: The Moral Life
  of the Person*, edited by Yunxiang Yan, Arthur Kleinman, Jun Jing, Sing Lee,
  Everett Zhang, Tianshu Pan, Fei Wu and Jinhua Guo, 36–77. Berkeley: University
  of California Press, 2011.
———. "The Chinese Path to Individualization." *The British Journal of Sociology*
  61, no. 3 (2010): 489–512.
Yang, Fei. "Jinhou Wunian Hongse Lüyou Jiang 'Hong' Bian Huaxia Dadi [Red
  Tour Popular across the Country in the Next Five Years]." www.people.com.cn,
  last modified February 25, 2005, http://travel.people.com.cn/GB/41636/41637/44
  670/44672/3202881.html.
Yang, Lan. "The Depiction of the Hero in the Cultural Revolution Novel." *China
  Information* 12, no. 68 (1998): 68–94.
———. "'Socialist Realism' Versus 'Revolutionary Realism Plus Revolutionary
  Romanticism.'" In *In the Party Spirit: Socialist Realism and Literary Practice*

*in the Soviet Union, East Germany and China*, edited by Hilary Chung, Michael Falchikov, Bonnie S. McDougall and Karin McPherson, 88–105. Amsterdam: Rodopi, 1996.

Yin, Hong. "Yiyi, Shengchan Yu Xiaofei—Dangdai Zhongguo Dianshiju De Zhengzhi Jingji Xue Fenxi [Ideology, Production and Consumption: A Political Economic Analysis of Contemporary Chinese Television Drama]." *Xiandai Chuanbo [Modern Communication]* 2001, no. 4 (2001): 1–7.

Yin, Hong, and Daihui Yang. "Zhongguo Dianshiju Yishu Chuantong [the Artistic Tradition of Chinese Television]." In *Zhongmei Dianshiju Bijiao Yanjiu* [???, edited by Chunjing Qu and Ying Zhu, 315–344. Shanghai: Shanghai Sanlian Bookstore, 2005.

Yu, Hongmei. "Dujie Women Shidaide Jingshen Zhenghou: Dui Dianshi Lianxuju 'Gangtie Shi Zenyang Lianchengde'Jieshoufankui De Sikao[Reading and Understanding the Spiritual Syndrome of Our Times: Reflections on the Reception of the Television Drama 'the Making of a Hero.']" In *Shuxie Wenhua Yingxiong [Writing About Cultural Hero: Cultural Studies at the Turn of the Century]*, edited by Jinhua Dai. 192–227. Nanjing: Jiangsu People's Press, 2000.

Zha, Jianying. *China Pop: How Soap Operas, Tabloids, and Bestsellers Are Transforming a Culture*. New York: New Press, 1995.

Zhang, Fa. "Hongse Jingdian: 2004 De Yizhong Wenhua Xianxiangde Jiedu [Red Classics: Interpretations of a Cultural Phenomenon in 2004]." *Wenyi Yanjiu [Literary and Art Research]* 2005, no. 4 (2005): 21–25.

Zhang, Xuejun. "E'gao 'Shanshande Hongxing,' Zuozhe Hu Daoge Xiang Baiyichang Daoqian [Author Hu Daoge Apologises to Baiyi Studio for Spoofing 'the Shining Red Star']." (2006), last modifued April 24, 2006. http://news.163.com/06/0424/10 /2FFHLNQ900011229.html

Zhang, Yanqin. "Lei Feng Zaoyu Le 'Hou Liuxing,' Dang Lei Feng Yushang Wangluo E'gao [Caught in the Post-Pop, When Lei Feng Meets the Online Spoofing Fad]." Last modified March 24, 2006. http://news.163.com/06/0324/17 /2D0E02650001124T.html.

Zhang, Yingjin. *Chinese National Cinema*. London: Routledge, 2004.

Zhang, Zhizhong. "Dingwei Yu Cuowei: Yingshi Gaibian Yu Wenxue Yanjiu Zhong De 'Hongse Jingdian' [Positioning and Mis-Positioning: TV Adaptations and Literary Research on the Red Classics]." *Wenyi Yanjiu [Literary and Art Research]* 2005, no. 4 (2005): 13–20.

Zhang, Zongwei. "Yiqi Shixian Zhangyang De Wenhua Shijian: Toushi 'Hongse Jingdian' Gaibian [A Drummed-up Cultural Event: On the Adaptation of the Red Classics]." *Dangdai Dianying [Contemporary Cinema]* 2007, no. 1 (2007): 74–79.

Zhao, Weiqing, Xinxun Wu, and Ni Yu. "Qi Sheng Shi Qu Nongcui Dianshi Shoushi Xiguan Diaocha Baogao [Survey Report on Rural Television Viewing Habits in Seven Provinces, Municipalities and Autonomous Regions] ." *TV Research* 201, no. 8 (2006): 38–40.

Zhao, Yong. "Shui Zai Shouhu 'Hongse Jingdian': Cong 'Hongse Jingdian' Ju Gaibian Kan Guanzhongde 'Zhengzhi Wuyishi' [Who is guarding the 'Red Classics': TV Adaptation Viewers' Political Unconsciousness]." *Southern Cultural Forum*, no. 6 (2005): 36–39.

Zhao, Yuezhi. "Caught in the Web: The Public Interest and the Battle for Control of China's Information Superhighway." *Info* 2, no. 1 (2000): 41–65.

———. "Neoliberal Strategies, Socialist Legacies: Communication and State Transformation in China." In *Global Communications: Towards a Transcultural Political Economy*, edited by Paula Chakravarty and Yuezhi Zhao, 23–50. Lanham: Rowman & Littlefield, 2008.

———. "Rethinking Chinese Media Studies: History, Political Economy and Culture." In *Internationalizing Media Studies*, edited by Daya Kishan Thussu, 175–195. London and New York: Routledge, 2009.

———. "From Commercialization to Conglomeration: The Transformation of the Chinese Press within the Orbit of the Party State." *Journal of Communication* 20, no. 2 (Spring 2000): 3–26.

———. *Media, Market and Democracy in China: Between the Party Line and the Bottom Line*. Urbana: University of Illinois Press, 1998.

Zhong, Xueping, and Ban Wang, edited by *Debating the Socialist Legacy and Capitalist Globalization in China*. London: Palgrave Macmillan, 2014.

———. *Mainstream Culture Refocused: Television Drama, Society, and the Production of Meaning in Reform-Era China*. Honolulu: University of Hawai'i Press, 2010.

Zhou, Xuelin. "'From Behind the Wall': The Representation of Gender and Sexuality in Modern Chinese Film." *Asian Journal of Communiction* 11, no. 2 (2001): 1–16.

Zhou, Xuetong. "Guanzhong Bu Fan 'Jiqing Ranshao De Suiyue' Lianbo Wubian [Viewers Not yet Had Enough: Five Reruns of 'Passion' Series in a Row]." www.people.com.cn/GB/wenyu/64/128/20020827/808984.html.

Zhu, Hong. "Huihuang De Chengjiu, Canlan De Weilai: Zhongguo Dianshi Shiye Fazhan Chengjiu [Brilliant Achievement, Bright Future: Development Trajectory of China's Television Industry]." *Dianshi Yanjiu [Television Studies]* 2006, no. 5 (2006): 10–12.

Zhu, Wei, and Jizhen Zhang. "'Yimeng' Shoushilu Yuju Yangshi Di'er: You Wang Rongying 2009 Nian Yangshi Huangjindang Dianshiju Shoushi Guanjun ['Yimeng' Jumped to Second Place in CCTV's Rating: Possible Number One in CCTV's 2009 Overall Primetime Drama Rating."] *Qilu Evening News*, Dec 8 2009, C02.

Zhu, Xiaodong. "Tongguo Hunyin De Zhili." In *Shenti De Wenhua Zhengzhixue [The Cultural Politics of the Body]*, edited by Ming'an Wang, 51–75. Kaifeng: Henan University Press, 2004.

Zhu, Ying, Michael Keane, and Ruoyun Bai, eds. *TV Drama in China*. Hong Kong: Hong Kong University Press, 2008.

Zhu, Ying. "Yongzheng Dynasty and Chinese Primetime Television Drama." *Cinema Journal* 44, no. 4 (Summer 2005): 3–17.

Zhu, Ying, and Chris Berry, eds. *TV China*. Bloomington and Indianapolis: Indiana University Press, 2009.

# Index

www.ingramcontent.com/pod-product-compliance
Lightning Source LLC
Chambersburg PA
CBHW021817270326
41932CB00007B/220